This up-to-date snapshot of European, Latin American and Asian regional integration is informed by a theoretical framing that touches the most important bases in the field of comparative regional studies. This book is a very useful and very readable addition to an important area of world politics and a vibrant field of scholarship.

Peter J. Katzenstein, *Walter S. Carpenter Professor, Jr. of International Studies, Cornell University, USA*

Are regional organisations in crisis, or are they a crucial part of the solution to addressing the challenges of contemporary crises? Saurugger and Terpan have assembled an impressive range of expertise to analyse the relationship between regionalism and crisis-response in Europe, Asia and Latin America. The result is a highly topical volume which is an important contribution to the burgeoning literature on comparative regionalism.

Thomas Christiansen, *Maastricht University, the Netherlands*

Crisis and Institutional Change in Regional Integration

Comparative regional integration has met with increasing interest over the last 20 years with the emergence or reinforcing of new regional dynamics in the EU, NAFTA, MERCOSUR and ASEAN.

This volume systematically and comparatively analyses the reasons for regional integration and stalemate in European, Latin American and Asian regional integration. It examines whether regional integration systems change in crisis periods, or more precisely in periods of economic crises, and why they change in different directions. Based on a neo-institutionalist research framework and rigorously comparative research design, the individual chapters analyse why financial and economic crises lead to more or less integrated systems and which factors lead to these institutional changes. Specifically it addresses institutional change in regional integration schemes, power relations between member states and the institutions in different policy domains, and change in individual or collective citizens' attitudes towards regional integration. Adopting an actor-centred approach, the book highlights which regional integration schemes are influenced by economic and financial crises and how to explain this.

This text will be of key interest to scholars, students and policy specialists in regional integration, European Politics, International Relations, and Latin American and Asian studies.

Sabine Saurugger is Professor of Political Science and Research Dean at Sciences Po Grenoble, France. Her research focuses on theoretical approaches to European integration, interest groups and public policy, and more recently, the interplay between politics and law in the European Union.

Fabien Terpan is Associate Professor of Public Law at Sciences Po Grenoble, France, visiting Professor at the College of Europe, Natolin, and the holder of a Jean Monnet Chair. He is also Deputy Director of the CESICE (Center for the study of international security and European cooperation) and has published widely on EU law, European external action, and the interplay between law and politics in the European Union.

Routledge Studies on Challenges, Crises and Dissent in World Politics

Series editors: Karoline Postel-Vinay
Centre for International Studies and Research (CERI), France
and
Nadine Godehardt
German Institute for International and Security Affairs, Germany

This new series focuses on challenges, crises and dissent in world politics and the major political issues that have surfaced in recent years. It welcomes a wide range of theoretical and methodological approaches including critical and post-modern studies, and aims to improve our present understanding of global order through the exploration of major challenges to inter/national and regional governability, the effects of nationalism, extremism, weak leadership and the emergence of new actors in international politics.

1 **Empires of Remorse**
Narrative, postcolonialism and apologies for colonial atrocity
Tom Bentley

2 **Crisis and Institutional Change in Regional Integration**
Edited by Sabine Saurugger and Fabien Terpan

Crisis and Institutional Change in Regional Integration

Edited by
Sabine Saurugger and
Fabien Terpan

Routledge
Taylor & Francis Group
LONDON AND NEW YORK

First published 2016
by Routledge
2 Park Square, Milton Park, Abingdon, Oxon OX14 4RN

and by Routledge
711 Third Avenue, New York, NY 10017

First issued in paperback 2017

Routledge is an imprint of the Taylor & Francis Group, an informa business

British Library Cataloguing in Publication Data
A catalogue record for this book is available from the British Library

Library of Congress Cataloging in Publication Data
Names: Saurugger, Sabine, editor. | Terpan, Fabien, editor.
Title: Crises and institutional change in regional integration / edited by Sabine Saurugger and Fabien Terpan.
Description: New York : Routledge, 2016. | Series: Routledge studies on challenges, crises and dissent in world politics ; 2 | Includes bibliographical references and index.
Identifiers: LCCN 2015042344| ISBN 9781138951839 (hardback) | ISBN 9781315667959 (ebook)
Subjects: LCSH: Europe–Economic integration. | Latin America–Economic integration. | Asia–Economic integration. | Financial crises.
Classification: LCC HC241 .C745 2016 | DDC 337.1–dc23
LC record available at http://lccn.loc.gov/2015042344

ISBN 13: 978-1-138-48814-4 (pbk)
ISBN 13: 978-1-138-95183-9 (hbk)

Typeset in Times New Roman
by Wearset Ltd, Boldon, Tyne and Wear

Contents

Figures

Tables

Contributors

Céline Belot is Research Fellow at the French National Council for Research (CNRS/PACTE) and teaches at Sciences Po Grenoble, University Grenoble Alpes (UGA). Her main publications focus on citizens' attitudes towards European Integration and European values. Most recent publication include 'Have European attitudes at last played a role at the European Parliament elections?' with V. Van Inglegom, *Revue européenne des sciences sociales*, 53(1), 49–78. She currently works on the relation between public opinion and public policies at the European level.

Olivier Dabène is Professor of Political Science at Sciences Po Paris and Senior Researcher at the Center for International Studies and Research (CERI). He is also the President of the Political Observatory of Latin America and the Caribbean (www.sciencespo.fr/opalc) and visiting professor in many Latin American universities. His main area of expertise is Latin American regionalism. His latest publications in English include *The Politics of Regional Integration in Latin America* (NY, Palgrave Macmillan, 2009) and 'Consistency and resilience through cycles of repoliticization', in *The Rise of Post-Hegemonic Regionalism. The Case of Latin America*, edited by Pia Riggirozzi and Diana Tussie, London, Springer, 2012, pp. 41–64.

Hanno Degner is a Senior Research Fellow at the Chair of International Relations, University of Konstanz, Germany. He studied Political Science at the University of Bremen (BA, 2009), and Public Administration and European Governance at the University of Konstanz (MA, 2011) and Sciences Po Grenoble (DNM, 2011). From 2012 to 2015, he worked as Doctoral Student at the University of Konstanz (Thesis Title: 'Crises and Integration. An Empirical-Analytic Study of European Integration in Response to Urgent Threats', Committee: Dirk Leuffen, Sabine Saurugger, Wolfgang Seibel).

Clarissa Dri is Professor of International Relations at the Federal University of Santa Catarina, Florianopolis, Brazil. She holds a PhD in Political Science from Sciences Po Bordeaux, France. Her main research interests are comparative regionalisms, Latin American foreign policies and legislative studies. Among her publications are *Parliamentary Dimensions of Regionalization* *and Globalization* (Palgrave Macmillan, 2013, co-edited with Olivier Costa and Stelios Stavridis) and *La construction du Parlement du Mercosur* (Larcier, 2014).

Kelly Gerard is Assistant Professor in the School of Social Sciences at the University of Western Australia. Her research interests span political economy, development and social movements in Southeast Asia. Her work has been published in *Globalizations, The Pacific Review* and *Contemporary Politics.* In 2014, she published *ASEAN's Engagement of Civil Society: Regulating Dissent* (Palgrave Macmillan). She is a member of the editorial review board of the book series *Challenging Governance* (Rowman & Littlefield) and an Associate Researcher of the Asia Research Centre, Murdoch University.

Isabelle Guinaudeau is Research Fellow at the French National Council for Research (CNRS/Centre Emile Durkheim) and Principal Investigator of the French Research Agency project Partipol. She explores questions related to party competition strategies, accountability and responsiveness, in particular at the EU level. Recent articles have been published in *Journal of Public Policy, French Politics* and *Journal of Elections, Public Opinion, and Parties*.

Axel Hülsemeyer is Associate Professor in the Department of Political Science at Concordia University in Montreal, Canada. He teaches International Political Economy with a focus on global and regional integration in trade and finance, as well as European Politics. He is the editor of *Globalization in the Twenty-First Century: Convergence or Divergence?* (Palgrave Macmillan, 2003); the author of *Globalization and the Adjustment of States: Federalism as an Obstacle?* (Ashgate, 2004) and *International Political Economy: A Reader* (Oxford University Press, 2010). A new co-authored book entitled *Citizen Discontent in the European Union: A General Phenomenon?* is under contract with Ashgate.

Christian Lequesne is Professor of Political Science at Sciences Po Paris and Senior Research Fellow at the Center for International Studies and Research (CERI). He is a visiting professor at the LUISS University, Rome; Charles University, Prague and Diplomatische Akademie, Vienna. He has published extensively on EU institutions, the relationships between the EU and its member states and the EU foreign policy. Among his last books *The member states of the European Union*, with S. Bulmer eds. (OUP, 2014).

Shaun Narine is an Associate Professor of Political Science and International Relations at St. Thomas University in Fredericton, Canada. He was a visiting fellow at the East West Center in 2000 and a Killam Postdoctoral Fellow at the University of British Columbia in 2000–2002. He has written extensively on multilateral institutions in the Asia Pacific, with a focus on ASEAN. He has also published work on Canadian foreign policy, humanitarian intervention and Western imperialism.

Kevin Parthenay holds a PhD in Political Science from Sciences Po Paris. A Research Fellow of the Center for International Research and Studies (CERI), he specialises in Central American foreign policies and regional integration. He worked for the French Ministry of Foreign and European Affairs, and for the Organization of American States (OAS) as an international observer of the Colombian 2010 general election. He currently supervises the Development and Partnership Division of the Political Observatory for Latin America and the Caribbean (OPALC). He is Academic Coordinator at Sciences Po and Associate Doctor at Sciences Po/CERI.

Sabine Saurugger is Professor of Political Science at Sciences Po Grenoble, and Senior Research Fellow at PACTE. She currently works on the politics of law in the EU and domestic administrative resistances to European integration. Recent publications include *Theoretical approaches to European integration*, Palgrave 2013 and journal articles in *European Journal of Political Research, West European Politics, Comparative European Politics, Journal of European Public Policy, Journal of Common Market Studies* and *European Foreign Affairs Review*.

Fabien Terpan is Associate Professor of Public Law at Sciences Po Grenoble, visiting Professor at the College of Europe and the holder of a Jean Monnet Chair. He is also Deputy Director of the CESICE (Centre d'études de la sécurité internationale et des coopérations européennes) and has published widely on EU law, European external action, and the interplay between law and politics in the European Union in journals such as *European Law Journal, Comparative European Politics, European Foreign Affairs Review* and *European Security*. Fabien Terpan is on the editorial board of *Studia Diplomatica* and *Politique et sociétés*.

Reuben Wong is Jean Monnet Chair and Director of Studies at the College of Alice and Peter Tan, National University of Singapore. He is the author of *The Europeanization of French Foreign Policy: France and the EU in East Asia* (Palgrave Macmillan, 2006), *National and European Foreign Policies* (co-edited with Christopher Hill, Routledge, 2011), and journal articles in the *Cambridge Review of International Affairs, Politique Européenne, Asia Europe Journal* and *EU External Affairs Review*. He serves on the Council of the think-tank SIIA, is Associate Fellow at the EU Centre Singapore and Senior Research Affiliate at the College of Europe in Bruges.

Preface

The idea for this book has two origins, one theoretical, the other empirical. On the theoretical aspect, the wish for writing a book on comparative regionalism emerged when one of the two editors of this collective volume worked on the chapter on comparative regionalism for her book on *Theoretical approaches to European Integration.* She was intrigued by the fact that most of the literature was extremely promising and a fascinating read, but very few of the edited volumes on comparative regionalism dealt systematically with the question of why different regional integration schemes reacted differently to exogenous challenges. Regional institutions abound, but since the systematic studies undertaken by Joseph Nye, Bruce Russett, Philippe Schmitter or Amitai Etzioni in the 1960s and 1970s, the complexity of contemporary world politics and the sheer abundance of conceptual frameworks developed to study them seemed to make it very difficult to undertake a systematic comparative studies of different regional organisations. The absence of these studies, however, made it difficult to teach comparative regionalism, beyond presenting in-depth case studies and going back to the origins of the conceptual frameworks published by the authors quoted above in the founding years of the *Journal of Common Market Studies*, at that time much more interested in comparative regionalism than with European integration alone.

The second reason is empirical. During study visits in Brazil and Argentina, the editors of this volume discussed regional integration with their colleagues from these emerging powers. We were struck by the desire to cut ties with European studies, presented as a dying power, whereas Latin America, Asia and South Africa were perceived to be on the rise. As understandable this position was politically, we nevertheless wanted to compare regional integration more scientifically. We are therefore very grateful to our colleagues over the globe, Australian, Brazilian, Canadians, French, German and Singaporean – only to mention their academic affiliation – for having accepted to follow us into this endeavour and to have reacted to our suggestions and demands with good humour. The challenges to produce a book that answers the question why some regional integration schemes deepen after financial and economic crises and why others react with inertia were important. The adventure was exciting and we hope that the readers will find the answers as stimulating as we do.

We would like to thank the editors of the Routledge Series on Dissent and Crises in World Politics, Karoline Postel-Vinay and Nadine Godehardt as well as the external reviewers for their constructive comments on the manuscript. The participants of the panel on 'Regional integration in times of crises' at the 2014 ECSA-C Conference in Montreal contributed to the manuscript with enthusiastic comments and constructive suggestions. A special thanks to Andrew Taylor and Charlotte Endersby for their warm welcome and professionalism at Routledge, to Marijn van der Wal for preparing the index, and to Anna Jeannesson for proofreading our chapters.

1 Regional integration in times of crises

Comparative regional integration approaches and institutional change[1]

Sabine Saurugger and Fabien Terpan

Financial and economic crises have a global impact. While this was already visible in the nineteenth and at the beginning of the twentieth century, when the collapse of national stockmarkets triggered economic crises in a large number of states, the most recent economic breakdowns and recessions – the 1980s in Latin America, the 1990s in Asia and, finally, the years 2000 in Europe and North America – have influenced not only states but also regional organisations. Institutional structures, as well as relations between member states and the citizens of these regional integration structures have been modified – either through strengthening these structures, and creating new opportunities for actors, or by weakening the relations between the main actors of regional integration.

The aim of this collective volume is to see whether regional institutions change in periods of economic and financial crisis and – if they do – analyse why they change to different degrees and in different directions. While the economic and financial crisis seems to lead the European Union to become more formal with its member state relations bringing the most powerful actors to the fore (Hodson *et al.* 2014), Asian and Latin American regional organisations appear to be influenced in a more limited way. Why do we observe the establishment of stricter rules in the European case, while neither Central and Latin American nor Asian institutional structures seem to be profoundly affected?

In this book we concentrate on the European Union (EU), the Association of South East Asian Nations (ASEAN), and Central and Latin American organisations: the Southern Common Market (MERCOSUR), the Central American Integration System (SICA) and the Union of South American Nations (UNASUR). By selecting three regional geographical areas we have favoured in-depth analysis rather than a wider regional spread including Africa or the interaction between regions (see Fioramonti 2012). The concentration on Europe, Latin America and Asia, allows us to deepen our understanding of three specific questions: If change occurs, does it strengthen regional integration, or do crises lead to progressively weaker regional integration? Is the strengthening or weakening of regional integration a consequence of the crisis or an endogenous process in which the crisis has very little influence? Finally, why do citizens react differently in all three regions: reactions ranging from increasing scepticism about integration projects to continued indifference?

These questions will be analysed more precisely with regard to three aspects: First, by looking at power relations between the member states and the regional organisations in different policy domains; second by focusing on institutional change in regional integration schemes, both with regard to formal and informal institutions such as legal rules but also practices and paradigms; and finally, by analysing change in individual citizens' attitudes or those of collective actors towards regional integration.

Taking up the theoretical questions, which have constituted the basis of comparative regionalism since the 1950s (Haas 1958; Etzioni 1965; Nye 1968; Schmitter 1970), this collective volume aims at deepening our understanding of contemporary transnational integration processes through comparing regional integration schemes. This echoes 'new regionalism' approaches (Söderbaum 2003; Hettne 2003; Breslin and Higgott 2003; Telo 2007; Sbragia 2008; Warleigh-Lack and Langenhove 2010), and contributes to the overall 'new regionalism' literature in three specific ways:

First, through in-depth studies of the concrete effects of economic and financial crises on state attitudes and institutional transformations. This will be done by explicitly concentrating on actors' behaviour, which allows us to go beyond the idea of purely institutional answers to external stimuli. The idea is to show how actors' perceptions and interactions create power games that either influence institutional changes or lead to inertia.

Second, through a comparative research design, which analyses transformations in Latin American, European and Asian regional integration: this will allow us to systematically develop hypotheses that guide the analyses in every chapter.

And finally, through a combination of 'new regionalism' approaches with the conceptual framework on institutional change stemming from new institutionalism.

While we start, without doubt, from a perspective anchored in 'European knowledge production' (Motsamai and Qobo 2012), the chapters of this book critically engage with this perspective, underlining the possibilities and the limits of its explanatory capacities in three geographical areas.

This introductory chapter presents the overall framework in which all chapters are anchored. Starting with general definitions of the concepts that are at the heart of this book: crisis and regional integration, it then draws on institutionalist approaches in order to elaborate a series of hypotheses that will be tested by the authors throughout the book. Finally, it gives an overview of the empirical puzzles in the three regional integration areas, which will be analysed in depth by the individual chapters.

Conceptualising crises and regional integration

The recurrent appearance of crises and the renewed interest in regional integration studies at the beginning of the twenty-first century, have produced new and exciting empirical insight into various types of regional integration – from North Africa, the Arab world, Latin America or Asia (Schulz *et al.* 2001; Telo 2007; Langenhove 2011). Economic and financial crises have affected food production and distribution, reduced social welfare provision, shrunk development funds, created contestation that spread over the planet and questioned the central role of Western powers in international relations through the emergence of new fora such as the G20, which includes the fastest growing economies of the developing world (Fioramonti 2012: 2). While case studies abound and analyses of possible future developments in regional integration emerge, this collective volume has a slightly different agenda. It aims at studying the responses of regional organisations established in three regional geographical areas to economic and financial crises from a systematically comparative perspective. This starts with an explanation of what we understand by the notion of crisis, followed by the establishment of a series of hypotheses based on in comparative regionalism studies.

Crises

Crises can take many forms and refer to political, military, social, ecological or economic and financial turmoil in a given context. In its most general sense, a crisis marks a phase of disorder in the seemingly 'normal' development of a system (Boin *et al.* 2005: 2). More specifically, the concept of 'crisis' refers to a situation which: (1) threatens the high priority goals of the decision-making unit, (2) restricts the amount of time available for response before the decision is transformed, (3) surprises the members of the decision-making unit by its occurrence (Hermann 1969). A crisis occurs when the core values or life-sustaining systems of a community come under threat. In this sense, a financial and economic crisis threatens citizens' job security and welfare benefits and thus undermines trust in the economic system. Crises induce a sense of urgency. Serious threats that do not pose immediate problems do not trigger a sense of urgency (climate change or pension systems are such examples) (Boin *et al.* 2005: 3). Only a threat that is perceived as urgent in the sense that non-action would be seen as leading to a worsening of the situation can be described as crisis, and the economic and financial crises under scrutiny certainly fall under this heading. Non-action on behalf of the government and financial actors was considered impossible, as it would have led to a worsening of the crisis, endangering the core values of the unit. Finally, in a situation of crisis, the perception of threat is accompanied by a high degree of uncertainty; uncertainty about the origins of the crisis, its analysis and the remedies that could be administered. Responding to the crisis is not a routine that institutions and governments apply to a well-known situation; rather it implies finding innovative solutions to unclear and complex problems.

In periods of crisis, as we will see in the individual chapters, the situation is characterised by an unusually high degree of uncertainty about the exact nature of the threat and the consequences of the decisions taken to counter the threat. In other words, crises are situations of overwhelming complexity and ambiguity about the problem encountered and the solutions envisaged (Hall 1993). But while crises are clearly exogenous, agency is needed to frame the understanding of the crises and to produce different, partially opposing solutions. Sense-making is one of the crucial processes that occur: 'Policy makers must recognise from vague, ambivalent, and contradictory signals that something out of the ordinary is developing' (Boin *et al.* 2005: 10). This understanding must then be transformed into a specific meaning. Policy-makers are expected to reduce uncertainty and provide an authoritative account of what is going on, why it is happening, and what needs to be done. They frame the understanding of the crisis and are in this context in competition with the media, stakeholders and other actors.

Hence crises are not only exogenous factors that, mechanically, trigger change. More specifically, they transform the understanding actors have of how to deal with issues, and enable actors whose interests have diverged from the mainstream paradigm to use the window of opportunity created by the crisis to influence the debate anew. It is thus crucial to understand which actors drive change and what types of strategies flourish in which kinds of institutional settings (Checkel 2007; Mahoney and Thelen 2010).

Analysing how actors made sense of the phenomena observed will be a central starting point in all chapters of this collective volume. The process in which agents make sense of crisis phenomena is considered to be a crucial part of the explanation as to why regional integration reinforces or, on the contrary, weakens or remains unchanged in times of turmoil. So, in this volume, we aim at placing specific emphasis on the complex interplay between policy-makers, experts and citizens to analyse why institutional change does or does not occur in reaction to financial and economic crises.

Comparative regionalism

The development of regionalism studies can schematically be divided into two waves going from 'old' regionalism to 'new' regionalism. Although some scholars argue that regionalism as an empirical phenomenon existed long before the beginning of European integration in the 1950s and cannot be considered a Western phenomenon (Acharya 2012), the first wave of regionalism studies emerged as a sub discipline of International Relations in the 1950s and is generally associated with European integration studied through the lenses of neofunctionalism. The second wave started developing in the late 1980s and is related to the process of globalisation (Breslin and Higgott 2003). Generally, 'new' regionalism differs from 'old' regionalism' in that it rejects Euro-centrism, perceived as mainly based on neofunctionalist explanations, which explain that integration is perceived as constantly reinforcing and enlarging from one policy area to another. 'New' regionalism instead adopts a pluralistic and global perspective (Söderbaum 2003). The distinction is not entirely neat, however, as the 'shadow' of neofunctionalism is said to also be present in the new theoretical approaches (Lombaerde 2011).

Beyond this 'constitutional' debate, comparative regionalism offers two worthwhile avenues to conceptually frame the collective volume's research question of whether financial and economic crises lead to more integration of formal and informal institutions in regional integration systems, or on the contrary whether they break up existing organisations and institutions and thus provide member states with increased autonomy. Comparative regionalism allows researchers to combine different conceptual frameworks, which is crucial, as regional integration schemes differ tremendously, as do their reactions to economic and financial crises. In this sense, comparative regionalism opens the possibility to 'import' an institutionalist approach into regional integration studies, which helps us develop a series of hypotheses as to why and to what extent different regions react differently to economic and financial crises.

A second avenue can be found in comparative regionalism's typology of region-ness, or degree of regionalisation (Hettne 2001), which is central to our choice of case studies: core regions, such as the European Union in this book, which are extremely well structured and allow their members to play an influential role on the world stage; intermediate zone regions, such as the Latin American regions analysed in this book, which imitate core regions to compete with them in the global economy; and, finally, peripheral zone regions, such as ASEAN, where political and economic institutions remain fragile and where member states' sovereignty is the main explanatory factor for regional activity or inactivity.

Explaining the impact of crises on regional integration

The chapters in this collective volume actively combine exogenous (crises) and endogenous variables (actors' use of the crises) with a view to explaining the transformation of regional integration schemes. Historical institutionalism allows us more specifically to formulate the hypotheses that are tested in the chapters, referring first to member states' evolving engagement or positions in regional integration in periods of crisis, second, to the impact of institutional density on institutional change, and finally, to the impact of citizens, whether through the forming of public opinion or civil society organisations, on member states' and institutional responses to crises.

In order to analyse the change in institutional structures with regard to regional integration in times of crisis, we combine insight from different new institutionalist approaches, based on an actor-centred research design.

Institutional change

We define institutions as

> a relatively enduring collection of rules and organized principles, embedded in structures of meaning and resources that are relatively invariant in the face of staff turnover and relatively resilient to the idiosyncratic preferences and expectations of individuals and changing external circumstances.
>
> (March and Olsen 2006: 3)

More specifically, it is possible to distinguish between *organisations* such as secretariats, parliaments or councils, consisting of 'persons, funds, and buildings that are meant to fulfil particular organisational tasks' (Héritier 2007: 5), on the one hand, and *formal* and *informal norms*, on the other. Formal norms refer to elements such as treaties, charters and other constitutional norms, rules established by the organisation's bodies, and hence can be understood as structures of relations between actors; informal norms refer to conventions, beliefs and ideologies (North 1990).

Understanding institutional change is a challenge often underlined by institutionalist approaches. While rational choice institutionalists explain change through exogenous shocks, which alter the context, both historical institutionalism and sociological institutionalism are said to be comparatively change-resistant in their explanation (Pierson 1993, Stacey and Rittberger 2003). The most recent literature using historical institutionalist approaches however, has pushed the question of institutional change to centre stage (Pierson 2004; Thelen 2003; Streeck and Thelen 2005; Hall 2008; Mahoney and Thelen 2010).

Why does change occur? If we start from the assumption that the establishment of institutions reflects a certain number of exogenous and endogenous conditions, then the shifts in these conditions will change the institutions. Crises are critical junctures, which introduce periods of uncertainty into longer periods of stability or so-called 'punctuated equilibria' (Baumgartner and Jones 1993). These long-term institutional structures that are present in all three regional contexts are the product of 'trust, successful performance, and coherence between policy ideas and organizational forms' (Boin *et al.* 2005: 125).

Two explanations can be found as to why crises suspend these equilibria: On the one hand, a crisis relaxes the structural constraints that keep institutions in place. It directs attention to previously unnoticed vulnerabilities. In these situations, decision-makers can count on wide-reaching support and develop unconventional risky policy options ('rally around the flag effect'). On the other hand, the routine way of working and thinking (cognitive frames) becomes discredited in the eyes of outsiders; room for alternatives suddenly emerges. This does not only concern a specific policy sector but can question the political system as a whole.

This means, more precisely, that institutional change occurs when problems of rule interpretation and enforcement open up space for actors to perceive as well as implement existing rules in new ways. This understanding of change allows us to consider exogenous shocks as independent variables leading to institutional change but also to take endogenous variables seriously. Thus, a change in the shared understanding of the impact specific institutions may have, can constitute an endogenous shock leading to institutional change. The notion of 'policy cycles' describes this process particularly well (Howlett and Ramesh 2003): While institutions in general are highly constraining in periods of stable politics (Duina 2007) and hence prone to path dependency, critical junctures, such as the economic and financial crisis periods under scrutiny in the studies of this collective volume, open up opportunities for change, or windows of opportunity induced by agents that seize this opportunity (Katznelson 2003, Genieys and Hassenteufel 2012).

Processes of change take multiple forms. Recent institutionalist analyses (Streeck and Thelen 2005; Mahoney and Thelen 2010) have described perspectives of change where change is not only the replacement of one institutional structure with another, but also a combination of old and new institutions inducing a new shared understanding of a specific institution. This can be understood as layering whereby new institutions are created on top of others, a process that involves amendments, revisions or additions; as conversion where old institutions are remodelled for new purposes; as drift, if the rules remain unchanged but their impact changes due to shifts in the environment; and finally displacement whereby existing rules are replaced by new ones (Streeck and Thelen 2005; Mahoney and Thelen 2010). This typology is particularly helpful when categorising the changes that took place in regional organisations during and after periods of crises. It develops a perspective of change in which change is not only the replacement of one institutional structure with another, but also a mixture between old and new ones or inducing a new shared understanding of a specific institution.

Two reform types are possible. On the one hand, a reformist approach whose aim is to change policies and redesign the institutional features of a public organisation in order to ensure a new fit with the changed environment. This reform type adds up to adopting lessons learned to restore faith in the sector by breaking with past practices. On the other hand, a conservative approach which defends and maintains the existing institutional essence in the face of pressure to change it. The core idea is that incremental improvement rather than radical redesign will close the performance gap and restore legitimacy (Boin *et al.* 2005: 126). This means adapting policy instruments and recalibrating organisational structures and routines to accommodate external pressure for change, as a means to preserve the institutional core, for example the prevailing policy paradigm and organisational mission (ibid).

In this volume, we define institutional change more precisely as change in (a) member state relations, (b) in 'institutional density' or (c) citizens' and collective actors' attitudes towards regional integration. Institutional change is hence our dependent variable, influenced by exogenous crises and the endogenous use of crises by change actors.

Our model therefore includes the two perspectives of institutional change identified by Adrienne Héritier (2007: 7–8): the 'process perspective', on the one hand, which looks at the factors driving institutional change and the correlations existing between these variables. On the other hand, the 'structural perspective', which concentrates on the levels and arenas in which institutional change occurs, but even more specifically on the types and behaviour of actors.

Change actors

The first possible explanation for change/non-change in regional integration in times of crisis pertains to change actors, and more specifically member states in the framework of this book. The behaviour of change actors is extremely difficult to conceptualise, however. These change agents are historically embedded and thus historically framed. Their strategies of change are likely to flourish in particular institutional environments, which also includes cognitive frameworks (McNamara 1998; Jabko 2006; Saurugger 2010). Thus, 'change actors' or 'policy entrepreneurs' are rarely confined to one particular category, but might use different types at different times, or simultaneously.

In the particular context of institutional change, actors' attitudes can be understood along two lines: first, they induce change when the specific cognitive context, the specific understanding of an issue, allows them to have an impact. More specifically, change agents have an impact when they are able to frame a problem in accordance with their paradigmatic position, or when the problem and solution frame is in accordance with their own ideal understanding. Second, change agents search to increase influence as well as legitimacy. This is linked to the fact that new institutional structures are not only designed to improve the decision-making processes, through increased efficiency, but also to make them more legitimate.

It follows from the above that actors possess different forms of power (Strange 1996). They can defend or share a specific cognitive frame that, at a particular moment, becomes the dominant paradigm that rules the way problems and solutions are interpreted. This becomes particularly visible when we look at the examples of how the EU responded to the economic and financial crises (increased austerity and more formal rules) or how non-state actors managed to introduce environmental and human rights concerns into ASEAN's political agenda. Power of course can also refer to a more classic understanding such as an actor's relative economic, political or military power in a specific context.

Actors can form coalitions in order to influence change. A number of chapters in the volume show that coalitional dynamics are central to understanding the change agents' strategies in periods of crisis. In order to understand institutional change, it is crucial to understand the coalitions these actors establish: 'The success of various kinds of agents in effecting change typically depends on the coalitions they are able to deliberately forge or that emerge unexpectedly in the course of distributional struggle' (Mahoney and Thelen 2010: 29).

These coalitions are embedded in special formal and informal frameworks that allow these networks to influence the change of regional organisations. In other words, the idea that the more integrated the institutional structures are, the less room for manoeuvre the national actors have, is embedded in the reasoning behind path dependency and institutional 'lock-ins' (Mahoney 2000). In this sense, historical institutionalism arguably predicts that in the event of an exogenous shock, the pre-crisis level of integration will, to a large extent, determine actors' attitudes.

We thus argue that the higher the relative power of state actors (cognitive, economic, political, military) before a crisis occurs, the higher the probability that these actors influence institutional change in a situation of crisis (H.1.).

Institutional density

Following the definition of institutions presented earlier as, on the one hand organisations, and on the other, formal and informal norms, we argue that actors, i.e. state and non-state actors, largely speaking evolve in more or less institutionalised contexts, understood as different degrees of 'institutional density'. 'Institutional density' is a dynamic concept, implying fluidity and movement. By 'institutional density', we understand the degree to which institutions created by regional organisations constrain, on the one hand member states in their domestic and international politics, and on the other individuals (public opinion) and collective groups of citizens (civil society organisations and interest groups).[2] Institutional density is affected by three variables: the regional organisation's functionality, the actors' degree of socialisation and the impact of regional organisations. 'Functionality' refers to the functions assigned by national governments to supranational actors. 'Degree of socialisation' refers to the degree of interaction between citizens, the elites and supranational bodies. 'Impact' addresses the political, economic and social influence of the integration process under examination on the members of the organisation.

The questions to be answered in this collective volume with regard to institutional density in the context of crises are: Which actors are leading the integration process, and why? Which mechanisms are in place? What functions do national governments assign to the regional organisation and what competencies are transferred to the supranational level? The assumption here is that regional integration processes are discontinuous ('stop-and-go') processes led by the governments of the member states.

This 'processes perspective' helps us to measure the 'structural perspective', in other words the levels of influence exercised by the specific regional integration processes under scrutiny – the global level, the internal functioning of the member states as well as non-member states – in political, economic or social terms. It is important to underline, however, that we do not presume that the organisation's impact is stronger if based on formal than on informal rules. It is precisely the strength and weaknesses of both formal and informal rules that will be analysed by the different authors in this book.

The elements developed here lead us to formulate the following hypotheses:

> The higher the institutional density in a situation of crisis, the higher the continued commitment of both institutions and member states in regional integration (H.2.). More precisely, we argue here that the higher institutional density in a situation of crisis, the higher the probability that agents will push integration forward (H.2.1.). With regard to the form of institutional change we argue that the higher institutional density in a situation of crisis, the higher the probability that path dependence occurs (H.2.2.).

Explaining citizens' attitudes

Finally, in order to analyse both individual as well as collective citizens' attitudes towards regional integration in crisis situations, and the possible influence this attitude exerts on the strengthening or loosening of integration processes, we analyse how individual and collective citizens' attitudes impact on institutional change and how these attitudes are influenced by regional integration.

Studying this crucial question of citizens' attitudes from a comparative perspective will contribute widely to the literature on comparative regionalism, as this puzzle has been studied to a certain extent in the EU but much less in the framework of other regional integration schemes (Fioramonti 2013; Chandra 2004; Patomäki and Teivanen 2002). For a detailed analysis of the empirical difficulty of comparing citizens' attitudes and values in regional organisations beyond the EU see Acharya and Johnston 2007.

In EU studies we find extensive research dedicated to public opinion, and Euroscepticism and their link to the European economy (for an overview see Loveless and Rohrschneider 2011). Four series of elements in particular explain citizens' attitudes to European integration. First, these attitudes refer to variables related to the instrumental self-interest of citizens. These include personal economic situation and the individuals' perceptions of their own economic status and national economic performance. On this basis, certain citizens (due to their education and occupation) can be identified as economic winners or losers from the processes of integration (Gabel 1998a; Kriesi *et al.* 2008). Winners are thus more likely than losers to support the integration process. As a consequence, this explanation essentially presupposes that the individuals perform a cost-benefit analysis, which determines their attitude towards integration. However, which economic factors are the most relevant for citizens is still a subject of debate (Loveless and Rohrschneider 2011).

The second group of variables is labelled 'social location'. In opposition to the previous arguably overly materialist explanation, this second group of variables attempts to account for the 'individuals' incremental political sophistication [which] created a value system of appreciation for the democratic organization … and eventually extended to support for the EU' (Loveless and Rohrschneider 2011). This 'process of sophistication was predicated on the notion that individuals' cognitive mobilization increased political awareness which lessened the "threat" of integration' (Loveless and Rohrschneider 2011). The basic idea is that when citizens (or at least some of them) become more politically sophisticated and cosmopolitan-oriented, their appreciation and support for the EU is likely to increase.

The third group of variables refers to national *vs*. European identity. There are two approaches to the identity of citizens. The first one attempts to identify the extent to which citizens associate themselves with their country and the extent to which they fear 'the other' (the level of hostility towards other cultures). The second approach aims to determine whether citizens identify themselves with their country or as Europeans. By this logic, strong national identities would result in negative attitudes towards integration. However, this conceptualisation suggests that the two identities are mutually exclusive, which is not always the case. Scholars differentiate between 'exclusive national identity' (citizens feel attachment only to their nation and not to Europe) and 'cumulative national identity' (according to which citizens can have a feeling of belonging to both the EU and their state) (Hooghe and Marks 2005). The former type of identity is likely to have a negative impact on citizens' attitudes towards the EU.

Finally, the fourth group of explanatory variables in relation to attitudes towards European integration is related to institutions and institutional performance (Loveless and Rohrschneider 2011). The overview claims that '[t]he most fertile branch of this argument has been that individuals' evaluation of the EU depends on the nation-state performance' (Loveless and Rohrschneider 2011). In other words, satisfaction with the performance of national institutions can be used as a proxy to determine the level of support for the EU as the two are considered to be positively correlated. Not everyone agrees with this. Cuenca argues that distrust in the national institutions (especially if national governments are perceived as corrupt) can actually lead to more support for the EU (Sanchez-Cuenca 2000).

While a large number of studies exist analysing the question of European citizens' attitudes towards integration, and more particularly the impact of the economic and financial crisis (Serricchio *et al.* 2013; Hobolt and Wratil 2015), few studies do so with regard to Latin American or Asian regional integration (for an exception see Roberts 2007). The conclusion of the Europe-centred studies is that the economic crisis did not substantially bring economic factors back in as an important source of citizens' attitudes towards integration, although the most pronounced increase in Euroscepticism has taken place in the countries most affected by the crisis. Overall, however, economic explanations alone seem to have limited analytical leverage. If economic and financial crises do not seem to have a strong influence on attitudes towards regional integration, other factors must explain why the level of support remains more or less stable. Linking this result to the institutional density explanations presented above, we therefore argue that the higher the institutional density, the higher citizens' support for increased regional integration in times of economic crisis (more formal and informal cooperation) (H.3.1.).

Even less empirical evidence exists with regard to the influence of regional integration on collective groups, such as civil society organisations during crisis situations. Although interest group studies have reached a new level of visibility in the EU (see Klüver *et al.* 2015), their reaction to crisis situations, whether in EU studies or in comparative regionalism studies is not yet well understood. In line with the hypothesis on citizens' attitudes formulated above, we could argue that economic and financial crises enhance the willingness of civil society organisations to engage in favour of integration (in specific policy fields), if institutional density is high. On the contrary, the less integrated a region is, the less civil society organisations feel inclined to commit to more activism at the regional level. Hence we argue in this context that the stronger the regional integration, the higher the probability that civil society organisations support increased regional integration in times of crises (H.3.2.).

We combine the three ideal-types of regional organisation presented earlier with these hypotheses in Table 1.1.

Table 1.1 Institutional change according to regional integration type

	Power relations among member states	*Institutional density*	*Citizens and collective non-state actors' attitude towards regional integration*
Core regions	+++	+++	+++
Intermediate regions	++–	++–	++–
Peripheral regions	+–	+–	+–

Economic and financial crises in regional organisations: the structure of the book

Several of the economic and financial crises of the end of the twentieth and the beginning of the twenty-first century match the definition of crises based on threat, urgency and surprise.

The 1997 and 2008 periods of financial and economic turmoil impacted on all ASEAN member states. In July 1997, Thailand was the first Asian country to be affected but very fast the crisis spread to other ASEAN members. Panic among lenders led to a large withdrawal of credit from these countries, causing a credit crunch and bankruptcies. In 2008, the global crisis – starting with the US subprime crisis – was transmitted to East Asia through the trade channel, and considerably slowed the growth of East Asian economies.

In Latin America, Brazil was affected by a financial crisis in early 1999, when a devaluation of the currency was decided, followed by another devaluation in 2001. Partially connected with the Brazilian financial crisis, the Argentinean economic crisis in 2001–2002 led to recession, widespread unemployment, the fall of the government, a default on the country's foreign debt and the end of the peso's fixed exchange rate with the US dollar. These two crises as well as the global crisis in 2008 had a serious impact on Latin American regional organisations.

In 2008–2009, following the financial crisis which started in the United States, the European Union and the Eurozone, in particular, were faced with a number of member states – Ireland, Greece, Portugal and Spain, followed later by Italy – which found it difficult to repay or refinance their government debt without the assistance of third parties, and experienced severe difficulty complying with the economic and financial control rules of the so-called Stability and Growth Pact (SGP). Although a group of states were more specifically affected, this crisis has been analysed as a Eurozone crisis.

Three sections of this book deal with the impact of these crises on regional integration. The first section looks at the impact of economic and financial crises on the European Union, a number of its member states and its public opinion. The chapters in the second section focus on crisis-induced change in Latin American regional organisations. The third and final section then concentrates on ASEAN, at the level of institutions and civil society, including the impact of major states not only within but also outside ASEAN (China and Japan in particular).

In the first section dedicated to the European Union, Hanno Degner starts by analysing the EU's institutional reaction to the sovereign debt crisis in the Euro Area 2010–2013 or, in short, the 'Euro Crisis'. The chapter analyses the causal impact of the 'Euro Crisis' on European Integration in the field of EMU institution building. It covers the time period from 11 February 2010, when the Euro Area Heads of State and Government issued their first formal statement on the Greek fiscal crisis, to 15 October 2013, when the ECOFIN Council approved the 'Single Supervisory Mechanism' as the first pillar of the new 'Banking Union' of the Euro Area (Council of the European Union 2013). The measures decided during this period represent a decisive step towards more integration in the field of EMU. The chapter concentrates on the causal mechanisms that link the Euro Crisis to these integration steps. It shows that the European Council and the Council of Ministers as well as the European Central Bank (ECB) have played decisive roles in the process of EMU reform.

Christian Lequesne takes a state-centred approach, questioning whether the power relations between the most powerful member states have changed throughout the crisis. He starts from the classic assumption that, since its origin, EU integration has been based on a compromise between two methods: the intergovernmental method allowing member states to keep their hands on final decisions, and the supranational method through which member states delegate the final decisions to European institutions. Germany has long supported the supranational method more, the UK the intergovernmentalist method and France a combination of the two. The aim of this chapter is to study how the economic and financial crisis influenced these member state attitudes towards European integration. Did France, Germany, the UK and Poland remain close to their initial integration paradigms or, on the contrary, did the crisis lead to a change in the political attitudes of the states, and ultimately to a power shift at the EU level?

Taking a meso-level approach, Axel Hülsemeyer analyses in his chapter how the crisis influenced both Germany's position and its public opinion. The chapter studies the position of the German government throughout the Eurozone crisis from April 2010 (Troika establishment) to March 2014 (legality of ESM). It proceeds in two steps: first, it traces three German policies areas (financial bailouts, parliamentary voting and Eurobonds) through coverage in the two largest German newspapers. It emerges that changes in governmental preferences were highest on bailout conditions and non-existing on Eurobonds. Second, the paper explains these moderate alterations. It holds that the constraining factor on the government is German public opinion – it is stricter than the government itself.

Finally, Céline Belot and Isabelle Guinaudeau analyse how macro-economic performance shapes citizens' support for the EU. Based on a longitudinal approach, necessary to understand the impact of the current crisis on citizens' attitudes, it uses multilevel analyses of Eurobarometer surveys and OECD data on economic performance. The authors argue in their chapter that citizens' support is considered a necessary condition for the deepening of regional integration. This need for legitimacy is increased due to the growing competences of regional institutions, and is particularly palpable in periods of crisis. This is particularly true with regard to economic crises, which challenge the original functions of regional integration and require coordinated responses. Understanding the effect of economic crises on citizens' support therefore appears crucial. Over a period of more than 40 years, citizens have tended to support the European Community less when the economic situation deteriorates. The authors observe a moderating effect of 'socialisation' through the existence of institutional density, as citizens are less prompt to call their support for the EU into question in economic hard times, the longer their country has been a member state; but this result holds only all things being equal. The EU is held increasingly responsible for macro-economic conditions, as it becomes more institutionalised and is delegated a growing number of powers. Public support for the EU may therefore be altered precisely when most acutely needed when cooperation or solidarity among member states is required in order to cope with an economic crisis. Variations over time (from the mid-1980s to today's economic crisis) in each of the EU-15 countries are analysed against the background of several measures of macro-economic performance, while controlling for the impact of classic factors including the national government popularity, the aggregate strength of national identity and EU-related events such as treaty ratifications, referendums or EU presidencies.

In the second section on Latin America, Kevin Parthenay argues in his chapter on institutional change that since the mid-twentieth century, the Central American region has been confronted with crisis situations that have significantly influenced interstate relations. With regard to the recent global economic and financial turmoil, this chapter argues that in the case of Central America, institutional change is not only the result of exogenous shocks but also unanticipated consequences that contribute to characterising change as incremental. Even if external context matters – in terms of financial dependence on international donors – endogenous factors matter too. The weak structure of state authority and legitimacy in the region have often led to transferring more power to supranational actors and helped those actors to strengthen their autonomy. Hence, the complex relations between states, regional institutions and international actors explain the institutional dynamics of Central American integration. Since the revival of regional integration in 1991, and the Tegucigalpa Protocol, informal processes and a counter-intuitive supranational logic that challenge the pervasive thesis of state predominance have guided the institutional dynamic. The product of such a singular process of institutional change has been the 'hybridisation' of the Central American Integration System, that is to say institutional transformation dynamics that emerge from two antagonistic realities (*intergovernmentalism* versus *supranationalism*). In this chapter, based on an in-depth empirical investigation in Central America, Parthenay uses a political sociology of regional integration (Saurugger 2013) in order to analyse institutional change at the regional level.

In the following chapter, Olivier Dabène adopts a more longitudinal approach. Contrary to Europe, where a single process of regional integration has experienced several waves of enlargement, Latin America is characterised by a succession of waves that saw the signing of several agreements launching or reactivating several distinct integration processes. Since the 1950s, Latin America has gone through four waves of regional integration, weaving a complex patchwork quilt. Each wave has been the product of a paradigm shift intersection with a disruptive event. Each entails a change in agendas and policies and some institutional adjustments. The fourth, and to date last, wave of integration has been shaped by a series of responses to crisis situations. Dabène examines this latest wave, focusing on the Union of South American Nations (UNASUR). Dabène considers UNASUR's peculiar 'post-trade' agenda largely as a product of emergency presidential summits convened to address crises, and thus concentrating on the question to what extent the answer to the crisis was driven by the most powerful states in the region. He focuses on three issues: one that was left out of UNASUR's agenda (trade), one that was added (defence) and one that has been there (democracy) since 2000. The chapters shows that trade has been excluded from the agenda mainly because the negotiations for the Free Trade Agreement of the Americas (FTAA) have failed. On the contrary, defence has been included because the U.S. has extended its war on terror to Latin America. Even if Brazil planned to address the issue, the Colombian crisis spill-over in 2008–2009 affected the timing and the content of the project. Finally, democracy was part of the initial priority of the South American summits. Yet, two crises, in Bolivia (2008) and Ecuador (2010), precipitated the adoption of a democracy clause and shaped its substance.

Finally, in her chapter, Clarissa Dri concentrates on a comparison between the 2001 Argentine crisis, which had a considerable political impact on Mercosur, and the 2008 international economic crisis. The 2001 crisis led Mercosur governments to take measures to reinforce integration, such as creating an international secretariat and reforming the dispute settlement system. In 2008, on the contrary, responses to the crisis were mostly national and no important political measures were taken by regional organisations. Dri argues that the attitudes to regionalism throughout time of two important Brazilian political parties can account for this state of affairs. The PSDB (Brazilian Social-Democracy Party) and PT (Workers' Party) have been in power in Brazil since 1994 and represent the traditional left-right divide. Whilst the 2001 crisis contributed to a one-off change in the PSDB's scepticism about Mercosur, the 2008 crisis consolidated the position of a nationalist-left faction within the PT. The chapter analyses these processes by interpreting official documents, press declarations and semi-structured interviews with members of both parties.

A third and last section analyses the influence of financial and economic crises on ASEAN. Here Reuben Wong's chapter questions the principal assumptions about 'crises' and the deleterious effects of crises on regionalism. Wong re-examines the dominant narratives concerning ASEAN's collective responses to the regional crises of 1997 by questioning the assumption of the book's conceptual framework, more precisely whether powerful state actors – in this case, Indonesia – play an instrumental role in influencing institutional change in a crisis situation.

In the case of the 1997 Asian Financial Crisis (AFC), Indonesia's ensuing regime change and democratic transition played a pivotal role in altering human rights dialogue within ASEAN and paved the way for the creation of more institutionalised human rights mechanisms. In contrast, notwithstanding the subsequent establishment of various regional frameworks such as the 1998 Regional Haze Action Plan (RHAP) and the 2003 Haze Agreement, Wong argues, progress in environmental governance has continually been at a glacial pace with Indonesia reluctant to undertake firm action against recalcitrant individuals and errant companies. Whilst there were differing outcomes in the two crises, both crises support the hypothesis that powerful state actors play an instrumental role in influencing institutional change in a crisis situation. On the other hand, ASEAN's ongoing efforts to reinforce institutional density are not yet conclusive.

Shaun Narine takes up this question and studies whether ASEAN has evolved in response to regional crises and uncertainties, and become an agent of regional integration in the aftermath of two major financial/economic crises. Concentrating on both crises – the Asian economic crisis of 1997–1999 and the world financial crisis of 2008 – Narine explains how ASEAN's institutional development in the twenty-first century is directly related to dealing with the consequences of the Asian economic crisis. He argues that ASEAN's efforts to create an ASEAN Community are rooted in a fairly weak sense of regional identity and political cooperation. Thus, the ASEAN Charter, the primary document of the new institutional structure, describes an institution that supports the historical ASEAN norms of respect for sovereignty and non-intervention while encouraging the growth of a more coherent and potentially influential ASEAN.

Kelly Gerard's chapter finally adopts a civil society centred approach. She argues that citizens in Southeast Asia are no strangers to crises – whether financial, economic or political. This chapter more specifically examines the role of the late 1990s crisis on Southeast Asian regionalism, and in particular on civil society advocacy targeting the Association of Southeast Asian Nations (ASEAN). As noted by other contributors to this volume, the crisis not only had far-reaching domestic economic and political consequences, it also had a lasting impact on Southeast Asian regionalism. The Asian economic crisis generated a legitimacy crisis for ASEAN, and sparked a reform process that will culminate with the establishment of the ASEAN Economic Community at the end of 2015. Alongside this market-building agenda, ASEAN member states have also made a series of commitments to reform the institution and make it more 'people-oriented', this being a significant break from ASEAN's historical style of regional diplomacy that saw it characterised as elitist and exclusive.

Drawing from interviews conducted with representatives from Southeast Asian civil society organisations, ASEAN and its member states, this chapter critically engages with the Association's apparent shift to widen its political structures. It demonstrates that the Asian Economic Crisis drove ASEAN's reform agenda and its claims to becoming 'people-oriented', all of which stimulated the interest of civil society organisations which saw it is as an opportunity to shape regional policy according to their objectives. ASEAN's reform agenda encouraged the regionalisation of advocacy as some organisations united to overcome historical divides and develop new regional platforms targeting ASEAN, particularly the Solidarity for Asian People's Advocacy network that has led the management of the annual ASEAN Civil Society Conference. However, enthusiasm for ASEAN's reform agenda quite rapidly waned as a consequence of ASEAN's targeted and predetermined consultations with civil society actors. Charting those channels for civil society actors to contribute to regional policy-making, the chapter argues that ASEAN's apparent drive to develop a more inclusive institution has been directed towards legitimising the development of the ASEAN Economic Community while marginalising dissenting actors.

The conclusion of the book presents an overall model of crisis-induced institutional change for regional organisations, based on the empirical evidence and theoretical results presented in the individual chapters of this book. While all the chapters answer individual questions raised in the introduction and test one or a combination of hypotheses, the conclusion will take a step back and present a systematic comparison between these three regional integration organisations and their reaction to the crises. Its objective is to help us grasp the multiple variables behind the different institutional, member state and public opinion/civil society answers to crisis situations.

Notes

1 We would like to thank Iva Kopraleva for outstanding research support on this chapter.
2 We would like to thank Renaud Dehousse for this suggestion.

References

Acharya, A. (2012). Comparative Regionalism: A Field Whose Time has Come? *The International Spectator: Italian Journal of International Affairs, 47*(1).

Anderson, C. and Reichert, S. (1995). Economic Benefits and Support for Membership in the EU: A Cross-National Analysis, *Journal of Public Policy, 15*(3), 231–249.

Bickerton, C. J., Hodson, D. and Puetter, U. (2014). The New Intergovernmentalism: European Integration in the Post-Maastricht Era. *Journal of Common Market Studies* DOI: 10.1111/jcms.12212.

Boin, A., Hart, P. T., Stern, E. and Sundelius, B. (2005). *The Politics of Crisis Management: Public Leadership Under Pressure*. Cambridge: Cambridge University Press.

Breslin, S. and Higgott, R. (2003). New Regionalism(s) in the Global Political Economy: Conceptual Understanding in Historical Perspective. *Asia Europe Journal, 1*(2), 167–182.

Checkel, J. T. (2007). Social mechanisms and regional cooperation: are Europe and the EU really all that different? In Acharya, A. and Johnston, A. I. (eds.). *Crafting Cooperation. Regional International Institutions in Comparative Perspective.* Cambridge: Cambridge University Press, 221–243.

Duina, F. (2007). *The Social Construction of Free Trade: The European Union, NAFTA, and Mercosur*. Princeton: Princeton University Press.

Etzioni, A. (1965). *Political Unification: A Comparative Study of Leaders and Forces.* New York: Holt, Rinehart and Winston.

Fioramonti, L. (ed.) (2012). *Regions and Crises: New Challenges for Contemporary Regionalisms*. London: Palgrave Macmillan.

Fioramonti, L. (ed.) (2013). *Civil Society and World Regions: How Citizens are Reshaping Regional Governance in Times of Crisis*. Lanham: Lexington Books.

Fligstein, N. (2009). Who are the Europeans and how does this matter for politics? In Checkel, J. T. and Katzenstein, P. J. (eds.). *European identity*. Cambridge: Cambridge University Press.

Gabel, M. (1998a). Economic Integration and Mass Politics: Market Liberalisation and Public Attitudes in the European Union. *American Journal of Political Science, 42*(3), 936–953.

Gabel, M. (1998b). *Interests and Integration – Market Liberalization, Public Opinion and European Union*. Ann Arbor: University of Michigan Press.

Genieys, W. and Hassenteufel, P. (2012). Qui gouverne les politiques publiques? *Gouvernement et action publique*, (2), 89–115.

Haas, E. B. (1958). *The Uniting of Europe*. Stanford, CA: Stanford University Press.

Héritier, A. (2007). *Explaining Institutional Change in Europe*. Oxford: Oxford University Press.

Hermann, C. F. (1969). Some Consequences of Crisis which limit the Viability of Organizations. *Administrative Science Quarterly*, 8, 61–64.

Hettne, B. (2001). Regionalism, Security and Development: A Comparative Perspective. *Comparing Regionalisms: Implications for Global Development*, 1–53.

Hettne, B. (2003). The New Regionalism Revisited. In Soderbaum, F. and Shaw, T. M. (eds.). *Theories of New Regionalism: A Palgrave Reader*. New York: Palgrave Macmillan.

Hooghe, L. and Marks, G. (2005). Calculation, Community and Cues: Public Opinion on European Integration. *European Union Politics, 6*(4), 419–443.

Howlett, M. and Ramesh, M. (2003). *Studying Public Policy: Policy Cycles and Policy Subsystems*. Oxford: Oxford University Press.

Inglehart, Ronald and Rabier, Jacques-René (1978). Economic Uncertainty and European Solidarity: Public Opinion Trends. *Annals of the American Academy of Political and Social Science*, 440, 66–87.

Jabko, N. (2006). *Playing the Market: A Political Strategy for Uniting Europe, 1985–2005*. Ithaca: Cornell University Press.

Katznelson, I. (2003). Periodization and Preferences: Reflections on Purposive Action in Comparative Historical Social Science. *Comparative Historical Analysis in the Social Sciences*, 270–301.

Klüver, H., Braun, C. and Beyers, J. (2015). Legislative Lobbying in Context: Towards a Conceptual Framework of Interest Group Lobbying in the European Union. *Journal of European Public Policy, 22*(4), 447–461.

Kriesi, H., Grande, E., Lachat, R., Dolezal, M., Bornschier, S. and Frey, T. (2008). *West European Politics in the Age of Globalization*. Cambridge: Cambridge University Press.

Lombaerde, P. D. (2011). The Good, the Bad and the Ugly in Comparative Regionalism: A Comment on Sbragia. *Journal of Common Market Studies, 49*(3), 675–681.

Loveless, M. and Rohrschneider, R. (2011). Public Perceptions of the EU as a System of Governance. *Living Reviews in European Governance, 6*(2).

Mahoney, J. (2000). Path Dependence in Historical Sociology. *Theory and Society, 29*(4), 507–548.

Mahoney, J. and Thelen, K. (2010). A theory of gradual institutional change. In Mahoney, J. and Thelen, K. (eds.). *Explaining institutional change: Ambiguity, agency, and power*. Cambridge: Cambridge University Press, 1–37.

Marsh, M. (1999). Policy Performance. In Schmitt, Hermann and Thomassen, Jacques (eds.). *Political Representation and Legitimacy in the European Union*. Oxford: Oxford University Press.

Mattli, W. (1999). *The Logic of Regional Integration: Europe and Beyond.* Cambridge: Cambridge University Press.

McNamara, K. R. (1998). *The Currency of Ideas: Monetary Politics in the European Union*. Cambridge: Cambridge University Press.

Motsamai, D. and Qobo, M. (2012). Regionalism in Africa: Development Crisis and the Growing Influence of Emerging Powers. In Fioramonti, L. (ed.). *Regions and Crises: New Challenges for Contemporary Regionalisms*. London: Palgrave Macmillan, 145–162.

Neumann, I. B. (2003). A Region-Building Approach. In Soderbaum, F. and Shaw, T. M. (eds.). *Theories of New Regionalism: A Palgrave Reader*. New York: Palgrave Macmillan.

Nye, J. S. (1968). *International Regionalism: Readings*. Boston: Little Brown.

Patomäki, H. and Teivainen, T. (2002). Critical Responses to Neoliberal Globalization in the Mercosur Region: Roads Towards Cosmopolitan Democracy? *Review of International Political Economy, 9*(1), 37–71.

Pedersen, T. (2002). Cooperative Hegemony Power, Ideas and Institutions in Regional Integration. *Review of International Studies, 28*(4), 677–696.

Pierson, P. (1993). When Effect Becomes Cause. *World Politics, 45*(4), 595–628.

Pierson, P. (2004). *Politics in time: History, institutions, and social analysis*. Princeton: Princeton University Press.

Roberts, C. B. (2007). Affinity and Trust in Southeast Asia: A Regional Survey. In H. Katsumata, H. and Tan, S. S. (eds.). *People's ASEAN and Governments' ASEAN.* Singapore: Rajaratnam School of International Studies, 84–92.

Sanchez-Cuenca, I. (2000). The Political Basis of Support for European Integration. *European Union Politics, 1*(2), 147–171.

Saurugger, S. (2013). *Theoretical Approaches to European Integration*. Basingstoke: Palgrave Macmillan.

Sbragia, A. (2008). Review Article: Comparative Regionalism: What Might It Be? *Journal of Common Market Studies, 46 (Annual Review)* 29–49.

Schmitter, P. C. (1970). *A Revised Theory of Regional Integration.* Cambridge: Cambridge University Press.

Schulz, M., Söderbaum, F. and Öjendal, J. (eds.) (2001). *Regionalization in a Globalizing World: A Comparative Perspective on Forms, Actors and Processes*. London: Zed Books.

Serricchio, F., Tsakatika, M. and Quaglia, L. (2013). Euroscepticism and the Global Financial Crisis. *JCMS: Journal of Common Market Studies, 51*(1), 51–64.

Soderbaum, F. (2003). Introduction: Theories of New Regionalism. In Soderbaum, F. and Shaw, T. M. (eds.). *Theories of New Regionalism: A Palgrave Reader*. New York: Palgrave Macmillan.

Stacey, J. and Rittberger, B. (2003). Dynamics of formal and informal institutional change in the EU. *Journal of European Public Policy, 10*(6), 858–883.

Strange, S. (1996). *The Retreat of the State. The diffusion of Power in the World Economy*. Cambridge: Cambridge University Press.

Streeck, W. and Thelen, K. (2005). Introduction: Institutional change in advanced political economies. In Streeck, W. and Thelen, K. (eds.). *Beyond continuity: Institutional change in advanced political economies*. Oxford: Oxford University Press.

Telo, M. (2007). *European Union and New Regionalism: Regional Actors and Global Governance in a Post-Hegemonic Era.* 2nd ed. Farnham: Ashgate.

Thelen, K. (2003). Comment les institutions évoluent: perspectives de l'analyse comparative historique. *Annuels*, 13–43.

Toshkov, D. (2011). Public Opinion and Policy Output in the European Union: A Lost Relationship. *European Union Politics, 12*(2), 169–191.

True, J. L., Jones, B. D. and Baumgartner, F. R. (1999). Punctuated-equilibrium theory: Explaining stability and change in American policymaking. *Theories of the policy process*, 97–115.

Waltz, K. N. (1979). *Theory of International Politics*. New York: McGraw-Hill.

Warleigh-Lack, A. (2006). Towards a Conceptual Framework for regionalisation: Bridging 'new regionalism' and 'integration theory'. *Review of International Political Economy, 13*(5), 750–771.

Warleigh-Lack, A. and Rosamond, B. (2010). Across the EU studies – New regionalism frontier: Invitation to a dialogue. *Journal of Common Market Studies, 48*(4), 993–1013.

Warleigh-Lack, A. and Van Langenhove, L. (2010). Rethinking EU studies: the contribution of comparative regionalism. *European Integration, 32*(6), 541–562.

Part I

European integration

2 European integration in response to the 'Euro Crisis' 2010–2013

Hanno Degner

Introduction[1]

Economic crises have often served as catalysts for regional integration (Henning 2013). The most advanced regional integration project, the European Union (EU)[2] (Fioramonti 2012: 3), is no exception in this regard; since its inception in the late 1950s, the EU again and again responded to severe crises with reforms that *deepened* European integration (cf. Kirt 2001: 25ff, Stone Sweet 2004: 236f, Lelieveldt and Princen 2011: 280–282, Kaelble 2012: 131, Schmitter 2012: 39). This corresponds to the vision of EU 'founding father' Jean Monnet (1978: 417): 'I have always believed that Europe will be built through crises, and that it would be the sum of their solutions'.

In line with the general objectives of the edited volume, the present chapter analyses the impact of the recent 'Euro Crisis' on institutional change in the EU. The following research question guides the investigation: *Why and how did the Euro Crisis reinforce the institutional density of the European Union?*

In order to answer this question and test the above-developed institutionalist theoretical framework on regional integration in times of crises,[3] the chapter relies on the method of 'process-tracing' (Beach and Pedersen 2013: 56ff, George and Bennett 2005, Bennett 2010). This allows for an in-depth investigation of the key actors, their preferences, actions and interactions within the context of the EU's political system, while proceeding in a systematic and theory-oriented way. Concerning data, the chapter bases its arguments on 'hard primary sources' (Moravcsik 1998: 82ff) such as official governmental documents and speeches, as well as documents by domestic actors, e.g. press releases. As regards 'soft primary sources' (ibid.), the chapter mainly relies on quality newspaper articles. Beyond that, secondary academic literature will be used as a further data source, as well as for triangulation purposes (cf. Marks 2007).

The chapter argues that institutional change in times of the Euro Crisis was mainly driven by powerful national governments and the respective national preferences they defended. Powerful domestic actors such as parliamentary factions, central banks, well-organised economic interest groups and major banks in turn shaped these national interests. Beyond that, the high density of the EU's institutional structure at the outset of the crisis directly and indirectly turned deeper European integration into the most preferable solution for important domestic actors in the most important EU member states.[4] The adopted legislative acts in response to the crisis combine 'reformist' and 'conservative' types of institutional reforms.

After this introduction, the second section introduces the case of the Euro Crisis and places it in its historical-political context. The third section lines out four major vulnerabilities of EMU that were unveiled by the crisis. The fourth section points out why the Euro Crisis represented a 'window of opportunity' for integration activists and Eurosceptics in the respective member states, and investigates 'national preference formation' on EMU institutional reform in response to the crisis. The subsequent fifth section analyses 'intergovernmental bargaining' on the ultimately adopted policies and shows that the crisis actually reinforced the institutional density of the EU. The sixth section summarises the findings.

The Euro Crisis 2010–2013 and its context

The Euro Crisis represents the most severe economic crisis the EU ever faced (Barroso 2014). It threatened the Union with an unorganised return to national currencies after a potentially chaotic breakdown of the Euro area, and even put the sheer existence of the European integration project into question (Gianviti *et al.* 2010: 7, Schuknecht *et al.* 2011, Chiti *et al.* 2012, Salines *et al.* 2012: 665). Politicians faced great time pressure to respond to this threat, while uncertainty about both the exact causes of the crisis and the consequences of the potential solutions on the negotiation table was high. The Euro Crisis thus fits neatly into the crisis definition developed above (Saurugger and Terpan 2016: 4).

The heated and multifaceted political debate on the Euro Crisis is mirrored in an equally lively – and still ongoing – academic discussion. The impact of the crisis on European integration has been analysed by, for instance, Scharpf (2011, 2013, 2014), Schimmelfennig (2012, 2014, 2015), Chiti and Teixeira (2013), Genschel and Jachtenfuchs (2013), Meunier and Gocaj (2013), and Niemann and Ioannou (2015).

The political context of the Euro Crisis was shaped by the 2007–2009 worldwide financial and economic crisis (Lane 2012: 55ff, cf. also Schelkle 2011), which *did not cause* the Euro Crisis to occur, but provided two important background conditions for its outbreak. These are: (1) a destabilised financial system (Howarth and Quaglia 2013: 342f, Quaglia 2013: 70) and (2) rapidly rising government debt across the EU (Kunstein and Wessels 2011: 311f, Lane 2012: 56). High deficits, particularly in southern EU member states, increasingly alarmed financial market actors who had just suffered enormous material losses of about 5 to 15 billion dollars during the 2007–2009 crisis (Adelson 2013).

The 'Greek Crisis' that unfolded in December 2009 ultimately *triggered* the Euro Crisis. Rapidly rising interest rates for Greek sovereign debt bonds, which mirrored the vanishing trust of financial market actors, pushed the country to the brink of default (Featherstone 2011). With the exception of the Greek prime minister, EU heads of state and government initially regarded the situation of Greece as an 'isolated problem' (Gammelin and Löw 2014: 69f). In view of growing market panic, however, chief executives gathered extraordinarily on 11 February 2010 and adopted a statement (Council 2010a) that emphasised the *European* dimension of the looming crisis for the first time (cf. Gocaj and Meunier 2013: 241, Pisani-Ferry 2013: 115). On that day, the Euro Crisis started.

Institutional deficiencies prevented the timely resolution of the Euro Crisis

As theoretically expected (Saurugger and Terpan 2016: 11), the suddenly unfolding crisis and the threat of an imminent insolvency of Greece and other southern European Euro area member states 'direct[ed] attention to previously unnoticed vulnerabilities' of the EU political system.

First of all, the management of sovereign debt crises was not foreseen as a potential task for the EU (Gocaj and Meunier 2013: 241f, cf. also Merkel 2010c, Barroso 2014). Most notably, the Union lacked an institutional emergency mechanism, which could have provided the necessary fiscal means to restore public finances in Greece and elsewhere after the outbreak of the Euro Crisis. By contrast, when the institutional design of the EMU with the 'Stability and Growth Pact' (SGP) at its core was fixed in the mid-1990s, the so-called 'no-bailout clause' was inscribed into EU primary law (Art. 125.1 TFEU). It explicitly prohibited direct fiscal transfers from EU member states and EU organs to Euro area countries in need; this was thought to effectively deter governments from excessive deficit spending (Heipertz and Verdun 2010: 3ff). The no-bailout clause was moreover combined with the SGP's 'excessive deficit procedure' (Art. 126 TFEU), which threatens member state governments with exuberant deficits with penalties and fines. Widespread concerns (cf. Heipertz and Verdun 2010: 74) on the credibility of this arrangement in an actual crisis situation were ignored. After the outbreak of the Euro Crisis, these concerns turned out to be legitimate, though. In a speech on 1 December 2011, Nicolas Sarkozy (2011) summarised the situation in the following way: 'Le Traité de Maastricht s'est révélé imparfait. Il prévoyait des mécanismes de préventions, mais bien lacunaires, des sanctions, peu appliquées et aucun instrument d'urgence. Nous avons dû tout réinventer, tout reconstruire'.

Second, besides the lack of an institutional emergency mechanism, the crisis revealed the institutional inability of member state governments and EU organs to reduce (or even avoid) macro-economic imbalances in the Euro area. This inability roots in the fundamental asymmetry of EMU: the centralised monetary policy of the independent European Central Bank (ECB) (Art. 127.2 TFEU) is not balanced by a correspondingly centralised 'economic government' or a 'fiscal authority' at the EU level (Schwarzer 2012b: 30, Scharpf 2014: 52–54). This is why, despite the existence of overarching framework policies like the EU's 'Lisbon Strategy' (cf. Borrás and Radaelli 2012), economic coordination in EMU did not take place before the outbreak of the Euro Crisis but in rudimentary forms (Heipertz and Verdun 2010: 78).

Third, EMU provisions generally proved unable to ensure sound public finances. In particular, the SGP's 'excessive deficit procedure' turned out to be ineffective in holding national governments accountable for their fiscal policies (De Grauwe 2008: 333). Consequently, many Euro area member states generally failed to stick to the respective 3 per cent and 60 per cent thresholds for government deficits and overall debt defined by the SGP between 1999 and 2010 (Hallerberg *et al.* 2009: 178).

Finally, the crisis revealed the lack of a harmonised system for financial market supervision in the EU in general and in the Euro area in particular. Despite the existence of a general legislative framework for the EU's single internal market for financial services (Quaglia 2013: 65ff), the supervision of the predominantly *transnational* financial market actors like banks and hedge funds (Schwarzer 2012a: 18) was mainly carried out at the *national* level, following divergent institutional models (Quaglia 2013: 67f). As a result, potential sources of market instabilities, especially cluster risks and overrated bank capital, were overlooked, and the risk of systemic financial crises was not accounted for (Buti and Carnot 2012: 901).

The Euro Crisis as a window of opportunity for integration activists and Eurosceptics

By revealing the four just discussed vulnerabilities, the Euro Crisis triggered a 'change in the shared understanding of effects' (Saurugger and Terpan 2016: 11) of the existing EMU institutions in early 2010. More concretely, the crisis largely discredited the existing system of EU fiscal and economic governance. German Chancellor Merkel (2010c), for instance, called the SGP provisions an 'insane' ('schwachsinniges') instrument for fiscal crisis management, and urged for the revision of both EU treaty provisions and EU secondary legislation (Merkel 2010a). In other words, the crisis instantaneously set institutional change in EMU on the political agenda. Already on 11 February 2010, the heads of state and government of the Euro area expressed their willingness to set up an institutional emergency mechanism for Euro area members in need (Council 2010b) and moreover recognised a need 'to strengthen and complement the existing [legal] framework to ensure fiscal sustainability in the euro zone and enhance its capacity to act in times of crises' (Council 2010b). It can thus be argued that the aim was to achieve institutional change in the sense of 'layering', i.e. the set-up of a new institution, 'conversion', i.e. the remodelling of existing institutions for new purposes, and in case also 'displacement', i.e. the replacement of existing institutions by new ones (Mahoney and Thelen 2010).

The fact that the European Council alone discussed the legislative details of the EU's crisis response in 20 of its 24 meetings between 11 February 2010 and 15 October 2013 underlines the high salience of institutional change in times of the Euro Crisis.[5] Moreover, not less than ten of these meetings were convened extraordinarily or informally. Thus, in line with the above-formulated assumption (Saurugger and Terpan 2016: 5), the Euro Crisis provided integration activists – but also Eurosceptics – in the respective member states with a 'window of opportunity' (Kingdon 1984) to approach their governments with proposals for EMU reforms.

Integration *preferences* on EMU-related policies have always diverged between the domestic actors across the EU (Pisani-Ferry 2006). This became visible once again after the outbreak of the Euro Crisis in February 2010, when the governments of Germany and the UK[6] initially resisted the French proposal of a joint European rescue mechanism for Greece in reaction to pressure by domestic actors.[7] However, repeated warnings from important German domestic actors, especially from the *Bundesbank,* not to break or circumvent the no-bailout clause 'increasingly fell on deaf ears in Berlin' in the following months.[8] The reluctant change in the German government's position was first explained with continuous lobbying efforts from most private German banks, which were heavily invested in Greek sovereigns; the banking sectors of Germany and France together accounted for an exposure of 119 billion dollars to Greece in February 2010. French banks like Crédit Agricole, which owned the Greek bank Emporiki, and Société Générale, which owned the Greek bank Geniki, were in a particularly vulnerable position, but German banks like Commerzbank and Hypo Real Estate also threatened to lose important parts of their capital base in the event of Greek default.[9] This is why German industrial associations feared a renewed credit crunch and the disturbance of the Single Market in case of non-action,[10] and consequently lobbied the German government as well. The large German industrial associations even issued joint press releases with their French, Italian and Spanish counterparts, in which they expressed their common interest in a 'quantum leap' towards more European integration in order to preserve the Euro and the Single Market more generally.[11] This arguably supports hypothesis H2.1, which would expect a positive correlation between institutional density, in this case the already achieved integration in the Single Market and the Euro area, and political entrepreneurship aiming at deeper integration in EMU.

Looking into the process in more detail, *Deutsche Bank* staff met the Greek finance minster in Athens on 4 February 2010, with the aim to develop a joint European rescue scheme for the country. This scheme involved bilateral loans from Germany and France via their national banks *Kreditanstalt für Wiederaufbau* (KfW) and *Caisse de Dépôts* (CDC). *Deutsche Bank* Chairman Josef Ackermann presented the plan to the German Chancellery on 26 February 2010.[12] In the following weeks, the German government – very reluctantly (Hübner 2012) – gave in to the idea of coordinated bilateral loans for Greece, issued *inter alia* by the KfW and the CDC, as they were flanked with a tight fiscal restructuring programme under supranational control (Gocaj and Meunier 2013: 241, Gammelin and Löw 2014: 71–81). Coincidentally, German Finance Minister Schäuble took up a proposal by *Deutsche Bank* chief economist Thomas Mayer (2009) on the development of a permanent intergovernmental 'European Monetary Fund' (EMF), with the support of the CDU/CSU fraction in the German *Bundestag.*[13]

On 9 May 2010, when the Greek Crisis ultimately threatened to spill over to other southern members of the Euro area, the German government finally accepted the creation of an emergency mechanism for the Euro area, the European Financial Stability Facility (EFSF) (Gocaj and Meunier 2013: 243).[14] This institution combined financial aid with comprehensive structural reform programmes and close oversight by the 'Troika', i.e. the Commission, the International Monetary Fund (IMF) and the ECB (Bulmer 2014: 1253f). Chancellor Merkel justified this decision, which *de-facto* circumvented the 'no-bailout clause' of the EU treaties (Art. 125.1 TFEU), with the extremely high material costs of any other political strategy, particularly the prevalence of the status quo and the communisation of national debts via 'Eurobonds' (Merkel 2010d). In fact, she considered the setting up the newly created EFSF, which can be regarded as an incidence of 'layering' (Salines *et al.* 2012: 675), as 'without any alternative' (in German: 'alternativlos') to ensure the stability of the Euro and the entire Euro area.

The fact that a stable majority of Germans (<60 per cent) continuously opposed bailout payments for over-indebted Euro area members (Oppermann 2012: 512, Bechtel *et al.* 2014: 7) illustrates that public opinion arguments cannot explain the changing position of the German government concerning the set-up of an institutional emergency mechanism. A path dependency approach, as expected by hypothesis H2.2. of the theoretical framework, suits the empirical evidence better: on the one hand, the high density of the EU's institutional structures implied high 'sunk costs', which fostered the German government's willingness to preserve the Euro area and take unpopular and materially costly decisions to this end. On the other hand, the high institutional density of the EU political system turned the question of an emergency mechanism into a question of the EU's survival in general: 'If the Euro fails, Europe fails' (Merkel 2010b).

The German government's agreement for the provision of the EFSF with the huge sum of 440 billion Euro 'surprised' the other governments, particularly the French one (Gammelin and Löw 2014: 81f). However, they soon had to realise that the German government was determined to use its role as the largest economy and creditor country in the EU to resolve the other three afore-described problems of European economic governance according to its own preferences; from March 2010 onwards, Germany pushed for EMU reforms that would ensure the implementation of the German idea of a 'stability culture' in the other Euro area member states (Bulmer 2014: 1254). To this end, the German government particularly insisted on improved economic coordination, strengthened fiscal rules and rule enforcement mechanisms, and the set up of a system for supranational banking supervision. As the *Financial Times* summarises it,[15] 'if Germany's original vision of the eurozone – no bailouts, no shared debts and, in some quarters, no Greece – was becoming unachievable, Berlin was going to ensure that shared burdens came with centralised control'.

The German political strategy to reform EMU mirrored the pre-existing proposals the *Bundesbank*, as well as numerous German academics,[16] which had advocated for tougher fiscal surveillance and strict banking supervision since the mid-1990s (Heipertz and Verdun 2004: 776).[17] In that sense, Germany pursued a 'conservative approach' (cf. Saurugger and Terpan 2016: 12) to resolve the other three unveiled problems besides the lack of an emergency mechanism.

As French politicians and domestic actors in the area of economic and fiscal policy generally strived for more political discretion in this regard (Jamet 2011: 9), they tried to cushion the German demand for fiscal and economic rigidity with their concept of a '*gouvernement économque*' (Howarth 2007).[18] This political strategy shared the German desire to deepen EMU, but differed with regard to the terms of integration: supranational ECB monetary policy would be counterbalanced by intergovernmental economic coordination, including fiscal transfers. 'Il faut avancer vers plus d'intégration européenne, tant au plan des politiques économiques, que des mécanismes visant la résolution de la crise actuelle. Une initiative telle que la création d'un marché des Eurobonds irait dans ce sens'.[19] The French approach to EMU reform was thus much more 'reformist' than the German one (cf. Saurugger and Terpan 2016: 11f).

Powerful domestic actors in other southern European member states like Greece, Italy, Portugal, Spain or Belgium supported the French strategy. Given the worse economic situation of their countries in comparison to northern member states like Germany, Austria, the Netherlands or Finland, they shared the French actors' interest for more political coordination with the ECB, the introduction of Eurobonds and less rigid rules for national fiscal policies, in order to sustain their demand-led growth model (cf. Schimmelfennig 2015: 183).

The position of many domestic actors in the UK diverged from this pro-integration stance, though. Important parts of the ruling Conservative party even demanded for the 'repatriation' of competencies to the national level, instead of further European integration in response to the crisis (at least insofar as the UK itself was concerned) (Gamble 2012). Less integration-sceptic actors, particularly banks and other financial market actors of the City of London,[20] by contrast approached their government with proposals for a more integration-friendly course, which aimed at preserving or even enhancing their business opportunities (Levitt 2012: 1275). The British government tried to reconcile these positions by fostering *differentiated integration* (Leuffen *et al.* 2013), i.e. further integration of the Euro area without the participation of the UK. Besides that, the British government distanced itself from the efforts to 'save the Euro' and reform EMU throughout the crisis (Allen 2011: 213). To please the integration-sceptics, Prime Minister Cameron (2010) moreover proposed a bill that turned every future treaty change into a topic for a public referendum in Britain. Later, in view of the continuous pressure of the EU-hostile faction in his party and several defeats of his government in House of Commons votes, most notably on European policy issues (Cowley and Mark 2013, Bennister and Heffernan 2015: 33), Cameron (2013) even announced an in-out-referendum on British EU-membership to be held in 2017 at the latest (Bennister and Heffernan 2015: 30). Yet, the government constantly reiterated its desire to stay an EU member and strengthen the Single Market (Lords 2014: 34–39).

Increasing the EU's institutional density in response to the Euro Crisis

The fact that powerful domestic actors managed to shape the positions of their governments in the subsequent EU level negotiations – and thus indirectly influenced institutional change in response to the Euro Crisis – corroborates hypothesis H1 for the phase of national preference formation. The subsequent paragraphs show that H1 also holds for the phase of intergovernmental bargaining during the Euro Crisis.

The diverging positions of the three most important EU member states on EMU reform and the crisis context actually turned this second phase in a very intense endeavour. *Financial Times* author Peter Spiegel summarises a series of interviews with participants in the following way[21]: 'From mid-level bureaucrats to prime ministers, they tell an unsettling tale of accidents, near misses and seemingly foolhardy brinkmanship'. Yet, as Spiegel continuous, in the end 'the Euro has been saved'.

The most important preparatory negotiations took place in the framework of the 'Van Rompuy Task Force on Economic Governance', an intergovernmental negotiation forum that was installed by the European Council on 25–26 March 2010. Within this forum, the 'Franco-German engine' (Leuffen *et al.* 2012) once again represented 'a privileged, inner negotiation core' (Dyson 2000: 80), like it did in the 1990s when EMU and the Euro were initiated. The German and French governments repeatedly issued joint proposals or statements to pre-structure EU negotiations (cf. Schelkle 2012). Examples include the joint Franco-German letter of 6 May 2010, in which the two governments demanded tighter budget surveillance in the Euro area, 'including more effective sanctions for excessive deficit procedures and strengthening the consistency between national budgetary procedures and the Stability and Growth Pact',[22] and the famous Deauville compromise of 18 October 2010, which *inter alia* included the proposal of quasi-automatic sanctions for member states that run excessive deficits (cf. Hodson 2011: 243f). The fact that Germany and France communicated their Deauville compromise on the very same day as Council President van Rompuy presented the results of his 'Task Force' in Brussels, is a symbol for Franco-German dominance in times of the Euro Crisis.[23]

However, 'despite the Merkozy label applied to early initiatives, Germany has been the predominant partner' (Bulmer 2014: 1255). In detail, macroeconomic coordination in the Euro area and the EU in total was strengthened by parts of the legislative 'Six Pack' on economic governance and the intergovernmental 'Euro Plus Pact' (Buti and Carnot 2012, Schwarzer 2012b), which mirrored in large part the preferred strategies of the *Bundesbank*, the CDU/CSU parliamentary faction in the *Bundestag*, and a majority in the German political and academic community (Mussler 2011: 56). Fiscal surveillance in the EU was tightened by other parts of the Six Pack, the additional legislative 'Two-Pack', as well as the intergovernmental 'Fiscal Compact' (Buti and Carnot 2012, Schwarzer 2012b). All these measures predominantly remodelled the existing

SGP provisions and can thus be regarded as incidents of institutional 'conversion' (cf. Salines *et al.* 2012: 671ff). Finally, the EU decided to set up a 'Banking Union' under the aegis of the ECB. This includes a 'Single Rule Book' for all financial institutions in the EU, a 'Single Supervisory Mechanism', as well as a 'Single Resolution Mechanism' for the restructuring or shutdown of faltering private banks in the Euro area and further participating EU member states (Wyplosz 2012, Goyal *et al.* 2013, Véron 2013). Arguably, these measures predominantly represent incidents of 'layering'. Beyond that, the Single Supervisory Mechanism also partially 'displaced' the pre-existing national financial market supervision authorities.

While Germany could not achieve all its policy goals, for instance the introduction of 'automatic' sanctions under the revised Stability and Growth Pact, the adopted decisions (and also the non-adopted ones, e.g. on Eurobonds, or on more political oversight over the ECB) demonstrate that it played 'both a dominant role and a leadership role' in the EU during the Euro Crisis (Bulmer 2014: 1255). Sociologist Ulrich Beck (2012) even proclaimed the advent of a lasting 'German Europe' (in German: 'Das deutsche Europa'). Correspondingly, The *Guardian* comments in early 2015: 'Like France's weakened president, François Hollande, [UK Prime Minister] Cameron is reduced to reacting to a policy agenda directed not from London, Paris or Brussels, but from Berlin'.[24] In line with H1 of the theoretical framework, the success of the German government in interstate negotiations can be attributed to its great economic power (Bulmer 2014: 1251ff) and to the fact that it represented the main contributor to the emergency mechanisms with 27.1 per cent of all aids (Bulmer 2014: 1255).[25] While France – like Germany and all other Euro area member states – held a veto position in most decisions, this political-institutional power source did only play a subordinate role in the negotiations.

The British government, by contrast, stood at the sidelines of intergovernmental negotiations throughout the Euro Crisis, and repeatedly found itself isolated amongst its partners. Its influence suffered from its exceptionally weak position in the domestic political arena (Bennister and Heffernan 2015: 36). Moreover, it could not make effective use of its *de-jure* veto power: When the British government threatened to veto the Fiscal Compact in order to achieve the repatriation of some competencies in social policy and labour market policy,[26] the Euro area member states did not give in, but rather adopted the Fiscal Compact as an intergovernmental treaty outside the EU's legal framework. At the same time, they offered all non-Euro area member states the opportunity to sign the treaty as well – which all, except the UK and the Czech Republic,[27] actually did (Buti and Carnot 2012, Schwarzer 2012b, Merkel 2011). While this symbolises the UK's weakness in intergovernmental bargaining during the Euro Crisis, it also highlights that the UK's influence on institutional change in response to the Euro Crisis was small, but not completely absent.

Against the backdrop of high urgency, the necessary time to reach consensus on EMU reforms was 'bought' by the ECB. Building on its independence and its monetary policy capacities, the central bank assumed the role of a 'lender of last resort' (cf. Hu 2014) by providing banks with *de-facto* unlimited liquidity, and by engaging in (secondary-market) purchases of sovereign bonds (Torres 2013, Henning 2015). The ECB's willingness to play an active role in the management of the Euro Crisis has become most visible on 26 June 2012, when ECB president Mario Draghi (2012) stated: 'the ECB is ready to do whatever it takes to preserve the euro. And believe me, it will be enough'. This guarantee was subsequently translated in the institutional form of the ECB's 'Outright Monetary Transaction' (OMT) programme in August 2012 (Yiangou *et al.*: 234).

Besides its activities on the financial markets, the ECB also 'engaged in strategic interaction with the governments of the euro area' (Henning 2015: 2, 6ff), in order to ensure that the underlying problems of EMU would actually be resolved by political reforms. Spiegel's interview partners consider German Chancellor Merkel's tacit acceptance of the ECB's institutional 'drift' during the crisis, and particularly her consent to the set-up of the OMT programme, to be:

> a reflection of how deep the crisis had grown that summer. But more importantly, it was the final move of a two-step dance between political leaders and central bankers that was crucial at every important turning point in the crisis.[28]

The Commission, by contrast, did not play an active or even activist role during the Euro Crisis (Schimmelfennig 2012: 407f). In fact, the EU's supranational authority was 'not very visible in early crisis management' (Puetter 2012: 172), and remained 'indecisive and uninspiring' later (Menz and Smith 2013: 202). Dermot Hodson (2013: 312) explains the lack of supranational activism by the Commission with reference to both 'structure' and 'agency'. With regard to the former, the author argues that the Commission did not pursue integrationist initiatives, e.g. the introduction of Eurobonds, for strategic reasons; knowing about the fierce opposition of important member states, most notably Germany, the Commission did not want to invest political capital in a hopeless battle. With regard to the latter, Hodson holds that the centre-right orientation of the Barroso Commission materialised in a preference for defending 'fiscal conservativism and light-touch financial regulation over further integration' (ibid.).

The supranational European Parliament (EP) played a similarly marginal role during the Euro Crisis.[29] This has most prominently been deplored by EP president Martin Schulz (2012): 'More and more decisions are taken without parliamentary involvement. Exceptional circumstances have become the norm'. Scholarly research underlines this point; in times of the Euro Crisis, Richard Bellamy (2013: 3) for instance claims that 'most policy responses … have privileged executive decisions over parliamentary scrutiny, technocratic solutions over democratic accountability'.

Conclusions

The present chapter investigated the EU's response to the Euro Crisis and traced the political process of its formulation between 2010 and 2013. It particularly aimed at answering the question why and how the crisis reinforced the institutional density of the European Union. Thereby, the chapter tested the above-developed institutionalist theoretical framework on regional integration in times of crises.

The empirical findings generally corroborate the theoretical claims. In line with hypothesis H1, institutional change in times of the Euro Crisis was mainly driven by powerful national governments, especially the German, and to a lesser degree, the French one. Powerful domestic actors in turn shaped the national interests; the findings show that integration activists in Germany and France profited the most from the 'window of opportunity' the Euro Crisis opened. Both parts of the 'Franco-German engine of the EU' correspondingly pursued policy change concerning EMU that implied *deeper* European integration, despite divergences on the institutional design of the measures. Due to its inferior bargaining power, the French government had to accept most German demands, especially the reinforcement of economic coordination in EMU, tighter rules for fiscal surveillance, particularly for Euro area members, and the set up of a harmonised system of banking supervision in the Euro area. Yet, France succeeded in realising minor parts of its longstanding ideal of a *gouvernement économique* for the Euro area, most notably the set-up of an institutional emergency mechanism, the EFSF, which later became the ESM. The British government, by contrast, played only a minor role in the negotiations on EMU reform in response to the Euro Crisis and fostered further *differentiated integration* in the Euro area without the UK. With this position, the government tried to reconcile the interests of the Eurosceptic Conservative party and the more integration-friendly stance of the City of London.

In line with hypothesis H2.1, the proposals of powerful German and French domestic actors predominantly implied *deeper* European integration. The findings show that this can plausibly explained with the high institutional density of the Euro area and the EMU at the outset of the crisis, which directly and indirectly turned deeper European integration into the most preferable solution for most actors. British domestic actors by contrast have not been as directly affected as their counterparts on the continent, as the UK does not make part of the Euro area. This is why they rather favoured the prevalence of the status quo or even *less* European integration, at least with regard to the UK, in response to the crisis.

The ultimately adopted legislative acts combine 'reformist' and 'conservative' types of institutional reforms, and moreover corroborate hypothesis H2.2. The EFSF and the ESM are policy innovations in the sense of 'layering'; the same accounts for most parts of the EU's newly established Banking Union. By contrast, most other parts of EMU reform in response to the Euro Crisis represent incidents of institutional 'conversion'.

As the Euro Crisis reinforced European integration to a degree that was 'almost unimaginable' (Barroso 2014) before its outbreak, Monnet's above-cited vision of a Europe that is build through crises has once again become reality. The debate on whether all the adopted measures can effectively prevent similar crises for the future (cf. Streek 2013, De Grauwe and Ji 2014) is far from over, though.

Notes

1 The author wishes to thank the editors of this volume, the participants of the Seventh Pan-European Conference on EU Politics, The Hague, Netherlands, and those of the Doctoral Colloquium of the Department of Politics and Public Administration, University of Konstanz, Germany, for their helpful comments on prior versions of this chapter. Moreover, Dirk Leuffen provided extremely valuable feedback on the author's larger PhD project, on which this chapter largely draws.
2 Being aware of the differences between the European Communities (EC) and the European Union (EU), the latter term is used throughout the manuscript to signify the European polity that was founded in 1957.
3 As hypothesis H3 mainly builds on research investigating the relation between Euroscepticism and the crises that affected the EU from 2008 onwards (cf. Loveless and Rohrschneider 2011, Serrichio *et al.* 2013), the present chapter cannot independently test it.
4 For reasons of space, the analysis of 'national preference formation' and 'intergovernmental bargaining' (Moravcsik 1993) in response to the Euro Crisis mainly focuses on France, Germany and the United Kingdom (UK), the three most important EU member states in both political and economic terms.
5 See the respective European Council Conclusions, online at www.european-council.europa.eu/council-meetings/conclusions.aspx?lang=en (last retrieved 30 September 2014).
6 The *Guardian*, 14 February 2010, online at www.theguardian.com/commentisfree/2010/feb/14/will-hutton-greece-euro?index=1 (last retrieved 15 February 2015).
7 Following calls from domestic economic actors, and in line with the French public opinion (Ifop 2010: 17), the French government pursued the idea of an as-big-as-possible rescue mechanism (possibly also backed by the ECB) from the start and throughout the Euro Crisis. The aim was to convince market actors that the Euro area was both financially able and politically willing to end the crisis. FT, 11 May 2014, online at http://on.ft.com/1skKrhL, and FT, 15 May 2014, online at http://on.ft.com/1t5oiGx (last retrieved 15 February 2015).
8 *FAZ*, 13 March 2010, p. 13.
9 *Wall Street Journal*, 17 February 2010, online at http://on.wsj.com/1nWbEKf (last retrieved 15 February 2015).
10 *FAZ*, 22 March 2010, online at www.faz.net/aktuell/wirtschaft/wirtschaftspolitik/eine-zumutbare-abgabe-koalition-will-banken-an-kosten-der-krise-beteiligen-1957667.html (last retrieved 15 February 2015).
11 See the joint declaration of the German BDI, the French MEDEF and the Italian Confindustria, 8 October 2011, online at www.bdi.eu/download_content/Gemeinsamer_Aufruf_von_BDI_Confindustria_MEDEF.pdf, as well as the joint deceleration of the *BDI, MEDEF, Confindustria*, the Spanish *CEOE* and the German *BDA*, 05.09.2012, online at www.medef.com/fileadmin/www.medef.fr/documents/Declaration_commune/declaration_commune_5sept12.pdf (last retrieved 15 February 2015).
12 *DIE ZEIT*, 26 May 2010, online at www.zeit.de/wirtschaft/2010–05/deutsche-bank-griechenland-rettungsplan (last retrieved 15 February 2015).
13 *FAZ*, 13 March 2010, p. 13.
14 As the threat of a failure of the Euro prevailed in 2011 and 2012, Germany even accepted the transformation of the temporary EFSF into the *permanent* European Stability Mechanism (ESM).
15 *Financial Times*, 15 May 2014, online at http://on.ft.com/1t5oiGx (last retrieved 15 February 2015).
16 *FAZ*, 10 July 2004, p. 13. FAZ, 12 July 2003, p. 13.
17 See the *Bundesbank*'s 'Jahresbericht 1995', online at www.bundesbank.de/Redaktion/DE/Downloads/Veroeffentlichungen/Geschaeftsberichte/1995_geschaeftsbericht.pdf (last retrieved 15 February 2015).

18 *Le Figaro*, 12 February 2010, p. 20, *Le Figaro*, 13 February 2010, p. 21 and *Le Figaro*, 17 February 2010, p. 14.
19 See MEDEF press release, 07 August 2011, online at www.medef.com/medef-corporate/salle-de-presse/communiques-de-presse/communiques-de-presse/categorie/2011/back/108/article/communique-de-presse-4.html (last retrieved 15 February 2015).
20 *FAZ*, 24 August 2013, p. 13.
21 *Financial Times*, 14 May 2014, online at www.ft.com/intl/indepth/how-euro-was-saved (last retrieved 15 February 2015).
22 See the joint Franco-German letter of 06 May 2010 by German Chancellor Angela Merkel and French President Nicolas Sarkozy to European Council President van Rompuy and COM President Barroso, online at www.ambafrance-uk.org/Franco-German-letter-to-EU-Council (last retrieved 15 February 2015).
23 Financial Times, 24 October 2010, online at http://on.ft.com/10lqsIZ (last retrieved 15 February 2015).
24 The *Guardian*, 6 January 2015, online at www.theguardian.com/world/2015/jan/06/angela-merkel-shows-cameron-world-stage-germany (last retrieved 15 February 2015).
25 See also *FAZ*, 3 February 2012, online at www.faz.net/aktuell/wirtschaft/standpunkt-deutsche-haftung-fuer-esm-bleibt-begrenzt-11841525.html (last retrieved 15 February 2015).
26 *Financial Times*, 9 November 2011, online at http://on.ft.com/1wYr2an (last retrieved 15 February 2015).
27 *Financial Times*, 22 September 2013, online at http://on.ft.com/1L3doYT (last retrieved 15 February 2015).
28 *Financial Times*, 14 May 2014, online at www.ft.com/intl/indepth/how-euro-was-saved (last retrieved 15 February 2015).
29 *SZ*, 16 January 2012, p. 3.

References

Adelson, Mark (2013). The Deeper Causes of the Financial Crisis: Mortgages Alone Cannot Explain It. *The Journal of Portfolio Management* 39(3), 16–31.

Allen, David (2011). Die EU-Politik der britischen Koalitionsregierung: Distanz vor Pragmatismus. *integration* 20(3), 197–213.

Barroso, José Manuel Durão (2014). *Valedictory speech by President Barroso.* SPEECH/14/707. European Parliament, 21 October 2014. Brussels: European Commission.

Beach, Derek and Pedersen, Rasmus B. (2013). *Process-Tracing Methods. Foundations and Guidelines.* Ann Arbor: University of Michigan Press.

Bechtel, Michael M., Hainmueller, Jens and Margalit, Yotam (2014). Preferences for International Redistribution: The Divide over the Eurozone Bailouts. *American Journal of Political Science* 58(4), 835–856.

Beck, Ulrich (2012). *Das deutsche Europa.* Berlin: Suhrkamp.

Bellamy, Richard (2013). The Democratic Deficit, Social Justice and the Eurozone Crisis. In Bellamy, Richard and Staiger, Uta (eds.). *The Eurozone Crisis and the Democratic Deficit.* London: UCL Europe Institute, 3–4.

Bennett, Andrew (2010). Process Tracing and Causal Inference. In Brady, Henry E. and Collier, David (eds.). *Rethinking Social Inquiry: Diverse Tools, Shared Standards.* Lanham: Rowman & Littlefield, 207–219.

Bennister, Mark and Heffernan, Richard (2015). The Limits of Prime Ministerial Autonomy: Cameron and the Constraints of Coalition. *Parliamentary Affairs* 68(1), 25–41.

Borrás, Susana and Radaelli, Claudio M. (eds.) (2012). *The Politics of the Lisbon Agenda. Governance Architectures and Domestic Usages of Europe.* Abingdon: Routledge.

Bulmer, Simon J. (2014). Germany and the Eurozone Crisis: Between Hegemony and Domestic Politics. *West European Politics* 37(6), 1244–1263.

Buti, Marco and Carnot, Nicolas (2012). The EMU Debt Crisis: Early Lessons and Reforms. *Journal of Common Market Studies* 50(6), 899–911.

Cameron, David (2010). *Intervention in the debate on the Queen's Speech, House of Commons.* London, 25 May 2010. Accessed 15 February 2015. www.publications.parliament.uk/pa/cm201011/cmhansrd/cm100525/debtext/100525-0003.htm – 10052511000379.

Cameron, David (2013). *EU speech at Bloomberg.* London, 23 January 2013. Accessed 15 February 2015. https://www.gov.uk/government/speeches/eu-speech-at-bloomberg.

Chiti, Edoardo, Menéndez, Augustín José and Teixeira, Pedro Gustavo (eds.) (2012). *The European rescue of the European Union? The existential crisis of the European political project.* Oslo: ARENA.

Chiti, Edoardo and Teixeira, Pedro Gustavo (2013). The Constitutional Implications of the European Responses to the Financial and Public Debt Crisis. *Common Market Law Review* 50(3), 683–708.

Council, European (2010a). *Statement by the Heads of State or Government of the European Union, Brussels, 11.02.2010.* Accessed 15 February 2015. www.consilium.europa.eu/uedocs/cms_data/docs/pressdata/en/ec/112856.pdf.

Council, European (2010b). *Statement of the Heads of State and Government of the Euro Area, Brussels, 11.02.2010.* Accessed 15 February 2015. www.consilium.europa.eu/uedocs/cms_data/docs/pressdata/en/ec/113563.pdf.

Cowley, Philip and Stuart, Mark (2013). *Cambo Chained. Or: Dissension amongst Coalition's Parliamentary Parties, 2012–2013. A Data Handbook.* Accessed 15 February 2015. http://nottspolitics.org/wp-content/uploads/2013/05/Cambo-Chained.pdf. Nottingham: University of Nottingham.

De Grauwe, Paul (2008). On the Need to Renovate the Eurozone. *International Finance* 11(3), 327–333.

De Grauwe, Paul and Ji, Yuemei (2014). *Disappearing government bond spreads in the eurozone – Back to normal?* CEPS Working Document No. 396/May 2014. Brussels: Centre for European Policy Studies.

Draghi, Mario (2012). *Speech by Mario Draghi, President of the European Central Bank at the Global Investment Conference.* London, 26 June 2012. Accessed 15 February 2015. www.ecb.europa.eu/press/key/date/2012/html/sp120726.en.html.

Dyson, Kenneth (2000). *The Politics of the Euro-Zone: Stability or Breakdown?* Oxford: Oxford University Press.

Featherstone, Kevin (2011). The JCMS Annual Lecture: The Greek Sovereign Debt Crisis and EMU: A Failing State in a Skewed Regime. *Journal of Common Market Studies* 49(2), 193–217.

Fioramonti, Lorenzo (2012). Introduction: Regionalism in Times of Crises. In Fioramonti, Lorenzo (ed.). *Regions and Crises. New Challenges for Contemporary Regionalism.* Houndmills: Palgrave Macmillan, 1–10.

Gamble, Andrew (2012). Better Off Out? Britain and Europe. *The Political Quarterly* 83(3), 468–477.

Gammelin, Cerstin and Löw, Raimund (2014). *Europas Strippenzieher. Wer in Brüssel wirklich regiert.* Berlin: Econ.

Genschel, Philipp and Jachtenfuchs, Markus (2013). *Vision vs. Process. An institutionalist account of the Euro-crisis.* Paper presented at the ECPR General Conference, 5–7 September 2013, Bordeaux.

George, Alexander L. and Bennett, Andrew (2005). *Case Studies and Theory Development in the Social Sciences.* Cambridge, MA: MIT Press.

Gianviti, François, Krueger, Anne O., Pisani-Ferry, Jean, Sapir, André and von Hagen, Jürgen (2010). *A European mechanism for sovereign debt crisis resolution: a proposal.* Bruegel Blueprint 10. Brussels: Bruegel.

Gocaj, Ledina and Meunier, Sophie (2013). Time Will Tell: The EFSF, the ESM, and the Euro Crisis. *Journal of European Integration* 35(3), 239–253.

Goyal, Rishi, Brooks, Petya Koeva, Pradhan, Mahmood, Tressel, Thierry, Dell'Ariccia, Giovanni, Leckow, Ross and Pazarbasioglu, Ceyla, IMF Staff Team (2013). *A Banking Union for the Euro Area.* IMF Staff Discussion Note February 2013. Washington DC: International Monetary Fund.

Hallerberg, Mark, Strauch, Rolf R. and von Hagen, Jürgen (2009). *Fiscal Governance in Europe.* Cambridge: Cambridge University Press.

Heipertz, Martin and Verdun, Amy (2004). The dog that would never bite? What we can learn from the origins of the Stability and Growth Pact. *Journal of European Public Policy* 11(5), 765–780.

Heipertz, Martin and Verdun, Amy (2010). *Ruling Europe. The Politics of the Stability and Growth Pact.* Cambridge: Cambridge University Press.

Henning, C. Randall (2013). Economic Crises and Regional Institutions. In Kahler, Miles and Macintyre, Andrew (eds.). *Integrating Regions. Asia in Comparative Context.* Stanford: Stanford University Press, 170–192.

Henning, C. Randall (2015). *The ECB as a Strategic Actor: Central Banking in a Politically Fragmented Monetary Union.* School of International Service Research Paper No. 1/2015. Washington: American University.

Hodson, Dermot (2011). The EU Economy: The Eurozone in 2010. *Journal of Common Market Studies* 49 (Annual Review), 231–249.

Hodson, Dermot (2013). The little engine that wouldn't: supranational entrepreneurship and the Barroso Commission. *Journal of European Integration* 35(3), 301–314.

House of Lords (2014). *Euro area crisis: an update.* House of Lords European Union Committee, Eleventh Report of Session 2013–2014. London: House of Lords.

Howarth, David J. (2007). Making and breaking the rules: French policy on EU 'gouvernement économique'. *Journal of European Public Policy* 14(7), 1061–1078.

Howarth, David J. and Quaglia, Lucia (2013). Banking on Stability: The political economy of new capital requirements in the European Union. *Journal of European Integration* 35(3), 333–346.

Hu, Kun (2014). The Institutional Innovation of the Lender of Last Resort Facility in the Eurozone. *Journal of European Integration* 36, 1–15.

Hübner, Kurt (2012). German crisis management and leadership – from ignorance to procrastination to action. *Asia Europe Journal* 9(2–4), 159–177.

Ifop (2010). *Les Européens face à la crise grecque.* Paris: Fondation pour l'Innovation Politique.

Jamet, Jean-François (2011). EU Economic Governance: The French View. In Jamet, Jean-François, Mussler, Werner and De Corte, Stefaan (eds.). *EU Economic Governance: The French and German Views.* Brussels: Centre for European Studies, 6–42.

Kaelble, Hartmut (2012). Europa in der Krise: Zivilisationskrise – Integrationskrise – Krisenmanagement. In Mergel, Thomas (ed.). *Krisen verstehen. Historische und kulturwissenschaftliche Annäherungen.* Frankfurt/Main: Campus, 131–145.

Kingdon, John W. (1984). *Agendas, Alternatives, And Public Policies.* Boston: Little, Brown.

Kirt, Romain (2001). Europa in der Krise – Leidet der Alte Kontinent am 'Buddenbrook-

Syndrom?' In Kirt, Romain (ed.). *Die Europäische Union und ihre Krisen.* Baden-Baden: Nomos, 17–39.

Kunstein, Tobias and Wolfgang Wessels (2011). Die Europäische Union in der Währungskrise: Eckdaten und Schlüsselereignisse. *integration* 20(4), 308–322.

Lane, Philip R. (2012). The European Sovereign Debt Crisis. *Journal of Economic Perspectives* 26(3), 49–68.

Lelieveldt, Herman and Princen, Sebastiaan (2011). *The Politics of the European Union.* Cambridge: Cambridge University Press.

Leuffen, Dirk, Degner, Hanno and Radtke, Kerstin (2012). Which mechanics drive the 'Franco-German Engine'? An Analysis of How and Why France and Germany Have Managed to Shape Much of Today's EU. *L'Europe en formation* 53(4), 47–83.

Leuffen, Dirk, Rittberger, Berthold and Schimmelfennig, Frank (2013). *Differentiated Integration. Explaining Variation in the European Union.* Basingstoke: Palgrave.

Levitt, Malcolm (2012). The City and EMU. *International Affairs* 88(6), 1261–1275.

Loveless, Matthew and Rohrschneider, Robert (2011). Public perceptions of the EU as a system of governance. *Living Reviews in European Governance* 6(2), 1–38.

Marks, Gary (2007). Introduction: Triangulation and the square-root law. *Electoral Studies* 26(1), 1–10.

Mayer, Thomas (2009). The Case for a European Monetary Fund. *Intereconomics* 44(3), 138–141.

Menz, Georg and Smith, Mitchell P. (2013). Kicking the Can Down the Road to More Europe? Salvaging the Euro and the Future of European Economic Governance. *Journal of European Integration* 35(3), 195–206.

Merkel, Angela (2010a). *Rede anlässlich der Eröffung des 61. Akademischen Jahres des Europakollegs Brügge.* Bruges, 2 November 2010. Accessed 15 February 2015. Translated manuscript online at www.bruessel.diplo.de/contentblob/2959854/Daten/.

Merkel, Angela (2010b). *Rede anlässlich der Verleihung des Internationalen Karlspreises zu Aachen an Donald Tusk, Premierminister von Polen.* Aachen, 13 May 2010. Accessed 15 February 2015. Translated manuscript online at www.aachen.de/de/stadt_buerger/aachen_profil/preise_auszeichnungen/karlspreis/preistraeger/karlspreis2010/reden_kp10/kp10_merkel_dt.pdf.

Merkel, Angela (2010c). *Rede zum Haushaltsgesetz 2010 vor dem Deutschen Bundestag.* Berlin, 17 March 2010. Accessed 15 February 2015. Translated manuscript online at www.bundesregierung.de/Content/DE/Bulletin/2010/03/27-1-bk-bt.html.

Merkel, Angela (2010d). *Regierungserklärung zu den Maßnahmen zur Stabilisierung des Euro vor dem Deutschen Bundestag.* Berlin, 19 May 2010. Accessed 15 February 2015. http://dipbt.bundestag.de/dip21/btp/17/17042.pdf.

Merkel, Angela (2011). *Regierungserklärung von Bundeskanzlerin Dr. Angela Merkel zu den Ergebnissen des Europäischen Rates am 8./9. Dezember 2011 in Brüssel vor dem Deutschen Bundestag.* Berlin, 14 December 2011. Accessed 15 February 2015. Translated manuscript online at www.bundesregierung.de/Content/DE/Bulletin/2011/12/135-1-bk-reg-erkl.html.

Monnet, Jean (1978). *Memoirs.* Garden City: Doubleday.

Moravcsik, Andrew (1993). Preferences and Power in the European Community: A Liberal Intergovernmentalist Approach. *Journal of Common Market Studies* 31(4), 473–524.

Moravcsik, Andrew (1998). *The Choice for Europe. Social Purpose and State Power from Messina to Maastricht.* Ithaca: Cornell University Press.

Mussler, Werner (2011). EU Economic Governance: the German View. In Jamet, Jean-François, Mussler, Werner and De Corte, Stefaan (eds.). *EU Economic Governance: The French and German Views.* Brussels: Centre for European Studies, 43–74.

Niemann, Arne and Ioannou, Demosthenes (2015). European economic integration in times of crisis: a case of neofunctionalism? *Journal of European Public Policy* 22(2), 196–218.

Oppermann, Kai (2012). National Role Conceptions, Domestic Constraints and the New 'Normalcy' in German Foreign Policy: the Eurozone Crisis, Lybia, and Beyond. *German Politics* 21(4), 502–519.

Pisani-Ferry, Jean (2006). Only One Bed for Two Dreams: A Critical Perspective on the Debate over Economic Governance of the Euro Area. *Journal of Common Market Studies* 44(4), 823–844.

Pisani-Ferry, Jean (2013). *La crise de l'Euro et comment nous en sortir.* Paris: Fayard/ Pluriel.

Puetter, Uwe (2012). Europe's deliberative intergovernmentalism: the role of the Council and European Council in EU economic governance. *Journal of European Public Policy* 19(2), 161–178.

Quaglia, Lucia (2013). Is European Union Governance Ready to Deal with the Next Financial Crisis? In Anheier, Helmut K. (ed.). *Governance Challenges and Innovations: Financial and Fiscal Governance.* Oxford: Oxford University Press, 63–87.

Salines, Marion, Glöckler, Gabriel and Truchlewski, Zbigniew (2012). Existential crisis, incremental response: the eurozone's dual institutional evolution 2007–2011. *Journal of European Public Policy* 19(5), 665–681.

Sarkozy, Nicolas (2011). *Discours sur les réponses gouvernementales et européennes face à la crise financière internationale.* Toulon, 1 December 2011. Accessed 15 February 2015. www.lefigaro.fr/politique/le-scan/2014/03/27/25001-20140327ARTFIG00086-le-discours-de-nicolas-sarkozy-a-toulon-en-2011.php.

Saurugger, Sabine and Terpan, Fabien (2016). Introduction. In Saurugger, Sabine and Terpan, Fabien (eds.). *Crisis and Institutional Change in Regional Integration.* ch. 1.

Scharpf, Fritz W. (2011). *Monetary Union, Fiscal Crisis, and the Preemption of Democracy.* MPIfG Discussion Paper 11/11. Köln: Max-Planck-Institut für Gesellschaftsforschung.

Scharpf, Fritz W. (2013). The Costs of Non-Disintegration: The Case of the European Monetary Union. In Eppler, Annegret and Scheller, Henrik (eds.). *Zur Konzeptualisierung europäischer Desintegration. Zug- und Gegenkräfte im europäischen Integrationsprozess.* Baden-Baden: Nomos, 165–184.

Scharpf, Fritz W. (2014). Die Finanzkrise als Krise der ökonomischen und rechtlichen Überintegration. In Franzius, Claudio, Mayer, Franz C. and Neyer, Jürgen (eds.). *Grenzen der europäischen Integration.* Baden-Baden: Nomos, 51–60.

Schelkle, Waltraud (2011). A tale of two crises: the Euro area in 2008/09 and in 2010. *European Political Science* 10(3), 375–383.

Schelkle, Waltraud (2012). Policymaking in Hard Times: French and German Responses to the Eurozone Crisis. In Bermeo, Nancy and Pontusson, Jonas (eds.). *Coping with Crisis. Government Reactions to the Great Recession.* New York: Russell Sage Foundation, 130–161.

Schimmelfennig, Frank (2012). Zwischen Neo- und Postfunktionalismus: Die Integrationstheorien und die Eurokrise. *Politische Vierteljahresschrift* 53(3), 394–413.

Schimmelfennig, Frank (2014). European Integration and the Euro Crisis: The Limits of Postfunctionalism. *Journal of European Integration* 36(3), 321–337.

Schimmelfennig, Frank (2015). Liberal intergovernmentalism and the euro area crisis. *Journal of European Public Policy* 22(2), 177–195.
Schmitter, Philippe C. (2012). European Disintegration? A Way Forward? *Journal of Democracy* 23(4), 39–46.
Schuknecht, Ludger, Moutot, Philippe, Rother, Philipp and Stark, Jürgen (2011). *The Stability and Growth Pact. Crisis and Reform.* Occasional Paper Series No 129/ September 2011. Frankfurt/Main: European Central Bank.
Schulz, Martin (2012). *Speech by EP President Martin Schulz to the European Council of 28 June 2012.* Brussels, 28 June 2012. Accessed 15 February 2015. www.europarl.europa.eu/the-president/en/press/press_release_speeches/speeches/sp-2012/sp-2012-june/pdf/speech-by-ep-president-martin-schulz-to-the-european-council-of-28-june-2012.
Schwarzer, Daniela (2012a). Economic Governance in der Eurozone. *Aus Politik und Zeitgeschichte* 62(4), 17–24.
Schwarzer, Daniela (2012b). The Euro Area Crises, Shifting Power Relations and Institutional Change in the European Union. *Global Policy* 3(S1), 28–41.
Serrichio, Fabio, Tsakatika, Myrto and Quaglia, Lucia (2013). Euroscepticism and the Global Financial Crisis. *Journal of Common Market Studies* 51(1), 51–64.
Stone Sweet, Alec (2004). *The Judicial Construction of Europe.* Oxford: Oxford University Press.
Streek, Wolfgang (2013). Nach der Krise ist in der Krise. Aussichten auf die Innenpolitik des europäischen Binnenmarktstaats. *Leviathan* 41(2), 324–342.
Torres, Francisco (2013). The EMU's Legitimacy and the ECB as a Strategic Political Player in the Crisis Context. *Journal of European Integration* 35(3), 287–300.
Véron, Nicolas (2013). *A Realistic Bridge Towards European Banking Union.* PIIE Policy Brief 17/2013. Washington DC: Peterson Institute for International Economics.
Wyplosz, Charles (2012). Banking union as a crisis-management tool. In Beck, Thorsten (ed.). *Banking Union for Europe. Risks and Challenges.* London: Centre for Economic Policy Research, 19–23.
Yiangou, Jonathan, O'Keeffe, Mícheál and Glöckler, Gabriel (2013). 'Tough Love': How the ECB's Monetary Financing Prohibition Pushes Deeper Euro Area Integration. *Journal of European Integration* 35(3), 223–237.

3 The Eurozone crisis and European integration

'New intergovernmentalism' as a valid theory[1]

Christian Lequesne

Introduction

As a polity, the European Union (EU) grew up since its creation in 1952 through a permanent interaction between two institutional methods: a *Supranational Method*, also called the Community Method, and an interstate method, also called the *Intergovernmental Method*, close from the one characterising diplomacy in the Westphalian international system.

European integration theories have devoted thousands of pages since the 1950s to assess which of the two methods has been dominant in the development of the EU polity. A lot of contributions have been written opposing mainly the neofunctionalist argument, insisting on the dominance of the Supranational Method, to the statist argument, focusing on the primacy of the Intergovernmental Method (Saurugger 2013; Rosamond 2000). Each of the two 'theoretical families' has never been a monolith and has provided its own nuances, according to the authors and to the phenomena they choose to focus on.

In the 1990s, EU scholars became less satisfied with the opposition of neofunctionalism to intergovernmentalism, and developed alternative theories. New approaches, like the multi-governance theory (Hooghe and Marks 2001) or neo-institutionalism (Bulmer 2009), introduced more eclecticism and, by the way, gave often more importance to the empirical dimension of the analysis (Saurugger 2013).

The economic and financial crisis of the EU, whose maximum intensity was reached between 2008 and 2012, reactivated the debates about the respective virtues of theories to understand the EU and the Eurozone (the 19 member states of EU using the currency Euro) as polities (Puetter 2006). It moves the EU again from the study of the policy-making, where it has been very much confined since the 1990s, to the study of the polity-making, where it was located between the 1950s and the 1980s.

The main objective of this chapter is to show, in accordance with the edited volume's conceptual framework, how the economic and financial crisis has produced institutional change in the EU and how this change had impacted the theoretical debate. It is structured in three sections.

In section 1, I will map the main features of supranationalism and intergovernmentalism as institutional methods (and not theories) to demonstrate that, in the long term, the EU polity can be explained as a recurrent balancing act between the two methods.

In section 2, I will show how the economic and financial crisis between 2008 and 2012 has produced change in the power of the EU member states, reinforcing the power of some and decreasing the power of others. The fluctuated power of the member states is one dimension of what Sabine Saurugger and Fabien Terpan name institutional density, conceived as ‘a dynamic concept, implying fluidity and movement’.

In section 3, I will show how the economic and financial crisis forces the EU scholars to reassess their theoretical approaches. The emergence of *de novo* institutions created by the member states to respond and manage the crisis makes the argument of a new intergovernmentalist theory valid. In this case, the substantive intergovernmentalism is not used to describe an institutional method, but is a theoretical account to explain the EU institutional change.

Supranational and intergovernmental methods: a balancing act in the long term

Analyses of the EU as institutional methods (not theories) take rarely into consideration the long period that consists in more than 60 years of historical experience. By method, I mean a process using a particular manner of building institutions. Even the so-called historical institutionalists do not consider much long-term history, when historians of European integration remain often too descriptive and show little interest for conceptualisation. The French political scientist Jean-Louis Quermonne (a lawyer by education) is one of the few institutionalists who have taken into account the long period (what he names *le temps long* in French) to understand the EU institutional methods (Quermonne 2008; see also Goetz and Meyer-Sahling 2009). My argument in this section is, when we precisely consider the long period, the development of the EU (or of the European Community before 1993) does not fit exclusively with the supranational method OR the intergovernmental method, but is a balancing act between both.

The Supranational Method

The Supranational Method, also known in the EU practitioners’ jargon as the *Community Method* (Dehousse 2011), bears on six institutional characteristics and practices.

The EU polity has specific supranational institutions able to assume a certain autonomy vis-à-vis the member states that have created them in signing interstate treaties. The supranational institutions can be run by politicians (like the Commission and the European Parliament), and by experts (like the Court of Justice and the European Central Bank). One important tenet of the Supranational Method is the right of initiative devoted to the Commission in the EU policy cycle. Except on CFSP issues, the Commission has the monopoly of drafting all policy proposals that will be further discussed and adopted by the member states and the European Parliament (Kassim 2013).

In the Supranational Method, the EU polity requires its own parliament separated from the parliaments of the constituent member states. The Supranational Method favours the development of a European Parliament – directly elected by the citizens of the member states – that exercises its proper legislative competences. Between 2009 and 2014, 89 per cent of the EU public policies have been adopted through a so-called co-decision procedure between the European Parliament and the member states (Pittela *et al.* 2014). Co-decision has become the norm of the ordinary legislative procedure in the EU (Ringe 2010).

The Supranational Method does not deny the role of states' representatives (ministers and officials) inside EU institutions: the European Council (heads of state and government), the Council of ministers (ministers) and the Committee of the Permanent Representatives (ambassadors to the EU). However, the Supranational Method tries to bypass the principle of national sovereignty within these institutions in organising decisions through majority and not unanimity rule. With the Supranational Method, the language of negotiations between the member states is the language of the majority. Even if the search for consensus has not disappeared in the practice of the Council of ministers, the majority rule constitutes the main incentive to reach consensus (Naurin and Wallace 2008).

The Supranational Method assumes that the EU – as one level of a multilevel polity – detains its own budget. If the EU budget represents only 1 per cent of the member states' GDP (142 billion euros in 2014), it is not exclusively funded by the member states' contributions but by a series of own resources: customs duties on imports, a levy on the Value Added Tax. As in a federal state, the treaties (equivalent to a constitution) also attribute exclusive policy competences to the central level. These exclusive competences devoted to the EU concern the customs union, the establishing of competition rules, the monetary policy, the conservation of marine biological resources, the common commercial policy and the conclusion of certain international agreements. In these policy areas, the member states have renounced to exercise their own policy competences to the sole benefit of the EU institutions.

With the Supranational Method, the member states agree that the polity produces a specific law – the EU law – accepted as superior to the national laws by the member states and whose compliance is compulsory. A European Court of Justice composed of European judges, like a constitutional or a supreme court in a federal state, is in charge of arbitrating conflicts of competences between the EU law and the national laws (Meeusen 2013). It is also the European Court of Justice that can impose to the member states the implementation of the EU law. Since the Treaty of Maastricht (1993), the European Court of Justice can impose fines to the incumbent states that do not comply with the EU law. The main result of this judicialisation is an EU law much closer in its effects from domestic laws than from international public law (Foster 2014).

Finally, the Supranational Method anticipates the possibility for the polity to add or revise policies from the existing ones. Several procedures exist. One applies just to the internal policies of the EU and consists in revising the competences without convening a specific conference of the member states. On the basis of proposals made by the Commission, the European Parliament and the European Council can agree upon policy changes. A unanimous ratification of the member states is in certain cases required and the treaties call it a 'simplified revision'. The other procedure consists in reforming the treaties after convening a Convention and an Intergovernmental Conference of member states. It is a heavier and longer procedure requiring at the end the ratification of the policy changes by all the member states, according to their respective constitutional practices.

The Intergovernmental Method

Differently from the Supranational Method, the Intergovernmental Method does not rest upon the principle of autonomy of the EU institutions vis-à-vis the constituent member states (Hoffmann 1966). Close from what exists in most of international governmental organisations, the Intergovernmental Method is characterised by five components.

The EU polity is reflecting what the member states are bargaining, because the EU institutions are agents at the service of member states considered as principals (Pollack 2002). The member states have a right of policy initiative at the EU level. In the field of CFSP for instance, the member states and not the EU Commission have the right of initiative.

In the Intergovernmental Method, the legislative power is concentrated in the hands of the institutions composed of member states – the European Council and the EU Council of ministers (Hayes Renshaw and Wallace 2006). Inside those institutions, the power is dominated by the 'big' member states. The policy-making also escapes for a large part any parliamentary power at the EU level.

In the Intergovernmental Method, the decisions agreed by the member states respect the principle of national sovereignty in using unanimity rather than majority voting. Each member state keeps a veto power, as it is the case in policy domains like CFSP, citizenship, enlargement policy, tax policy. It does not mean that there is no deliberative dynamic. As for the supranational institutions, negotiating and bargaining are normal modes of political exchange inside the intergovernmental institutions (Naurin and Wallace, 2008).

In the Intergovernmental Method, there is no compulsory EU law having a direct effect on the national laws. The European Court of Justice has no power to exercise a judiciary control, as it is the case for CFSP and CSDP (Garbagnati-Kebel 2006).

Finally, the Intergovernmental Method does not necessarily require a reform of the EU treaties to add new policy competences to the existing ones. There is a possibility to develop new policies on an ad hoc basis through interstate treaties, as the Prüm Convention on the stepping up of cross-border cooperation, signed in May 2005 between Austria, Belgium, France, Germany, Luxemburg, the Netherlands and Spain and the Treaty on Stability, Governance and Coordination signed in March 2012 by all member states except the Czech Republic and the United Kingdom.[2] In these cases, the policy changes affecting the polity are mainly referring to international public law.

The balancing act

In the long period, the development of the EU polity is a recurrent balancing act between the Supranational Method and the Intergovernmental Method. What scholars name *European integration* is the outcome of permanent interactions between both methods. The resulting polity is a hybrid with no equivalent among domestic and international institutions. It explains why scholars often use periphrases to qualify this polity, as William Wallace when he wrote that the EU was 'more than an international regime and less than a federation' (Wallace 1983). Being a hybrid polity does not mean that this polity cannot be compared to other existing models. There is a huge difference between underlying this hybridisation and stressing the so-called *sui generis* nature of the EU. The latter does not make sense, as all polities can be regarded as *sui generis*.

To demonstrate empirically that the EU polity is a balancing act between the Supranational Method and the Intergovernmental Method, it is useful to look at the policy level. The making of policies in (and not by) the EU since 1952 can all be located in a continuum going from the Supranational Method to the Intergovernmental Method, with regular crossings and overlaps. There is a pole of pure intergovernmentalism represented by the CFSP and the CSDP at one tip of the continuum and a pole of pure supranationalism represented by the exclusive competences of the EU at the other tip.[3]

All the other policy issues are located in between, at a distance that is more or less far from the two poles. It is confirmed by the vast number of 'share competences' that the Treaty on the Functioning of the European Union mentions in its article 4. A 'share competence' is the legal name to describe policy overlaps between the Supranational Method and the Intergovernmental Method.

Four observations can be raised about the effects of the two institutional methods on the EU polity, when we consider long-term period.

First, the EU member states have been more prepared to delegate to the supranational institutions (the centre) the management of their economic interdependence than the management of their security. Interestingly, a comparison with most of the federal states existing in the world shows an opposite trend: the security and defence issues are often central competences when economics is more under the competences of the federated states (Burgess 2006). The difficulty to delegate the security issues is more difficult for military issues, a significant example of failure being the project of the European Defence Community in 1954. It is not at all the same trend for police and immigration issues. Since the Treaty of Amsterdam (1997), the member states have accepted to move immigration, police and control of borders issues, which were ruled by the Intergovernmental Method (the Third Pillar of the Maastricht Treaty) to the supranational pole (Bremberg 2015).

Second, if the Supranational Method applies more to the management of economic issues than security issues, we can observe counter-examples going in the direction of the Intergovernmental Method, as tax harmonisation for example, ruled by unanimity in the Council of ministers. None of the institutional reforms that took place since the Single European Act, in 1986, was able to modify this situation.

Third, the examples of re-nationalisation of EU policies have been rare despite political debates in favour of such an evolution in some member states, like the United Kingdom or the Netherlands. Since the Single European Act (1986), we can find obvious examples of policies that moved from the Intergovernmental Method to the Supranational Method, as the policy on justice and home affairs or some aspects of economic policy (Schimmelfennig 2015a: 3). There are less obvious examples of the opposite movement, except some issues of the Common Agricultural Policy, which moved from exclusive competences to shared competences under the Treaty of Lisbon (Skogstad and Verdun 2010).

Finally, there is a strong influence of the 28 domestic politics of the member states on the pendulum between the Supranational Method and the Intergovernmental Method. For this reason, it is senseless to study EU integration without investing in parallel the domestic politics and the polities of the member states (Bulmer and Lequesne 2013).

If the EU polity can be considered empirically as a balancing act between the two methods, why do theories lose then so much time to demonstrate theoretically the superiority of neofunctionalism on intergovernmentalism or vice-versa? The answer to this question is because theories often focus on periods and policy domains where one method has been more pregnant that the other to explain the development of the EU polity. This is precisely why theories, to move forward, have to avoid catching entirely the Supranational Method or the Intergovernmental Method to explain the development of the EU polity, but have to find new tools to explain the interactions between both, as I will demonstrate in section 3.

The impact of economic crisis on member states' power

In their introduction to this book, Saurugger and Terpan formulate the hypothesis that 'the higher the relative power of actors, the higher the probability that these actors influence institutional change' in regional integration. I will consider this hypothesis in insisting on the causal impact of 'domestic politics' (Bulmer 2015). In the case of the economic and financial crisis of 2008, institutional change is not so much the result of how regional institutions *constraint* member states, but of how member states were able to influence the crisis domestically. To measure the impact of the crisis on what Saurugger and Terpan name 'institutional density', we must absolutely consider the capacity of each member state to cope efficiently or not with the crisis and to influence or not policy decisions. I am deliberately choosing the case of four member states usually classified in the category of the 'big' – Germany, France, Poland and Spain – to demonstrate this causality.

Germany: the empowerment of the 'virtuous' economy

Since the 1990 reunification, Germany is the most populated member state of the EU (82 million inhabitants) and the fourth economy in the world. The costs of the 1990 reunification had negative effects on the macro-economic situation of Germany, which was considered at the end of the 1990s as the 'sick man/economy of Europe'. After ten years of salary restriction and welfare austerity, the country recovered his position in 2010, just after the start of the economic crisis. Simon Bulmer has showed how 'Germany has played a prominent role in advocating solutions to the Eurozone crisis' (Bulmer 2014: 1253). Chancellor Merkel's first diagnostic in 2009 was that Greece had an internal problem and had to follow the EU rules in order to resolve it (Jones 2014). Only in spring 2010 was the recognition by Berlin that the crisis needs a European emergency arrangement, because of the risk of contamination.

> As the scale of the Eurozone crisis became apparent, with rescues afforded to, successively Ireland (autumn 2010), Portugal (spring 2011), Greece again (summer 2011), with the risks of spill-over to Spain and Italy, plus the bailout of Cyprus in 2013, German policy was forced to evolve.
>
> (Bulmer 2014: 1253)

It is during this long second phase that the CDU/CSU – FDP government argues for fiscal discipline and strict conditionality to be imposed on the recipients of the rescue funds. This policy, as we will see in section 3, produces results in inspiring the creation of new institutions at the EU level. France in particular found compromises with Germany but without being able to rebalance the general philosophy of fiscal discipline and conditionality towards less austerity. It was explicit when the right-wing Nicolas Sarkozy was president, but also when the left-wing François Hollande took office after the May 2012 presidential election (Lequesne 2014). If the new socialist President articulated a discourse on the necessity not to forget growth, his government – confronted to a strong public deficit (4.1 per cent in 2010) – was not able to oppose in EU negotiations the fiscal orthodoxy established in Berlin and shared by a certain number of Northern countries like the Netherlands, Denmark and Poland. There is then evidence that Germany – which recovered itself from the slow down of its economy – has played, through its policy actions, both a dominant and a leadership role in the Eurozone crisis. The economic crisis makes Germany the de facto hegemon of Europe not through an explicit political project to dominate Europe, but because of its economic position and the impossibility for the other member states to impose credible and convincing alternatives (Paterson 2011; Lequesne 2015). Considering the necessity raised by Saurugger and Terpan not to limit the analysis of institutional density to governmental decisions, the German position at the EU level was reinforced by the broader concern of German institutions and German public about EU representation and legitimacy.

At the German domestic level, debates about the Greek crisis involved three German institutions which have based their legitimacy on the 1949 Basic Law: first, the German parliament (*Bundestag*) and the Federal Court of Justice (Bundesverfassungsgericht) which have often convergent strategies; and second, the German *Bundesbank*.

In 2009, the Federal Court of Justice of Karlsruhe ruled on the constitutionality of the Lisbon Treaty, 'holding again the Treaty was in conformity with the Basic Law' (Bulmer and Paterson 2013: 1399). In the absence of a European *demos*, the German Federal Court required new legislation to be passed to grant the *Bundestag* appropriate powers before the ratification of the Treaty of Lisbon (Auel and Höing 2014). Similar parliamentary conditionality has arisen from judgements directly inspired by the measures decided at the EU level to cope with the Eurozone crisis: one on the European Financial Stability Facility (in 2011) and the other on the European Stability Mechanism and the Fiscal Compact (September 2012). The European Stability Mechanism, for instance, 'was declared compatible with the German Basic Law, but any increase in its resourcing would have to receive the explicit approval of the Bundestag' (Bulmer and Paterson 2013: 1399). The German *Bundesbank* also plays a role in the German political debate, as the largest shareholder of the European Central Bank and a highly respected institution in the public opinion. The new president appointed in February 2011, Jens Weidmann (Chancellor Merkel's former economic adviser), criticised several times during the crisis the lack of economic convergence in the Eurozone and the necessity to think about the exit of default members, looking particularly at Greece. In July 2012, he opposed publicly the ECB Board of Directors' decision to buy Spanish and Italian bonds to keep interest rates in these countries capped at manageable levels (Linn 2012).

These institutional positions emphasised some reactions among the German public against letting the German taxpayer financing the deficits of the so-called 'badly managed' Southern EU member states. It gave birth in February 2013 to a new political party, *Alternative für Deutschland* (AfD), hunting votes among the electorates of the Chancellor's party CDU and the Liberal party FDP who considered that the Eurozone has become a real burden for the German taxpayer. AfD got 7 per cent of the votes in the European elections of June 2014 and entered four regional parliaments in 2014 and 2015 (Brandenburg, Thüringen, Saxe and Hamburg). It has become a competitor for the German governments, both during the CDU/CSU/FDP coalition (2009–2013) and the CDU/CSU/SPD 'Great Coalition' after 2013.

Both the good state of the German economy and the changing debate about Europe in the German public opinion are variables to understand why the German government was keeping firm on its model of fiscal orthodoxy in EU negotiations. More than ever, Germany appeared to itself but also to the partners the powerful member state able to give the tone to institutional density in the EU (Kundnani 2014; Schimmelfennig 2015b, Lequesne 2015).

France: not wealthy enough to impose an alternative scenario

France is a country that has a long tradition of co-leading the EU with Germany (Krotz and Schild 2013), and, in some policy issues like defence, with the UK. France, a long time defender of Keynesianism in Europe, was not totally resistant to the neoliberal norms that penetrated Europe after the mid 1980s (Jobert 1994, Hall 2012). Parts of the bureaucratic and political elites (both right and left) became convinced that fiscal discipline is a valid argument and that France did not do enough to control its public budget under deficit since 1974. It does not mean that the French elites were suddenly sharing a neoliberal line and that the pro-austerity argument was successful to impose a decrease of the French public deficit, because of strong veto players in the French society (Algan *et al.* 2009).

In the first phase of the economic crisis (2009–2011), President Nicolas Sarkozy assumed the necessity to work in the same direction than the German Chancellor Merkel upon the creation of fiscal rules to make the Eurozone more sustainable. It immediately created in France an opposition to the 'Merkozy' tandem, President Sarkozy being accused of following what Merkel wanted and renouncing to play the established role of an independent leader in the Gaullist tradition (Lequesne 2013). In the perspective of the presidential election of 2012, the Socialist candidate François Hollande understood the political importance for his campaign to distinguish his economic views from the German economic orthodoxy. His discursive claim to give more importance to growth in the EU was mostly an instrument to differentiate himself from 'Merkozy' and to give the impression that France was not just following Berlin. After Hollande succeeded in the May 2012 election, he asked the European Council to adopt in June 2012 a 'European Pact on Growth' but, for the rest, did not renegotiate the Fiscal Compact signed by Sarkozy. The French Parliament ratified the Fiscal Compact with a large majority in October 2012 (Lequesne 2014). There are at least two explanations to that decision. A first explanation is ideological: Hollande chose prime ministers (Jean-Marc Ayrault, and then Manuel Valls) and ministers of finance (Pierre Moscovici, and then Michel Sapin) who belong to the centre-left of the Socialist Party and accept the idea of cuts in the public spending. The second explanation has to do with the relationship between the state of the French domestic economy and the ability of the French government to influence institutional change in the EU. Due to structural difficulties aggravated by the crisis (a decrease of firms' competitiveness and 10 per cent unemployment rate), Hollande's France was not in a position to impose to the EU a credible alternative economic model to the German one. This economic vulnerability has been correlated to a political one: the raise of the far right party Front National that proposed the withdrawal of France from the Eurozone and a return to the French Franc. The National Front got the largest number of seats in the European elections of June 2014, sending 23 deputies to the European Parliament. Due to these weaknesses directly linked to the governance of the economic crisis at the domestic level, France's traditional role of co-leading power in the

EU decreased when Germany imposed itself as the leading power that influences the direction of institutional change in Europe (Fabbrini 2013). This equation resulting from the economic crisis also explains why France decided – under Sarkozy as under Hollande – to adopt a higher profile compared to the rest of the EU (UK included) regarding the foreign and military interventions abroad. These domains are exactly the ones where Germany – due to its history – is not prepared to compete with France (Lequesne 2015). This French strategy of assertiveness in external foreign policy is a form of compensation to the difficulty to influence institutional change in the economic and financial domains.

Poland and Spain: the opposite effects of the crisis on power

Spain and Poland have often been compared as countries of a similar size inside the EU, having both experienced democratic transition and a strong support of their public opinion towards the EU as a way to modernise both their state and society. The differentiated effects of the economic crisis on each country have impacted their respective capacity to influence institutional change.

The Spanish crisis began in 2008. The main cause of Spain's crisis was an enormous housing bubble and the accompanying artificial and unsustainably high GDP growth rate. In 2009, Spain entered officially in recession. The consequences were a strong economic downturn, a severe increase in unemployment and bankruptcies of major companies. The Socialist government of José Luis Zapatero started austerity measures, but did not ask for EU loans in the first years of the crisis. It is only in 2012 that the Conservative government of Mariano Rajoy was unable to bailout its financial sector and had to apply for a €100 billion rescue package provided by the European Stability Mechanism (ESM). Spain felt suddenly in the category of the 'left behind' states of the EU (Garcia Cantalapiedra and Pacheco Pardo 2014). The jump of the unemployment rate (50.7 per cent for those younger than 25 years old in January 2012) forced young people – including qualified ones – to migrate to other EU member states, especially Germany. Movements of undignified people grew up in Madrid and in the main cities of the country, leading to the creation of a new left-wing party *Podemos* opposed to the strong conditionality imposed by the EU institutions. In the EU negotiations, the position of Spain changed from a proactive country supporting all new steps of European integration to one submitted to conditionality from the northern countries, and especially from Germany. The economic crisis has changed the power of Spain, moving from a member state considered virtuous to a member state under EU monitoring. In October 2012, the so-called Troika (European Commission, ECB and IMF) started negotiations with Spain to establish an economic recovery programme in exchange to additional financial loans from the European Stability Mechanism. The effect of the crisis on the decrease of the Spanish power in the EU has been direct. Mariano Rajoy's government implemented the austerity measures but also started in parallel a strategy of nation branding, named *Marca Espana*, to recover a good image abroad, especially among the EU investors.[4] The main objective was that Spain escaped as soon as possible the group of 'thick economies' of the Eurozone to recover a leverage on the EU institutional change (Garcia Cantalapiedra and Pacheco Pardo 2014).

Contrary to Spain, Poland is one of the EU member states that have been the least impacted by the economic and financial crisis in the period 2008–2012. The reasons are both institutional and economic. The institutional factor is the non-participation of Poland to the Eurozone, despite the political commitment of the centre-right government of Donald Tusk to adopt the Euro (Pomorska and Vanhoonacker 2012). Keeping a capacity to play on the devaluation of the zloty was an advantage all over the economic crisis, despite the contradiction with the political objective to join the Eurozone. The economic factor is the cautiousness of the Polish banks vis-à-vis the purchase of toxic assets in the decade preceding the crisis. Contrary to other countries like Ireland, Greece or Spain, the Polish prudential rules were conservative enough to avoid major risks on the foreign financial markets.

The Polish government led by Prime Minister Tusk adopted during the crisis a position on institutional change close from the German one. The Civic Platform (PO), his party, understood that the support to the more powerful member state of the EU was a way to reach a main objective: being recognised as a 'big' member state. In terms of strategy, the discourse of Polish leaders played an instrumental role, especially during the Polish Presidency of 2011 where Poland suffered from being excluded from the Eurogroup negotiations (Lauenroth and von Ondarza 2014). The Polish minister of Foreign Affairs, Radoslaw Sikorski, did not hesitate to repeat publicly that in the face of the economic crisis, Poland was considering itself as 'North European' country, which meant in the camp of the 'responsible' Germany and other member states as the Netherlands and Finland (Jokela 2015). In a discourse in Berlin in November 2011, Sikorski asked for a further strengthening of institutional change in the EU, proposing a merger of the posts of the Presidents of the European Council and the European Commission. He even advocated the direct election of the President by the European demos. Warning that EU was standing at the brink of a disaster, he spoke strongly in favour of active power of its Western neighbour: 'I will probably be the first Polish foreign minister in history to say so, but here it is: I fear German power less than I am beginning to fear German inactivity'.[5] As Pomorska and Vanhoonacker rightly observe:

> The speech was a clear expression of the Polish desire to be part of the European core and also an illustration of how Poland, since its accession in 2004, has increasingly been turning towards the EU rather than the United States, with Germany becoming its major partner.
>
> (Pomorska and Vanhoonacker 2012: 78)

For Poland, the rapprochement with Germany during the economic and financial crisis was an instrument to increase its own power in the EU. This strategy has borne fruit as Poland started to be considered more not simply as a 'new' member state of Central Europe, but as a 'big' member state with a political ambition regarding institutional change. In the French *White book on Defence and National Security* published in 2013, Poland is mentioned as a worthy partner for a future European Defence Policy (Livre blanc sur la défense et la sécurité nationale, 2013). Former President Giscard d'Estaing published in 2014 a book where he suggested a new start for the Eurozone around a limited number of 12 states. The only Central and East European State included in Giscard's list was Poland (Giscard d'Estaing 2014: 127). The rapprochement with the 'earnest' Germany was the political mean that the Polish government used to consolidate this strategy of empowerment, expecting political dividends at the EU level (Kaminska 2014).

This comparative analysis is important to demonstrate how the member states remain main units to be taken into account in the analysis of institutional change in the EU. Understanding the EU polity requires the necessity to open the box of domestic politics and to do in parallel comparative politics (Bulmer and Lequesne 2013). More than ever, understanding institutional change in the EU requires an analysis of 'how problems in domestic preference formation have become standalone inputs into European integration process' (Bickerton *et al.* 2015). It imposes an interest not only for the negotiations taking place in Brussels but also in each member state.

The economic and financial crisis is a good example of how the member states' polities influence their respective capacity to impose institutional change in the EU. Power arises both from a capacity to impose decisions in the intergovernmental game and to present a 'respectful image'. Analysing institutional density in regional integration as the degree to which regional institutions constrain member states in their domestic and international politics is clearly not enough. We must also admit that domestic politics constraints institutional change.

De novo institutions and the theory of new intergovernmentalism

This section is not using the term intergovernmentalism to qualify a method but a theory. The economic and financial crisis has reactivated among EU scholars the project to elaborate 'grand theory' instead of concentrating exclusively on the 'less grandiose issues' of EU policies or EU governance (Bulmer 2015: 289). In this refreshing debate, Bickerton *et al.* bring a solid theoretical argument about what they call new intergovernmentalism defined as a way to explain the 'new phase in European integration' that represents the Post-Maastricht era (Bickerton *et al.* 2015: 3).

Bickerton *et al.* formulate six hypotheses, each of which is related to a particular aspect of the new intergovernmentalism:

1 Deliberation and consensus have become the guiding norms of day-to-day politics;

2 Supranational institutions are not hard wired to seek ever-closer-union;
3 Where delegation occurs, governments and traditional supranational actors support the creation and empowerment of *de novo* institutions;
4 Problems in domestic preference formation have become standalone inputs into European integration process;
5 The differences between high and low politics have become blurred;
6 The EU is in a state of disequilibrium.

Not all six hypotheses have the same explanatory value, as further empirical studies shall demonstrate. Some critics of new intergovernmentalism have emerged in the literature, insisting that the theory is not very new compared to what Stanley Hoffmann and Andrew Moravcsik have analysed in the past under the label of intergovernmentalism or liberal intergovernmentalism (Schimmelfennig 2015a). I do not share this critic for one main reason: Hoffmann and Moravcsik's theories were mainly attempts to refute the influence of the Supranational Method and, then, the validity of neofunctionalism as a theory. With new institutionalism, we are not anymore in this binary opposition, as the theory is reconciling the power of the member states (linked to domestic politics argument) without denying the influence of the supranational method. It is an interesting attempt to theorise the balancing act between the Supranational Method and the Intergovernmental Method.

Schimmelfennig is right when he says that it is useful to take into account the 'policy characteristics' to theorise the balancing act (Schimmelfennig 2015b, 2). Let's take the Economic and Monetary Union (EMU) as an example. EMU is typically a policy resulting from the balancing act between the Supranational Method and the Intergovernmental Method. According to the Treaties, the monetary policy is 'supranationalised' with an independent central bank – the European Central Bank (ECB) – in charge of controlling inflation in the member states' economies. The main rationale behind this policy choice, responding to a strong German demand in the 1990s, was to disconnect the control of inflation from electoral politics (Fabbrini 2013). On the other hand, the macro-economic policies (the 'E' component of EMU) have remained a coordination between the member states using the Intergovernmental Method. Regarding EMU, the Treaty of Lisbon has confirmed the intergovernmental nature of the EU economic policy, in deciding, as Sergio Fabbrini writes, that these policies should be pursued through *soft law*, not *hard law*' (Fabbrini 2013: 1008).

The crisis of 2008–2012 has re-launched, among the EU leaders, a political debate about the *coherence* between a supranational monetary policy and intergovernmental macro-economic policies. It is here that new intergovernmentalism appears very relevant as a theory. The institutional change to move towards more macro-economic coherence has consisted for the member states in creating *de novo* intergovernmental bodies, but with clear links with the existing supranational institutions (Bickerton *et al.* 2015: 11). Three *de novo* institutions have been created by the EU states to respond to the crisis, using intergovernmental agreements rather than a formal reform of the existing EU Treaties: the European Financial Stability Facility (EFSF) in 2010 to assist the member states that were unable to finance their public debt; the European Stability Mechanism (ESM), a permanent structure that replaced the EFSF in 2012; and finally the Fiscal Compact (formally the Treaty on Stability, coordination and governance in the European Union) signed by 25 member states in 2012 to impose fiscal discipline to the national budgets (Verdun 2015).

New intergovernmentalism helps to explain the 'ambivalent relationship between *de novo* institutions' and existing supranational institutions provided by the EU Treaties (Bickerton *et al.* 2011: 11), reinforcing the logic of crossing, overlaps and hybridisation between the Intergovernmental Method and the Supranational Method. Let's take the example of the *Fiscal Compact* to understand this ambivalence. It is formally an intergovernmental treaty between 25 member states to make sure that the national budgets of the Eurozone members remain in balance or in surplus, but not in deficit (the so-called Golden Rule). The Golden Rule, resulting from a purely intergovernmental treaty, shall however work in accordance with join principles proposed by a supranational institution, the EU Commission. In the same vein, according to the *Fiscal Compact*, it is another supranational institution – the European Court of Justice – that can decide financial sanctions against member states that do not respect the Golden Rule (Treaty on Stability, Governance and Coordination 2012). By the way, the *Fiscal Compact* creates for the Court of Justice itself difficulties in the interpretation of EU law. In their Pringle case of 2012, the European judges stated that 'the general principle of effective judicial protection does not preclude the conclusion … of an agreement such as the Treaty establishing the European stability mechanism' between a limited number of EU member states whose currency is the Euro.[6]

The positions of the Heads of State and Government, when they addressed the crisis also support the relevance of new intergovernmentalism as a theory. German Chancellor Merkel, for instance, made her institutional choice clear in the discourse she pronounced in November 2012 at the College of Europe in Bruges. She stated that time has not to be wasted anymore in debates about the benefits of the supranational or intergovernmental methods of integration. For her, the EU can establish intergovernmental frames that give responsibilities to the existing EU supranational institutions. This is what Chancellor Merkel calls the Union Method – in German *die Unionsmethode*.[7] President Sarkozy goes in the same direction when he said, in a speech in Toulon on 2 December 2011, that 'the reform of Europe is not a march towards supranationality … The integration of Europe will go the intergovernmental way because Europe needs to make strategic political choices' (quoted in Fabbrini 2013: 1012). The positions of major EU leaders are useful to investigate more the causality of hybridisation between the Supranational Method and the Intergovernmental Method catched by new intergovernmentalism. Two causal factors can at least be identified. The first has to do with controversial domestic politics on the management of the Eurocrisis, which makes the empowerment of supranational institutions more difficult to present in terms of public justification and legitimacy. This is what we saw in Section 2, in particular about Germany. The second causal factor is the increased requirement, with the economic crisis, of differentiation in negotiation and implementation (Leuffen *et al.* 2012). Concerning negotiation first, only 19 EU member states on 28 are participating to the Eurozone and some of them (like the United Kingdom, Denmark and Sweden) are not interested in a full membership to EMU for reasons of domestic politics. It explains why the UK but also Czech Republic (which was governed by a Eurosceptic majority in 2012) were not interested to negotiate the *Fiscal Compact*. Having an intergovernmental treaty rather than reforming the existing treaties was the mean for the other member states to bypass the reluctance of Prague and London and to get, at the end, a decision (Fabbrini 2013). Regarding implementation, *de novo* institutions also offer some effectiveness to the member states that signed it. To take again the example of the *Fiscal Compact*, contrary to the EU treaties that require ratification of all member states according to their respective constitutional rules, the intergovernmental treaty can enter in force when 50 per cent of the signing member states have ratified it. This derogation to classic EU law shall be analysed as a guarantee for the member states to get effective decisions for the Eurozone.

The creation of *de novo* institutions in the EU to manage the economic and financial crisis demonstrates that EU theories have to avoid reducing the power relationships between member states and supranational institutions to a zero sum game. As Simon Bulmer wrote in a comment to an early draft of this chapter, theory is very often a 'matter of taste'.[8] Considering the theoretical box, new intergovernmentalism seems to be the tastiest tool to explain the effects of the economic and financial crisis on institutional change.

Conclusion

This book is about regional institutional change in periods of economic and financial crises. The EU offers an excellent case study to reflect on this phenomenon as it has experienced between 2009 and 2012 a lot of institutional changes resulting from a difficult economic and financial crisis. As a conclusion, I would like to come back on two questions that Saurugger and Terpan invite us to think about in this volume.

The first is the power relations between the member states and the regional organisation in the different policy domains. A clear conclusion of this chapter is that member states matter and that the capacity of them to resist or, at the opposite, to be deeply affected by the economic and financial crisis has direct influence on their capacity to exercise power in the regional organisation. Germany, as a member state not only 'big' but also able to adapt its economic policies to the crisis influenced the search for solutions at the EU level and increase, by the way, its empowerment at the regional level. We must think more about the causality of what Saurugger and Terpan name institutional density when member states are concerned. Institutional density is not only the degree to which institutions created by regional organisations constraint member states, but also the degree to which domestic politics of the member states constraint regional organisations.

The second question raised by Saurugger and Terpan is the institutional change in the regional integration schemes themselves, both with regard to formal and informal institutions. The economic and financial crisis has confirmed a long-term trend in the building of the EU polity, which is a balancing act between supranational and intergovernmental methods of integration. In this regard, there is always a risk considering too much the relationship between crises and institutional changes in regional organisations as a break. The institutional response to the economic and financial crisis in the EU can only be understood if we replace the angular momentum in a long-term perspective. Crisis does not bring necessarily radical institutional changes but make more visible existing trends, as the balancing act between the Supranational Method and the Intergovernmental Method.

Finally, the economic and financial crisis had an impact on the theoretical debate about regional integration. Regarding the EU, forces EU studies to consider more seriously the EU as a polity and not only a governance or a policy regime, and to reassess the theoretical toolbox. New intergovernmentalism, as developed by Bickerton *et al.*, fits particularly well with the institutional changes during the crisis. It invites the scholar to escape the theoretical trap consisting in searching a theory to validate either the superiority of the Supranational Method or the superiority of the Intergovernmental Method. New intergovernmentalism (as a theory and not a method) offers a good perspective to reflect on the balancing act between the Supranational Method and the Intergovernmental that characterises the EU polity during the crisis and more generally in the long-term perspective.

Notes

1 I would like to thank Simon Bulmer (University of Sheffield), Sergio Fabbrini (University LUISS Rome) and Sabine Saurugger (Sciences Po Grenoble) for their useful comments on the earlier version of the chapter.
2 Czech Republic finally signed the Fiscal Compact in May 2014 after a change of government and majority in Prague.
3 According to article 3 of the Treaty on the Functioning of the European Union, the exclusive competences of the EU concern the following and limited policy issues: customs union; the establishing of the competition rules necessary for the functioning of the internal market; monetary policy for the member states whose currency is the euro; the conservation of marine biological resources under the common fisheries policy; the common commercial policy.
4 www.marcaespana.es.
5 To read Sikorski's discourse in Berlin on 28 November 2011, see www.mfa.gov.pl/resource/33ce6061-ec12-4da1-a145-01e2995c6302:JCR.
6 Pringle Case C-370–12, European Court of Justice, 27 November 2012.
7 Merkel kritisiert EU Parlament und Kommission, *Euractiv*, 2 November 2010.
8 Simon Bulmer's comment, email to the author, 18 May 2015.

References

Algan, Yann, Cahuc, Pierre and Zyberberg, André (2009). *La fabrique de la défiance, et comment s'en sortir?* Paris: Albin Michel.

Auel, Katrin and Höing, Olivier (2014). Parliaments in the Euro-Crisis: Can the Losers of Integration still Fight Back? *Journal of Common Market Studies*, 52/6, 1184–1193.

Bickerton, Christopher, Hodson, Dermot and Puetter, Uwe (2015). The New Intergovernmentalism: European Integration in the Post-Maastricht Era. *Journal of Common Market Studies*. Early View (journal website), 1–20.

Bremberg, Niklas (2015). The European Union as Security Community-Building Institution: Venues, Networks and Cooperative Security Practices. *Journal of Common Market Studies*, 53/3, 674–692.

Bulmer, Simon (2009). Politics in Time meets the politics of time: historical institutionalism and the EU timescape. *Journal of European Public Policy*, 16/2, 307–324.

Bulmer, Simon (2014). Germany and the Eurozone Crisis: Between Hegemony and Domestic Politics. *West European Politics*, 37/6, 1244–1263.

Bulmer, Simon (forthcoming). Understanding the New Intergovernmentalism. Pre- and Post-Masstricht EU Studies. In Bickerton, Christopher, Hodson, Dermot and Puetter, Uwe (eds.). *The New Intergovernmentalism: States and Supranational Actors in the Post Maastricht Era*. Oxford: Oxford University Press, 290–301.

Bulmer, Simon and Lequesne, Christian (eds.) (2013). *The member states of the European Union*. Oxford: Oxford University Press.

Bulmer, Simon and Paterson, William (2013). Germany as the Reluctant Hegemon? Of Economic Strength and Political Constraints. *Journal of European Public Policy*, 20/10, 1387–1405.

Burgess, Michael (2006). *Comparative Federalism: theory and practice*. London: Routledge.

Dehousse, Renaud (ed.) (2011). *The Community Method: obstinate or obsolete?* Basingstoke: Palgrave Macmillan.

Fabbrini, Sergio (2013). Intergovernmentalism and Its Limits: Assessing the European Union's Answer to Euro Crisis. *Comparative Political Studies*, 46/9, 1003–1029.

Foster, Nigel (2014). *EU Law*. Oxford: Oxford University Press.

Garbagnati-Kebel, Maria-Gisela (2006). The jurisdiction of the European Court of Justice in respect of the CFSP. *The International and Comparative Law Quarterly*, 55/1, 77–120.

Garcia Cantalapiedra, David and Pacheco Pardo, Ramon (eds.) (2014). *Contemporary Spanish Foreign Policy*. Abingdon: Routledge.

Giscard d'Estaing, Valéry (2014). *Europa. La dernière chance de l'Europe*. Paris: XOEditions.

Goetz, Klaus and Meyer-Sahling, Jan-Hinrik (2009). Political Time in the EU: dimensions, perspectives and theories. *Journal of European Public Policy*, 16/2, 180–201.

Hall, Peter (2012). The Economics and Politics of the Euro Crisis. *German Politics*, 21/4, 355–371.

Hayes Renshaw, Fiona and Wallace, Helen (2006). *The Council of ministers*. Basingstoke: Palgrave Macmillan.

Hoffman, Stanley (1966). Obstinate or obsolete? The Fate of the Nation-State and the Case of Western Europe. *Daedalus*, 95/3, 862–915.

Hooge, Liesbet and Marks, Gary (2001). *Multilevel Governance and European Integration*. Lanham: Rowman & Littlefield.

Jobert, Bruno (ed.) (1994). *Le tournant néolibéral en Europe: idées et recettes dans les pratiques gouvernementales*. Paris: L'Harmattan.

Jokala, Juha (2015). Finland and the Eurozone Crisis. In Swedish Institute for European Policy Studies, *Same, same but different. The Nordic EU Member States during the Crisis*. Stockholm: SIEPS, 26–49.

Jones, Erik (2014). *The Year the European Crisis ended*. Basingstoke: Palgrave Macmillan.

Kaminska, Joana (2014). *Poland and EU Enlargement. Foreign Policy in Transformation*. Basingstoke, Macmillan.

Kassim, Hussein (2013). *The EU Commission in the twenty-first century*. Oxford: Oxford University Press.

Krasner, Stephen D. (1983). *International Regimes*. Ithaca: Cornell University Press.

Krotz, Ulrich and Schild, Joachim (2013). *Shaping Europe; France, Germany and Embedded Bilateralism from the Elysée Treaty to Twenty-First Century*. Oxford: Oxford University Press.

Kundnani, Hans (2014). *The Paradox of German Power*. London: Hurst.

Lauenroth, Anne and von Ondarza, Nicolai (2014). Playing the service provider, gaining in trust. Institutional Aspects of the Polish Council Presidency. In Karolewski, Ireneusz Pawel, Mehlhausen, Thomas and Sus, Monika (eds.). *Poland's EU Council Presidency. Navigating Europe through Stormy Waters*. Baden Baden: Nomos, 43–66.

Lequesne, Christian (2013). A New Socialist President in the Elysée: Continuity and Change in French EU Politics. *Journal of Common Market Studies*, 51, Annual Review, 1–13.

Lequesne, Christian (2014). La politique extérieure de François Hollande: entre interventionnisme libéral et nécessité européenne. *Sciences Po Grenoble Working Paper*, 23.

Lequesne, Christian (2015). L'Allemagne et la puissance. *Revue d'Allemagne et des Pays de Langue Allemande*, 47/1, 5–13.

Leuffen, Dirk, Rittberger, Berthold and Schimmelfennig, Frank (2012). *Differentiated Europe. Explaining Variations in the European Union*. Basingstoke: Palgrave Macmillan.

Linn, Matthew (2012). Gamble on ECB but only with money you can lose. *Market Watch*, 5 September.

Livre Blanc sur la Sécurité et la Défense Nationale (2013). French Ministry of Defence. Accessed 29 June 2015. http://fr.calameo.com/read/000331627d6f04ea4fe0e.

Meeusen, Johan (2013). *Judging Europe's judges: the legitimacy of the European Court of Justice*. Oxford: Bloomsbury.

Naurin, Daniel and Wallace, Helen (eds.) (2008). *Unveiling the Council of the European Union: games governments play in Brussels*. Basingstoke: Palgrave Macmillan.

Paterson, William (2011). The Reluctant Hegemon? Germany Moves Centre Stage in the European Union. *Journal of Common Market Studies*, 39, Annual Review, 57–75.

Pittela, Gianni, Vidal-Quadras, Alejo and Papastamkos, Georgios (2014). *Activity Report on Codecision and Conciliation 14 July 2009–30 June 2014*, Brussels, European Parliament, DV\1031024EN.doc.

Pollack, Mark (2002). *The engines of European integration: delegation, agency and agenda setting in the European Union*. Oxford: Oxford University Press.

Pomorska, Karolina and Vanhoonacker, Sophie (2012). Poland in the Driving Seat: A Mature Presidency in Turbulent Times. *Journal of Common Market Studies*, 50, Annual Review, 76–84.

Puetter, Uwe (2006). *The Eurogroup: how a selective circle of finance ministers shape European economic governance*. Manchester: Manchester University Press.

Quermonne, Jean-Louis (2008). *L'Union européenne et le temps long*. Paris: Presses de Sciences Po.

Ringe, Niels (2010). *Who decides and how? Preferences, uncertainty and policy choice in the European Parliament*. New York: Oxford University Press.

Rosamond, Ben (2000). *Theories of European Integration.* Basingstoke: Macmillan.

Saurugger, Sabine (2013). *Theoretical approaches to European Integration.* Basingstoke: Palgrave Macmillan.

Schimmelfennig, Frank (2015a). What's new in New Intergovernmentalism? A Critique of Bickerton, Hodson and Puetter. *Journal of Common Market Studies*, Early View (journal website), 1–8.

Schimmelfennig, Frank (2015b). Liberal intergovernmentalism and the euro area crisis, *Journal of European Public Policy*, 22/2, 177–195.

Skogstad, Grace and Verdun, Amy (eds.) (2010). *The Common Agricultural Policy: Policy Dynamics in a Changing Context.* London: Routledge.

Verdun, Amy (2015). A historical institutionalist explanation of the EU's responses to the euro area financial crisis. *Journal of European Public Policy*, 22/2, 219–237.

Wallace, William (1983). Less than a Federation, more than a regime: the Community as a Political System. In Wallace, Helen, Wallace, William and Webb, Carole (eds.). *Policymaking in the European Community.* London: John Wiley and Sons, 403–436.

4 The transformation of Germany's position in the Eurozone crisis

From Greek bailouts to Eurobonds[1]

Axel Hülsemeyer

Introduction

The present Eurozone crisis appears to have divided the member countries within the single currency into three groups: (a) the majority of states uninvolved in the current crisis; (b) the members receiving (or having received) financial aid; and (c) the countries financing the latter. Germany as the largest EU economy[2] is the main contributor in the third group; it has been involved from the outset, as the number of countries asking for financial assistance – to varying degrees and with different amounts of assistance involved – grew from one to five.[3]

As a domestic concern with national lending institutions developed into a sovereign-debt calamity, as well as a broader banking predicament, the German government financially contributed to ailing economies primarily through the inception of Eurozone-wide rescue funds, as well as on occasion with bilateral aid. (Continued access to these resources is based upon stringent criteria related to the size of the public sector and the liberalisation of state regulations – the term 'austerity' has become synonymous for it in public parlance.)[4]

Since the German government is a rare illustration of a Eurozone member state where the *same* chancellor (i.e. the head of government) has presided since the inception of the currency crisis, the question arises whether or not its approach to the crisis has changed over time, despite often intense international pressure to show greater flexibility, but also equally strong countervailing domestic considerations.

The chapter maintains that such a shift has indeed moderately occurred, particularly on the timeframe permitted by debtor member states to implement the financial measures imposed. Germany's stance is generally positive towards further institutionalisation at the EU level, from the launch of the European Stability Mechanism (ESM) to the contours of a Banking Union, to be administered by the European Central Bank (ECB). Conversely, the government (like the other northern European creditor countries such as the Netherlands and Finland) remains firmly opposed to the mutualisation of debt through the issuance of so-called Eurobonds. Note that both of these aspects are captured by hypothesis H2 of the edited volume's Introduction (i.e. the EU's high institutional density leads the German government to continued engagement).

I hold that this temperate transformation of the German government's position can most plausibly be explained by the constraints of domestic public opinion. While some member states, as well as news outlets like the *Economist*, find German leadership in the Eurozone crisis wanting, a large majority of citizens[5] approve of what they regard as the Chancellor's firm position towards debtor countries.

The evolution of the country's position originates in the financial and economic crisis; it would not have occurred in its absence. The ostensible weakening of the single currency has heightened resolve for increased institutionalisation, but only on Germany's (and other creditor countries') terms. In this sense, hypothesis H1 of the book's introductory chapter (i.e. that Germany's prior economic and political power within the EU leads it to influence the Eurozone crisis) can be confirmed, but with a caveat: as domestic public opinion, while in principle pro-European, has grown more hostile to further financial bailouts, the policy commitments of Germany will likely reflect little change.

The structure of the analysis is as follows: before analysing the German government's change through the Eurozone crisis, the crisis itself needs to be identified briefly to demonstrate the extent of Germany's political and financial participation in the crisis, resulting in a typology; this will be completed in the first section. In the second section, I discuss the methodology with which one could possibly identify the causal relationship of domestic public opinion as constraining the German government's stance in the Eurozone crisis over time. The third section is devoted to the empirical aspects of the country's involvement, and section four subsequently deals with the causality. In the conclusion, I summarise the findings and speculate on Germany's future position.

A brief history of the Eurozone crisis

There were two sets of *causes* for the Eurozone crisis: first, the global financial crisis from 2006 until 2008 had begun in the U.S. housing market through the issuance of so-called subprime mortgages. As in the United States, there are also European commercial banks that primarily focus on the mortgage market. These lending institutions, most of them housed in member states of the Eurozone, came under heightened scrutiny, both by credit rating agencies, as well as by the governments.

The second set of causes was European-made, as some governments began to bail out their own commercial banks, beginning in Ireland and cascading through a number of Eurozone countries. Thus, what had arisen as a domestic concern for some Eurozone governments with their own main commercial banks spiralled into a sovereign-debt crisis (i.e. several governments spent more money on bank bailouts than their budget could withstand).[6] This being so – and both Ireland and Spain fell into this predicament – the situation in Greece had a different cause. The trigger here was not the banking sector, but the realisation of the incoming Papandreou government in September 2009 that previous administrations had disguised the level of borrowing.[7] The size of the budget had to be revised to an annual deficit of 12 per cent and an accumulated debt of over 120 per cent. Put differently, the new government already had a sovereign-debt crisis from the beginning.[8]

The *consequence* for countries engulfed in a sovereign-debt crisis (i.e. whether Ireland or Greece) is that the so-called bond yields (i.e. the government financing costs) spread between debtor and creditor member states of the Eurozone. Since governments issue bonds (mostly of a ten-year maturity) in order to raise capital on the financial market, they depend upon these bonds being purchased by investors – equivalent to the concern with stocks dispensed by publicly-traded companies. If a state experiences financial difficulties, bond investors would demand a higher premium to offset their financial risk of, say, buying Greek bonds in the current environment. As a result, a state's borrowing costs go up – bond financing costs of close to 7 per cent are deemed economically unsustainable.[9]

This means that such a country would need access to loans at a cheaper rate than what it can obtain in the financial market in its situation.[10] In April 2010, the Eurogroup (i.e. the finance ministers of the Eurozone members) established the so-called Troika (comprising the ECB, the European Commission and the International Monetary Fund [IMF]) specifically for dispersing bailout money to Greece.[11] Representatives of the Troika negotiated these bailouts, which were tied to specific conditions related, for instance, to the size of the public sector, the size of pensions, the retirement age or the liberalisation of the labour market. The financial aid was given in instalments, each of which was only handed out if the Greek government made agreed-upon progress to implement these conditions.

The German government's financial contribution in the sovereign-debt crisis became clear, given the funding the three kinds of sources established for the various bailouts: first, the European Financial Stabilisation Mechanism (EFSM) is the only one administered by the EU itself, and as such it falls into the responsibility of the Commission, which in turn uses its budget as collateral for borrowing up to €60 bn. Member states participate according to the capital key weightings by the ECB – for Germany, this means a bit more than 27 per cent.[12]

Second, the European Financial Stability Facility (EFSF) is a treaty established outside of the European Union by the Eurozone countries in May 2010 with its headquarters in Luxembourg.[13] The EFSF can issue bonds or other debt instruments on the market with the support of the German Finance Agency[14] to raise the funds for the loans to Eurozone debtor countries. The emission of such bonds is then guaranteed by the Eurozone members again in proportion to their share in the paid-up capital of the ECB.[15] In October 2012, the temporary EFSM and EFSF were rolled into the permanent European Stability Mechanism (ESM), which can raise capital of up to €700 bn – again based upon the ECB-inspired contributions by the Eurozone members.[16] Controversial in Germany was the amount for which the government – and therefore the budget – would have to guarantee loans. The recipient countries (i.e. Ireland; Spain and Portugal) have 30 years to repay their loans – regardless of whether all three have left the bailout in the meantime – and the previous EFSF and the ESM are considered separate for repayment. On this basis, the German finance ministry identified in early August 2013 that German guarantees for the EFSF add up to €211 bn, and for the ESM additional guarantees of up to €190 bn.[17] Table 4.1 depicts a typology of the German institutional and financial links to the Eurozone.[18]

There has been quite some variation among the five countries (Greece; Ireland; Spain; Portugal and Cyprus – which I cover below) that officially had asked for financial assistance through the Troika. Ireland was the first country to leave its bailout programme after three years in December 2013, followed shortly thereafter by Spain (which exited after 1.5 years) in January 2014. Further, Portugal withdrew from its bailout phase in June 2014. This leaves Greece – where the Eurozone crisis began.[19]

Analytically separate – but empirically overlapping – from the sovereign-debt problem is the banking crisis (i.e. commercial banks do not lend, and/or do not have enough funds to lend, to consumers). There are three aspects to it, all of which have implications for the size of the German government's financial contribution. First, the ECB uses its budget to buy in large measure the bonds of countries with a sovereign-debt crisis from the private investors who hold these bonds. Through this, the European Central Bank attempts to reduce the borrowing costs of said governments, i.e. to effectively narrow the bond yields between Eurozone governments.

Second, the Eurozone member states have charged the ECB with implementing and overseeing a new Banking Union – and it is, at the time of writing, in the process of hiring about 1,000 new staff for this very purpose. The ECB's principle role is to apply so-called stress tests on each commercial bank in the Eurozone. These tests could be taking a given bank's balance sheet as the basis to assume, say, a 7 per cent drop in the home country's gross domestic product (GDP). The question then is how long this commercial bank can withstand such a scenario. The purpose of these stress tests is to determine which commercial banks can be saved, and which ones need to be wound down. Apart from such an initial assessment, these banks require continuous monitoring to ascertain that their financial health remains intact.

And third, there are now new rules in place for commercial bank rescues, identified in a liability cascade of six steps, advocated by the ECB: (1) the shareholders of a bank will receive a lower dividend than expected; (2) the creditors of said bank will have to write off a portion of these demands; (3) deposits of over €100,000 are always unsecured; such savers will lose a part of these deposits; (4) each commercial bank will be contributing to so-called national resolution funds, which are drawn upon; (5) the respective Eurozone member state will pay most of money not raised thus far; and (6) only as a last resort will any remainder of the funds come from the ESM (to which Germany contributes about one third).

This new process is labelled as 'bail-in' because the first four stages only concern a given commercial bank itself; only in the last two phases would tax payer's money be used, and even then solely at the domestic level at the beginning.[20]

Methodology

The Eurozone crisis differs from the two other economic crises covered in this volume: unlike the situations in Latin America and in Southeast Asia, the difficulties of the single currency in Europe are ongoing. Consequently, there are no academic sources available. Instead, the sourcing has to rely exclusively on the portrayal in the media (whether print or visual) or the press releases by the governments involved – although the latter are typically of less analytical value.

The dependent variable (DV) is the degree of change of Germany's policy during the 'Eurozone crisis'. The most plausible independent variable (IV) is a shifting domestic public opinion about further German bailout funds and the conditions placed upon them on recipient countries. Thus, a decline in domestic public opinion is then expected to constrain the options of the government to approve further bailout funding.

The timeline for this chapter is a five-year period that begins prior to the first bailout package for Greece, i.e. with the inception of the Troika in April 2010, and it ends in March 2014 with the ruling of the *Bundesverfassungsgericht* (German Constitutional Court) that upheld the legality under the German constitution of the ESM – which itself had been established in October 2012.

The sources through which the DV is traced are the reporting of the two main (in terms of copies sold) daily national newspapers in Germany: the conservative *Frankfurter Allgemeine Zeitung* and the slightly left-of-centre *Süddeutsche Zeitung*. In order to determine whether a given article or news agency report qualifies, I use two closely related means: first, Boolean operators (i.e. *UND/ODER/NICHT* – AND/OR/NOT) enable the connection of the keywords I selected: *Deutschland* (Germany); *Eurozone* (Eurozone); *Rettungsschirm* (EU rescue package, i.e. EFSF and ESM); and *Stabilitätspakt* (stability pact). I have connected these terms in different combinations with the purpose of finding as many relevant articles as possible. Second, the so-called truncation allows enhancing the search by using symbols to replace letters in words.[21] For my purposes, this is useful in cases where either there can be multiple terms (e.g. *deutsch** captures *deutsche* [+ noun] and *Deutschland*) or different spellings of the same keyword exist; this is particularly common in the German language (e.g. *Eurokrise* and *Euro-Krise* through *Euro*Rise*). After this, I then focused the search through content filters available in the newspaper databases (e.g. *Deutsche Haltung zu EWU-Rettungsmaßnahmen* – German position on means to rescue the European Economic Union). I examined these newspaper reports with software packages – one of the more common ones is called WordScores – developed for textual analysis (see e.g. Bei *et al.* 2008; Cardie and Wilkerson 2008; Monroe and Schrodt 2008; Van Atteveldt *et al.* 2008; Krippendorff 2013).[22] Therefore, the two German newspapers are part of the reference section for the entire timeframe, and I cannot mention individual articles throughout the analysis, due to the sheer volume of sources.

The material for the IV comes from the *Politbarometer*, which is conducted typically once a month (on occasion twice a month) by the polling firm

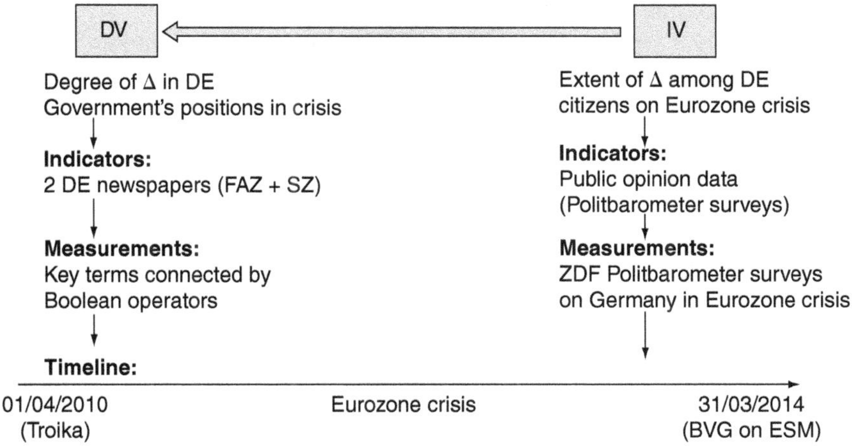

Figure 4.1 Methodology.

Forschungsgruppe Wahlen (Research Group Elections) on behalf of the public broadcaster *ZDF*. These surveys – existing since 1977 – naturally cover a variety of topics. Yet, citizen views on whether or not the German government should contribute to further bailouts, or if Greece can be trusted to meet austerity conditions, are among the questions – depending on the current political and economic topics – polled regularly.[23]

Empirical information: the newspapers

In general terms, the 2009 statistical data showed that almost two-thirds of all German exports still went to the member states of the EU (62.9 per cent), with less having accounted for the country's total imports from the bloc (58.3 per cent). With respect to the Eurozone, the consulting firm McKinsey maintained in January 2012 that Germany has profited from being in the single currency more than other members, with almost half the Eurozone's 2010 growth of 3.6 per cent having fallen on the German economy.[24] These data indicate why the German government continues to be invested in the bloc's, and especially in the Eurozone's, fiscal recovery.

The *German position* is conveyed by three main actors: first and foremost, Chancellor Angela Merkel, who is the only EU leader to have been in power throughout the Eurozone crisis.[25] Second, the Finance Minister Wolfgang Schäuble, who speaks not only on behalf of his ministry and as the most influential member of the Eurozone group of finance ministers, but also through both for the German government.[26] Third, during the second term of Chancellor Merkel, her political party governed with the small pro-business Liberal Party as the junior partner. Its then leader Guido Westerwelle was also the Foreign Minister at the time of the German debate on the first and second Greek bailouts. His position enabled him to be outspoken in this respect.

Thematically, I separate the positions of the German government into the following three categories:

- From Greece to Cyprus: Changing Financial Assistance
- Votes on Eurozone bailouts in the *Bundestag* (German parliament)
- Eurobonds (i.e. the mutualisation of debt among Eurozone countries)

Chronologically, these three sets necessarily overlap. Thus, they only serve an *analytical* purpose in order to show where the German governmental position has changed, when and why – and where it has not done so at all. (This entails the government's ability to garner domestic and/or Eurozone-wide support for its positions.)

From Greece to Cyprus: changing financial assistance

From the time of parliamentary approval of the first Greek bailout package in May 2010 via the altered rules for Cyprus in March 2013 to the quickly silenced debate on a fourth Greek bailout in August 2013, the German government's view softened over the course of this time. At the outset of the first €80 bn Greek package over three years[27] by Eurozone economies – of which Germany contributed €22.4 bn – Angela Merkel had suggested to her Eurozone colleagues to strengthen the so-called 'stability policy' (that stipulates the conditions under which a recipient country faces financial penalties for budgetary non-compliance), even if this meant reopening the Treaty of Lisbon for this purpose. In addition, the time available for recipient countries (in the current case: Greece) to reduce their sovereign debt should be considerably shortened.

When the German parliament began debating approving additional funds, Finance Minister Schäuble suggested that the commercial banks that held Greek state debt must be incorporated into the solution by delaying their claims against the Greek government by seven years.[28] The finance ministry also proposed sending a *Sparkommissar* (loosely a 'savings commissioner') to Athens to monitor compliance by the Greek government, and to be able to directly influence the country's budget. In light of critique by her Eurozone colleagues, Chancellor Merkel scrapped this idea entirely, leading to a first 'softening' of the German position by the end of January 2012.

In May 2012, Foreign Minister Westerwelle warned Greece in the wake of its impending general election that financial aid may be terminated if the new government were to renege on its budgetary consolidation. Doing so would also threaten its membership in the Eurozone. Yet, in October 2012, the German government had reversed its course of making the country's continued belonging to the single currency dependent upon its sustained austerity measures. Instead, Angela Merkel and Mr Schäuble declared in several public engagements that they *unbedingt* (i.e. definitely) wanted to keep Greece in the Eurozone.

By March 2013, the government's attention was briefly taken over by the financial difficulties of Cyprus. The island's woes were of a very different nature from Greece. The Cypriote commercial banking sector was 7.2 times larger than the country's GDP – compared to 3.2 for Germany. The vast majority of customers in its banks were wealthy Russian citizens. Chancellor Merkel announced financial aid, but the approval would be contingent upon first demanding contributions from the respective banks' shareholders, as well as account holders with more than €100,000. However, this new policy of 'bail-in' (i.e. a bailout by the Eurozone is only a last resort) initially became a public relations disaster, as allegedly also small account holders were required to contribute. (This prompted Chancellor Merkel in mid-March 2013 to repeatedly reassure German savers that funds up to €100,000 remain protected anywhere in the EU.)

After this Cypriote intermezzo, the government's focus returned to Greece for two occasions: first, in Angela Merkel maintained in early July that calls by the IMF for a Greek 'haircut' (i.e. creditors writing off part of their demands) were unnecessary, for she was confident that the country's government was by now positioned to service its sovereign debts. Instead, she called for a credible central banking authority that would be able to earn the trust of investors.[29] Second, Wolfgang Schäuble mused in a speech in mid-August that a third bailout programme for Greece would be necessary. Yet, given that the federal election would be in November, Chancellor Merkel denied that any concrete figures were on the table, and that this was only a personal view by the finance minister.

Hence, compared to the strict stance of the German government at the beginning of the first Greek financial package, its position had softened in the sense of becoming less dogmatic over more than three years.

Voting on Bailouts in the Bundestag

Parliamentary voting is not a policy area per se like the bailouts in section 3.1 or Eurobonds in section 3.3. However, I have included it here because it gives a sense of shifting voting – and as a corollary a slightly modified German position – the longer the Eurozone crisis continues, and the more difficult it becomes to explain to domestic voters continued support for ailing member state economies. With altered voting patterns came also particular debates that were unthinkable a few years earlier, as well as the involvement of the German Constitutional Court.

The German constitution requires that the *Bundestag* vote on the disbursement of public funds outside the national territory – in this case to other Eurozone members.[30] The government naturally has a majority in parliament, but an important public measurement is the so-called *Kanzlermehrheit* (i.e. chancellor's majority), which means the absolute majority of all eligible members. It is an indication of whether or not the chancellor commands his/her own coalition. Beyond this, matters related to the EU typically have broad support among political parties of otherwise different persuasions. Thus, even on domestically controversial continued German bailout contributions, the German government always aims for wide *Bundestag* support.

The initial test of this arose in May 2010 with the guarantee of €22.4 bn for the first Greek rescue package. Given that the ruling coalition of Christian Democrats and Liberals was joined by the opposition Greens, as well as by the Left Party (made up partly by members of the former GDR socialists), a comfortable passing of the bailout credit was already beyond doubt. An effort by Chancellor Merkel to win the support of the main opposition, the Social Democrats (SPD), ultimately failed on the precise language used to have the financial markets contribute to the fallout of the crisis. The latter demanded a *Transaktionssteuer* (i.e. a tax on all banking transactions), which in turn was unacceptable to the pro-business Liberal Party. Ultimately, the SPD resolved to simply abstain from the vote.

The second parliamentary vote took place only 1.5 years later in September 2011. The issue was the extension of the German liability to the main bailout mechanism at the time, the EFSF to €211 bn – up from the previous €123 bn. Since the main opposition of Social Democrats and Greens had signalled their support early on, the passage of the increase was never in doubt. However, thus far, not a single Euro had been called in by the then ailing economies – among them Ireland, Portugal, and of course Greece.[31]

At the end of February 2012, the governing coalition for the first time missed the chancellor's majority in a European vote, in this case on new funding for Greece. Since the majority of the opposition of Social Democrats and Greens again voted in favour, the passing was ensured; however, the political signal of Mrs Merkel failing to keep her coalition in line here was not lost on the opposition.

Against the backdrop of the financial woes across several southern European countries, the German parliament agreed in June 2012 on an *EU-Fiskalpakt* (i.e. an EU fiscal compact). The idea was to ask Chancellor Merkel to press for a European rule on the maximum deficit any member state could budget, since Germany already had such a limit enshrined by law.[32] Yet, in December 2012, an altered Greek loan programme came before the *Bundestag*. The interest rate the country had to pay was lowered and the timeline for repayment was extended. The parliamentary debate circled around the additional €130 bn the adjusted programme was envisaged to cost the German budget in the worst-case scenario (i.e. if Greece were unable or politically unwilling – after an election – to service its debt). Although the programme passed with 473 votes, the ruling coalition had not accomplished the *Kanzlermehrheit* again, this time by a larger margin (only 297 members in favour of its total of 311 MPs).

The concern with Greece was replaced in the first half of 2013 by the financial difficulties of Cyprus. Since the island accounts for merely 0.3 per cent of the EU's GNP, a number of parliamentarians held that the country does not deserve German loan guarantees. However, the Constitutional Court denied such a claim in April 2013, and allowed the aid package to go ahead. Immediately thereafter, the *Bundestag* approved the €10 bn aid package for Cyprus with 487 votes (i.e. with a majority of opposition Social Democrats and Greens in favour – despite the impending national election in September 2013).

However, the manner in which financial aid to ailing banks is henceforth dispensed had changed markedly with the Cypriot case; with account holders over €100,000, as well as the shareholders being first in line (see the detailed explanation of this cascading approach above).

Eurobonds: mutualising Eurozone debt

This is the aspect of German Eurozone policy in which its position has staunchly remained the same throughout (i.e. in the roughly 1.5 years between late-2010, when the 'Eurobonds' first arose as a topic for discussion, until mid-2012, when the government refused to have any further debate on the topic). Chancellor Merkel's and Finance Minister Schäuble's argumentation against Eurobonds is twofold.

First, *substantively*, they insist that the mutualisation of debt among Eurozone countries would make mediocre performance effectively the norm. The mutualisation of debt, favoured by Italy's then Prime Minister Monti, would thereby also raise the borrowing costs in the creditor countries. Particularly in Germany as the largest of the latter, higher interest rates for its economy and limiting its creditworthiness was unacceptable to the government. Instead, Merkel and Schäuble proposed that the initial monetary union was not sufficient, and that it needed to be supported by a *Stabilitätsunion* that gave the Union the final say over fiscal and budgetary policy in the member states.[33] *This* was in their view (and to which the Dutch or the Finnish could not have agreed more) the real problem; thus, Eurobonds could be at the very *end* of the process, but most definitely not at the beginning, since the latter would merely remove all urgency for ailing member state economies to make structural reforms and to impose budget control.

The second argument by the German government against Eurobonds was *legal*. Their issuance would not only contravene the Treaty of Lisbon, which would have to be reopened. Importantly, it would also necessitate an alteration of the member states' constitutions. The *Bundesverfassungsgericht* had made it clear in its ruling on the constitutionality of the German contribution to the ESM that any further transfer of the country's competences to the EU (such as constructing Eurobonds) would demand changing its constitution.

Domestic public opinion: causality?

The plausibility of German public opinion demonstrably constraining the ability of the government to take a tough stance on bailout funding and the conditions for it would presume a direction of 'cueing'. Rather than the government leading public opinion through explanation and actions, public opinion itself can serve as a 'scapegoat' for the government.

For reasons of analytical consistence, I organise the information on domestic public opinion in a similar *thematic* fashion as the newspaper information on the DV. Thus, I separate the following three categories:

- Domestic views on Greek bailouts
- Citizen opinions on the German government in the Eurozone crisis
- German polling on introducing Eurobonds

Equally as in Part III, I recognise that these classifications naturally overlap historically.

Domestic views on bailouts

Since days before this chapter's official timeline, the *Politbarometer* polling shows that the German public was consistently against apportioning additional funding to highly indebted Eurozone countries in general, and to Greece in particular. Not surprisingly, the same holds true for any loosening of the agreed upon austerity conditions. Depending on the concrete topic, majorities remained throughout between about two-thirds and roughly four-fifths of the citizenry.

On 26 March 2010, 68 per cent of Germans were opposed to financial aid for Greece with German credit (with 29 per cent in favour). On 17 December 2010, this sentiment was extended by 62 per cent to all highly indebted member states (with 32 per cent in favour). On 28 January 2011, 64 per cent were opposed to contributing to indebted Eurozone countries by extending the EFSF (29 per cent in favour). On 10 June 2011, additional loan guarantees for Greece was opposed by 60 per cent (with 33 per cent in favour). On 9 September 2011 (i.e. ahead of a vote by the *Bundestag* to increase the EFSF later that month), 76 per cent were against this scheme – and thereby an increase of the German loan guarantees to €211 bn (with only 18 per cent in favour). On 27 January 2012, 73 per cent opposed additional funds for the EFSF – for which Germany because of its economic size would have to shoulder the largest amount (only 21 per cent were in favour).

As the Troika was negotiating in Athens, on 10 February 2012, two-thirds (66 per cent) doubted Greece's will to save and restructure (with 27 per cent believing in the country's genuine attempt). Yet, 62 per cent expected negative repercussions for the German economy, should Greece default on its loans (with 18 per cent having anticipated a positive effect). Following a Greek election, the *Politbarometer* published a special issue on 18 June 2012; in it 54 per cent were against allowing Greece more time to repay its loans (but 37 per cent were in favour). However, Greek attempts to also negotiate an easing of its austerity terms were opposed by 78 per cent (with only 13 per cent in favour). Yet, after the Greek election, those in favour of the country remaining in the Eurozone jumped to 66 per cent – from 36 per cent a week prior to the election (only 26 per cent were now opposed). But the public opposition in Germany to any watering down of the Greek austerity terms remained high. On 24 August 2012, two-thirds (67 per cent) were against giving Greece two more years (with 29 per cent in favour); with respect to additional financial aid, 72 per cent were against it (with only 22 per cent in favour). Consequently, 61 per cent now favoured a Greek exit from the Eurozone (with 31 per cent maintaining the country should remain in the single currency).

This was coupled with low confidence in the Greek government. Related to the bailouts, on 14 September 2012, 78 per cent were in favour of the so-called fiscal compact – which is designed to curb the deficit allowed by Eurozone countries; please see above (with 15 per cent against). Against the very creation of the permanent ESM for helping debtor members was consistently opposed by almost two-thirds (62 per cent), with only 33 per cent in favour. On 16 November 2012, 79 per cent expected that Greece would not meet its agreed obligations; even with more loans and additional time (only 17 per cent were optimistic). Although a large majority was expected in the *Bundestag* in favour of additional credit for Greece, on 30 November 2012, 69 per cent of the public held that the country itself had not done enough to get out of its crisis (only 19 believed otherwise).

Citizen opinions on the German government in the Eurozone crisis

Unlike views held in some indebted Eurozone countries of the German government in general, and of Angela Merkel in particular, the degree of satisfaction of the domestic population with the chancellor's management of the Eurozone crisis remained high, at times reaching a two-thirds approval rating.

On 17 December 2010, 61 per cent viewed the job of Mrs Merkel in the Eurozone crisis as generally positive (with 29 per cent as negative). On 9 September 2011 (i.e. ahead of a *Bundestag* vote to increase the EFSF – and thereby a rise of the German loan guarantees to €211 bn), 50 per cent viewed the work of the government in the Eurozone crisis as generally negative (with 38 per cent in support). On 28 October 2011, on the heels of a Greek 'haircut', 51 per cent were satisfied with the chancellor's handling of the Eurozone crisis (with 40 per cent having seen this differently). On 10 February 2012, 69 per cent considered Angela Merkel's crisis management as generally positive (with 23 per cent holding the opposite view).[34] On 12 April 2012, 70 per cent approved Angela Merkel's handling of the Eurozone crisis (with 22 having a more negative view). At a recent meeting of the European Council (the Heads of State and Government in the EU), critique had emerged on Germany's austerity stance. Despite this, 63 per cent of Germans were satisfied with Mrs Merkel's Eurozone crisis policy (with 20 per cent being more critical).

German polling on introducing Eurobonds

The debate on mutualising the sovereign debt in the Eurozone did not begin until well into the second year of the crisis. Highly indebted member states began to see this as way to reduce their burden, whereas the German government continued to maintain that this would only reduce the incentive for structural reforms. This is exactly how about four-fifth of the domestic population viewed it.

Consistent with Angela Merkel's opposition to Eurobonds, the vast majority of Germans remain staunchly opposed to them. First asked on 25 November

2011, 79 per cent rejected them (with only 15 per cent in favour). A virtually identical picture emerged half a year later on 25 May 2012 with 79 per cent opposed to the introduction of Eurobonds (with only 14 per cent in favour). As a German-inspired common fiscal policy for the Eurozone was being discussed, 51 per cent were still opposed to Eurobonds under any circumstances on 13 July 2012. A further 24 per cent were only in favour if, and only if, a fiscal union were created first (only 12 per cent were in favour).

Conclusion

The argument advanced in this chapter had two aspects: first, it identified the areas in which the German governmental position changed and in which it remained the same from the inception of the Troika in April 2010 to the confirmation of the legality of German contribution to the ESM in March 2014. While there was movement on the conditions for financial assistance, the German stance on Eurobonds remained unchanged.

Second, it sought to explain these observed results. It was my contention that domestic public opinion is the most plausible account, relying on the German *Politbarometer* opinion polls. Concomitantly, this part ranged from the domestic views on Greek Bailouts to the German public's stance on Eurobonds. Generally, the country's citizens tend to be more unforgiving on member states receiving German bailout money than the government. Consequently, the approval rating of the Merkel government for sticking to its austerity message is high. Table 4.1 graphically displays the empirical findings on the DV and the IV, and their relation.

It shows that that the opinion polls in most cases preceded the German government's decision on the respective topics and the *Bundestag* votes. Therefore, German public opinion indeed appears to constrain government decisions in the Eurozone crisis. Although some decisions taken in parliament contravened public opinion, they often also resulted in a loss of the 'chancellor's majority'.

However, a caveat is nonetheless in order on these results. In the absence of public statements that the government specifically took certain positions in the Eurozone *because of* views in its public – and no government would possibly provide such unequivocal evidence – I cannot beyond doubt establish that the causal arrow indeed goes in the direction I suggested at the outset. Thus, this chapter technically can only establish a correlation between these two phenomena.

By January 2015 Greece was again in the headlines. A parliamentary election on 25 January had altered the political landscape by giving the left-leaning Syriza party its first victory in parliament. It was elected on the promise to end the German-inspired austerity measures, as it charged these had been crippling the Greek economy for four years.[35] Its leader and new Prime Minister Alexis Tsipras, having formed a coalition with the right-wing populist ANEL party, vowed to reverse all previous public sector and pension cuts, but keep Greece in the Eurozone. Not surprisingly, this sent his government on a collision course with the Eurogroup of finance ministers.

Table 4.1 Empirical findings

Topic	*IV (public opinion)*	*DV (decisions by DE government)*
Greece (+ CY)	26/03/2010: 68% against DE financial aid to GR 17/12/2010: 62% against DE aid to any debtor 28/01/2011: 64% against increasing EFSF for GR 10/06/2011: 60% against new loan for GR 09/09/2011: 76% against increasing EFSF for GR 27/01/2012: 73% against increasing EFSF 18/06/2012: 78% against easing austerity for GR 24/08/2012: 72% against new aid for GR 14/09/2012: 78% in favour of fiscal compact	05/2010: parliamentary approval of DE financial aid to GR (1st bailout package) 09/2011: parliamentary approval of extending EFSF 12/2012: parliament eases austerity for GR 02/2012: parliament approves new aid for GR 06/2012: parliament demands EU fiscal compact 05/2013: new change from bailout to bail-in with CY banks
Eurobonds	25/11/2011: 79% against Eurobonds 25/05/2012: 79% against Eurobonds 13/07/2012: 51% against Eurobonds; 24% in favour only with fiscal compact	11/2010: government rejects Eurobonds 06/2012: government rejects Eurobonds 06/2012: parliament demands EU fiscal compact
DE view of its government in the Eurozone	17/12/2010: 61% in favour of Merkel in Eurozone 10/02/2012: 69% in favour of Merkel in Eurozone 12/04/2012: 70% in favour of Merkel in Eurozone	

Note
The 'parliamentary approval' is part of the DV, for the votes in the *Bundestag* are introduced by the German government.

Throughout this time, German public opinion also remained steadfast. According to *Politbarometer* surveys between 30 January and 12 June 2015, 70–80 per cent of Germans wanted the Greek government to stick to all previously agreed austerity measures and opposed any further financial assistance if it did not adhere to the former.

To strengthen its position vis-à-vis its creditors, the Syriza-led coalition called a referendum, in which Greek citizens on 5 July 2015 overwhelmingly (61.31 per cent, at a turnout of 62 per cent) supported the so-dubbed 'anti-Merkel' side, asking the government to renegotiate the terms with the German-led donor countries. Yet, the 19 Eurozone members demanded that Mr Tsipras have a detailed list of privatisations in the Greek economy approved by parliament *and* implemented within less than a week. Only *if* this was to materialise – going against the Greek referendum – would negotiations for a third Greek bailout even begin.

German public's opinion and the stance of its government remain in step in the latest reverberations of the Eurozone crisis.

Notes

1 I wish to thank Sabine Saurugger for her continued support throughout and Sarah Tarry for her help in improving this chapter. Of course, any remaining errors are solely my responsibility.

2 In 2012, the country accounted for 20.6 per cent of EU GDP and 26.73 per cent of the Eurozone's GDP.

3 In the meantime, Ireland (December 2013), Spain (January 2014) and Portugal (June 2014) have left their respective bailout packages. Since the financial conditions for Cyprus were rather different (see below), this leaves Greece under Troika supervision.

4 In addition, several German (and French) commercial banks own the majority of the bonds issued by Greek governments at a time when the country's growth rate was one of the highest in Europe, i.e. prior to the current difficulties.

5 Chancellor Angela Merkel was re-elected for a third consecutive time in September 2013, for the first time in post-war Germany having a party fall just short of an absolute majority.

6 The term 'bailout' means that public (i.e. taxpayer's) money is being used to come to the rescue of private actors (in this case: commercial banks) in the economy. For instance, General Motors also was a recipient of U.S. bailout funding in the aftermath of the global financial crisis.

7 To get an idea of how this 'cooking the books' process remained undetected for some time, consider the Greek (state) railway. The incoming transport minister discovered that there apparently were more employees than customers. The previous government had the railway issue shares, all of which the government then bought. The losses of the railway through this procedure were a financial transaction, rather than an increase of the budget deficit. It therefore did not appear on the state budget balance sheet; that the Greek statistics office was not independent, but a government agency at the time, aided this disguise.

8 Among the five so-called Maastricht criteria – based upon which countries ultimately become Eurozone members – are requirements for a deficit/GDP ratio of no more than 3 per cent and for debt not exceeding 60 per cent of GDP.

9 Thus, the yields of bonds (i.e. their financing cost) spread between Eurozone countries; Germany could borrow money for about 1 per cent, while the costs for debtor-countries are much higher.

10 Such financial aid was not immediately forthcoming, as European creditor countries were initially debating whether or not to incorporate the IMF in such an endeavour.
11 However, once set up, Troika representatives have also negotiated the conditions for financial aid to the four other countries that had asked for such help: Ireland, Spain, Portugal and Cyprus.
12 France is the only other Eurozone country with slightly more than 20 per cent.
13 The chief executive officer of the EFSF is Klaus Regling, a former Director General of the European Commission's Directorate General for Economic and Financial Affairs, having previously worked at the IMF and the German Ministry of Finance. He continues on with the European Stability Mechanism (ESM) into which the EFSF has turned in October 2012.
14 The *Deutsche Finanzagentur* (German Finance Agency) is a financial services company owned by the Federal Republic of Germany; it is headquartered near the ECB in Frankfurt.
15 The €440 bn lending capacity of the Facility may be combined with loans from the EFSM – and with up to €250 bn from the IMF.
16 The ESM now covers all new bailouts, although the EFSF and EFSM continue to handle money transfers and programme monitoring for the previously approved bailout loans to Ireland, Portugal and Greece.
17 Up until April 2014, the country also pays almost €28 bn in cash into the ESM.
18 There has been a debate – primarily in the Anglo-Saxon print media – on whether or not Germany has profited from the Eurozone crisis [Das 2013; Reisenbichler and Morgan 2013]. The two sets of positions are inconclusive. I discard them here, as the purpose of this chapter is the extent of change of Germany's position in the Eurozone crisis; not if it benefited from it.
19 The country also received the largest amounts of financial assistance: a first bailout of €110 bn (including €80 bn in bilateral aid from Eurozone countries – with €23 bn of it from Germany), as well as further loan guaranties through the EFSF. The second bailout amounted to €100 bn through the EFSF. The Greek government in part utilised these amounts to be able to pay its public sector wages, but it created a vicious circle of budget deficits, high unemployment and low growth.
20 This cascade has first been used when Cyprus asked the EU for financial assistance for its banking system (which given the very small size of its economy is large). It is the approach taken to all commercial banks from now on. Note that 'small savers' – those with deposits of less than €100,000 – remain protected from any financial contribution to the rescue fund.
21 Although different databases use different symbols, the most common is the asterisk (*).
22 These programmes first count a 'bag of words', exemplified by the above key words connected with Boolean operators in different combinations. After this initial step, attention has to be placed on the substantive meaning of a sentence. For instance, 'The German stance in the Eurozone crisis has changed a great deal since 2010' and 'the German position on the Euro crisis has only marginally altered since early 2010'. These two sentences contain the same vocabulary, but have essentially the opposite meaning.
23 There are two other frequently used polling sources: first, the *Allensbach Institut für Demoskopie* (i.e. Allensbach Institute for Public Opinion Research) covers public opinion from a German perspective. Second, the Eurobarometer surveys on behalf of the European Commission instead combine all EU member states. In both outlets, European integration receives attention only *in general* (rather than on the German position). In addition, Gros and Roth (2011) report that these datasets are methodologically not compatible because Allensbach utilises 'trust' where the Eurobarometer tends to use 'support'. The Allensbach Institute also collapses three terms ('no trust at all', 'barely trust', and 'not so much trust') into one negative category, with the

positive group only being 'very big trust' – effectively inflating negative tendencies. For the above reasons, I ignore both polling sources in this chapter.

24 However, this was necessarily helped by southern Eurozone countries not having reported any growth at all for 2010.

25 Merkel was first elected Chancellor in November 2005, governing with so-called 'Grand Coalition' of the two largest political parties in Germany (i.e. her Christian Democratic Union (CDU) – along with its Bavarian sister party Christian Social Union (CSU) – and the Social Democratic Party of Germany (SPD). Angela Merkel was re-elected in November 2009, presiding over a coalition of her CDU/CSU with the liberal Free Democratic Party (FDP) as her junior partner. She was re-elected a third time in November 2013 by a margin just a few seats short of an absolute majority – a phenomenon foreign to electoral systems of proportional representation. Merkel governs again with a grand coalition. In March 2014, she became the longest serving incumbent head of government in the EU.

26 Schäuble is closely associated with chancellor Merkel. He served in all three terms of her government, as interior minister in the first, and then as finance minister in her second and third terms as Chancellor.

27 The total sum was 110 bn, for 30 bn came from the IMF.

28 Since public opinion in the Eurozone's creditor countries was against giving Greece such a 'break', Schäuble turned this into a 'voluntary' contribution of these commercial banks.

29 Interestingly, the Banking Union – under the auspices of the ECB – has become a reality one year later, subjecting commercial banks in the 28 member states to so-called stress tests.

30 The German parliament comprises 598 members – although the proportional arithmetic between the political parties can slightly increase its size.

31 In fact, since the EFSF could borrow money at the banks for cheaper than it loaned these funds to, say, Greece, this scheme was beneficial for the donor countries. Of course, it did not have to remain that way.

32 This ultimately came to pass. Member states by now are obliged to submit their budgets for approval to the European Commission. The latter can in principle reject a submission and demand alterations.

33 This proposal became reality in the 'Treaty on Stability, Coordination and Governance in the Economic and Monetary Union' (TSCG), known variously as the Fiscal Compact or Fiscal Stability Treaty. As an intergovernmental treaty, it is a stricter version of the previous 'Stability and Growth Pact'. The TSCG entered into force in January 2013 for 16 countries, and by April 2014, all 25 signatories (i.e. without the Czech Republic and the UK) had ratified it.

34 Domestically as well is the chancellor the most popular politician with 77 per cent finding that she did a good job (with only 19 per cent having held the opposite view).

35 Somewhat ironically, prior to the election, the Greek economy was at last able to return to the financial markets to issue ten-year bonds. This supposedly should have bode well for the previous prime minister Antonis Samaras – but his conservative New Democracy lost 53 seats, obtaining its worst result ever in terms of seats won, and coming in a distant second with 76 seats.

References

Bei, Yu, Kaufmann, Stefan and Diermeier, Daniel (2008). Classifying Party Affiliation from Political Speech. *Journal of Information Technology & Politics* 5(1): 33–48.

Cardie, Claire and Wilkerson, John (2008). Text Annotation for Political Science Research. *Journal of Information Technology & Politics* 5(1), 1–6.

Das, Satyajit (2013). Debt crisis has left Germany vulnerable. Accessed 8 August 2015. www.ft.com/intl/cms/s/0/07434b7e-3a54-11e3-b234-00144feab7de.html#axzz30aV7fUmE.

Frankfurter Allgemeine Zeitung (1 April 2010–31 August 2014). According to various keywords connected by Boolean operators.

Gros, Daniel and Roth, Felix (2011). *Do Germans Support the Euro?* (CEPS Working Document No. 359, December 2011). Accessed 8 August 2015. www.ceps.eu.

Krippendorff, Klaus (2013). *Content Analysis: An Introduction to Its Methodology*. 3rd edition. Thousand Oaks, CA: Sage.

Monroe, Burt L. and Schrodt, Philip A. (2008). Introduction to the Special Issue: The Political Analysis of Political Text. *Political Analysis* 16(4), 351–355.

Politbarometer (2010a). Zwei Drittel der Bürger gegen deutsche Kredite für Griechenland (März II, 26 March 2010). Accessed 8 August 2015. www.forschungsgruppe.de/Umfragen/Politbarometer.

Politbarometer (2010b). Mehrheit gegen stärkere Finanzhilfen für verschuldete EU-Staaten (Dezember II, 17 December 2010). Accessed 8 August 2015. www.forschungsgruppe.de/Umfragen/Politbarometer.

Politbarometer (2011a). 82 Prozent sehen Gefahr für Stabilität des Euro (Januar II, 28 January 2011). Accessed 8 August 2015. www.forschungsgruppe.de/Umfragen/Politbarometer.

Politbarometer (2011b). Mehrheit gegen weitere Finanzhilfen für Griechenland (Juni, 10 June 2011). Accessed 8 August 2015. www.forschungsgruppe.de/Umfragen/Politbarometer.

Politbarometer (2011c). Deutliche Mehrheit gegen Erweiterung des Euro-Rettunsschirms (September I, 9 September 2011). Accessed 8 August 2015. www.forschungsgruppe.de/Umfragen/Politbarometer.

Politbarometer (2011d). Mehrheit: Angela Merkel macht beim Euro ihre Arbeit eher gut (Oktober II, 28 October 2011). Accessed 8 August 2015. www.forschungsgruppe.de/Umfragen/Politbarometer.

Politbarometer (2011b). Massive Ablehnung von Eurobonds (November II, 25 November 2011). Accessed 8 August 2015. www.forschungsgruppe.de/Umfragen/Politbarometer.

Politbarometer (2012a). Mehrheit gegen Aufstockung des Euro-Rettungsschirms (Januar II, 27 January 2012). Accessed 8 August 2015. www.forschungsgruppe.de/Umfragen/Politbarometer.

Politbarometer (2012b). Mehrheit zweifelt am Sparwillen Griechenlands (February, 10 February 2012). Accessed 8 August 2015. www.forschungsgruppe.de/Umfragen/Politbarometer.

Politbarometer (2012c). Deutsche klar gegen Eurobonds (Mai, 25 May 2012). Accessed 8 August 2015. www.forschungsgruppe.de/Umfragen/Politbarometer.

Politbarometer (2012d). Mehrheit gegen Lockerung der Sparvorgaben für Griechenland (Extra, 18 June 2012). Accessed 8 August 2015. www.forschungsgruppe.de/Umfragen/Politbarometer.

Politbarometer (2012e). Euro-Krise gewinnt stark an Bedeutung (Juli, 13 July 2012). Accessed 8 August 2015. www.forschungsgruppe.de/Umfragen/Politbarometer.

Politbarometer (2012f). Griechenland: Zwei Drittel gegen mehr Zeit (August, 24 August 2012). Accessed 8 August 2015. www.forschungsgruppe.de/Umfragen/Politbarometer.

Politbarometer (2012g). Fiskalpakt ja – ESM nein (September I, 14 September 2012). Accessed 8 August 2015. www.forschungsgruppe.de/Umfragen/Politbarometer.

Politbarometer (2012h). Inzwischen klare Mehrheit für Verbleib Griechenlands im Euro (Oktober II, 26 October 2012). Accessed 8 August 2015. www.forschungsgruppe.de/Umfragen/Politbarometer.

Politbarometer (2012i). Vier Fünftel bezweifeln, dass Griechenland die Sparziele zukünftig einhalten wird (November I, 16 November 2012). Accessed 8 August 2015. www.forschungsgruppe.de/Umfragen/Politbarometer.

Politbarometer (2012j). Knappe Mehrheit für einen Bankrott von Griechenland (November II, 30 November 2012). Accessed 8 August 2015. www.forschungsgruppe.de/Umfragen/Politbarometer.

Politbarometer (2013a). Eurokrise Angst um Ersparnisse nimmt zu (März II, 22 January 2013). Accessed 8 August 2015. www.forschungsgruppe.de/Umfragen/Politbarometer.

Politbarometer (2013b). Deutliche Mehrheit sagt: Euro-Austritt wäre schlecht für Deutschland (April I, 12 April 2013). Accessed 8 August 2015. www.forschungsgruppe.de/Umfragen/Politbarometer.

Politbarometer (2014). EU: Desinteresse an Prsonalie Juncker (Juni II, 27 June 2014). Accessed 8 August 2015. www.forschungsgruppe.de/Umfragen/Politbarometer.

Politbarometer (2015a). Mehrheit für Verbleib Griechenlands im Euro – aber gegen Schuldenerlass (Januar II, 30 January 2015). Accessed 8 August 2015. www.forschungsgruppe.de/Umfragen/Politbarometer.

Politbarometer (2015b). Griechenland: Große Zweifel an Umsetzung der Reformliste (Februar, 27 February 2015). Accessed 8 August 2015. www.forschungsgruppe.de/Umfragen/Politbarometer.

Politbarometer (2015c). Massive Kritik an der griechischen Regierung (März, 13 March 2015). Accessed 8 August 2015. www.forschungsgruppe.de/Umfragen/Politbarometer.

Politbarometer (2015d). Verhandlungen über griechische Reformmaßnahmen (Juni, 12 June 2015). Accessed 8 August 2015. www.forschungsgruppe.de/Umfragen/Politbarometer.

Reisenbichler, Alexander and Morgan, Kimberley J. (2013). How Germany Won the Euro Crisis. *Foreign Affairs* Snapshot 20 June. Accessed 8 August 2015. www.foreignaffairs.com/articles/139520/alexander-reisenbichler-and-kimberly-j-morgan/how-germany-won-the-euro-crisis.

Süddeutsche Zeitung (1 April 2010–31 August 2014), according to various keywords connected by Boolean operators.

Van Atteveldt, Wouter, Kleinnijenhuis, Jan and Ruigrok, Nel (2008). Parsing, Semantic Networks, and Political Authority Using Syntactic Analysis to Extract Semantic Relations from Dutch Newspaper Articles. *Political Analysis* 16(4), 428–446.

5 Economic crisis, crisis of support?

How macro-economic performance shapes citizens' support for the EU (1973–2014)

Céline Belot and Isabelle Guinaudeau[1]

Introduction

Citizens' support is nowadays considered to be a necessary condition for the strengthening and deepening of regional integrations. This need for legitimacy is heightened given the growing competences of regional institutions, and is acutely palpable in periods of crisis, as institutions come under threat. This is particularly true in times of economic crisis, which challenge regional integrations in their initial functions and require coordinated responses. Yet, a substantial number of EU studies focus on the role of economic factors on EU support: as soon as the end of the 1970s, Inglehart and Rabier had unveiled the link between public support for European integration and economic performance (1978), and their work has since been taken up by numerous authors. Under some circumstances at least, citizens appeared to consider the EC responsible for economic concerns and supported it more when these conditions improved – and less when they deteriorated. Public support for the EU may therefore be altered precisely when most acutely needed, in times of economic recession, rising inflation, debt and/or unemployment, or when financial solidarity among member states is required in order to cope with an economic crisis.

This is why it appears crucial, in a volume on how regional integration systems change in times of economic and financial crisis, to consider how such crises – defined as an unexpected phase of 'turmoil', whose occurrence surprises decision makers, threatens their high-priority goals and requires a quick response before the decision is transformed (see definition in Introduction for further detail) – affect citizens' support for regional integration, which would have further consequences on the integration process. In the case of the EU, this question has become particularly relevant in the context of the economic and debt crisis that has affected the member states since 2008. This crisis of historical amplitude, that has triggered fading growth (even recession in many cases), rising unemployment, growing deficits and public debts, and the need for bailouts of historic size, is undoubtedly an eloquent example of how crises occur out of the blue, threaten core goals, in this case job security, welfare benefits and living conditions, and require a quick policy response.

This crisis is of unprecedented nature. However, regional integration in Europe has already been confronted with several economic crises of smaller amplitude and scope before: dramatic deterioration in the macro-economic conditions occurred in all European countries in the context of the 1973–1974 and 1979 oil crises, in many of these countries following the collapse of steel prices in 1975, as well as in the early 1990s, due to global factors (in particular the Gulf war and the subsequent economic slowdown), to the German reunification and to the monetary crisis that led to the ejection of the British pound and of the Italian Lira from the European exchange rate mechanism.

These previous crises provide the opportunity to put the current episode into perspective with an analysis of how macro-economic conditions affect public support for the EU over time. As we will argue in more detail later on, the available literature, although well-developed, does not provide a clear picture of this relationship. On the one hand, empirical results are of mixed nature, as conclusions vary according to the countries, period, (dependent and independent) variables and model specifications of the study. On the other hand, the contributions mainly come from the 1990s and only few of them cover the recent years, so they require an update. This is all the more important as the context, the process and the level of integration have evolved a lot over time, and are barely comparable to those of, for instance, the 1973–1974 economic crisis, in particular with respect to the end of the 'permissive consensus', to the rise of Euroscepticism and to the high level of integration achieved.

We propose to address these challenges with an analysis of how economic performance impact citizens' support over the whole 1973–2014 period, with a special focus on the short-term context of the economic crisis triggered in 2008 and on the longer term, from 1973 onwards. This allows an assessment of the consequences of the Great Recession on support for the EU and on the future course of integration by comparing whether the implications of economic fluctuations vary over time, notably in the course of the process of integration and institutionalisation.

We first provide an overview of the literature and of the available findings. After having described trends in input and output-based EU-support over time, we take a step back and seek to shed light on the contrasting evidence of an impact of economic conditions on EU support, by explaining variations. More specifically, we ask whether this impact is more significant than before, due to member states' citizens becoming aware of the expansion of European policies and attributing more responsibility to the EU over time, or whether the deepening of integration and the growing identification with the EU tend to moderate the effects of the economy on support. Studying the links between economic conditions and EU support over a period of 40 years covering several economic crises and numerous economic ups and downs allows us to evaluate whether the impact is as significant over this period that has witnessed an acceleration of the process of integration, as it was in the 1970s and 1980s.

Economic conditions, regional integration and citizens' support for this process

The link between citizens' support for European integration and economic conditions has been under scrutiny since the end of the 1970s. In their pioneer work on this topic, Inglehart and Rabier reported, with respect to the decline in support in the mid-1970s:

> the recession and inflation of the 1970's ... were worldwide phenomena that probably were affected only marginally by any actions taken by the European Community institutions. However, the publics concerned here did seem to attribute prevailing economic conditions to their membership in the European Community.
>
> (Inglehart and Rabier 1978: 75)

This effect seems plausible, as economic development, growth and welfare initially belonged – with peace – to the core motivations for European integration and have emerged, as war among member states has become less and less likely, as one of, if not people's main expectation of the EU.

This idea has been taken up and further developed in numerous publications. With the new downturn in support in the context of the economic crisis of the early 1990s, the economic approach to support even became '*the dominant approach for explaining public opinion toward European integration*' (Anderson 1995: 114). Using aggregate data, both at the European and national levels, researchers observe the effects of growth, unemployment and inflation (Anderson and Kaltenthaler 1996), sectorial gains and losses (Smith and Wanke 1993), the extent of commercial exchange inside the EC and national EC budget costs and benefits (Eichenberg and Dalton 1993) on citizens' support. Support appeared to not only be affected by bad economic performance as measured by all these indicators, but also by subjective perceptions of economic performance (Gabel and Whitten 1997; Marsh 1999).

Despite the number of available analyses, this literature provides only mixed-evidence for an impact of economic performance on EU support. While authors converge in their assessment of a degraded climate of support for integration in the context of the 1973–1974 economic crisis, the fall in support at the beginning of the 1990s has been analysed as resulting mostly from identity problems due to the end of the Soviet bloc (Gamble 1995) and the spectacular rise in Euroscepticism as 'post-Maastricht blues', induced by considerations of predominantly political nature. As Anderson puts it, '*the relationships between national economic performance and support for integration are overwhelmingly positive but by no means breathtaking*' (Anderson 1995: 125; see also Bosch and Newton 1995). The results are more generally much contrasted, depending on the country and years covered, the dependent and independent variables selected for analysis, as well as the model specification. Anderson and Reichert (1995) observe, for instance, a stronger impact of budget return than of trade among member states on EU support. Eichenberg and Dalton's observation (1993) of a stronger effect of inflation, while unemployment and GDP did not seem to matter (see Mahler *et al.* 2000: 441 for a similar finding), has been contradicted in a subsequent study by Anderson and Kaltenthaler in which unemployment matters most (1996), and in Eichenberg and Dalton's later study, that indicates a fading impact of all economic factors (2007). In a study published two years later, Gabel even observes a reverse effect, with better performance – less unemployment and inflation and more growth – being associated with less EU support (Gabel 1998: 86). A more recent account established a (negative) effect of unemployment and inflation, but no effect of growth and trade (Çiftçi 2005).

Against this backdrop, and as the EU has evolved towards political Union with growing powers that has been increasingly perceived, politicised and contested, scholars have turned to alternative factors, in particular related to identity, and some studies have concluded that EU support is more affected by the strength and the exclusive character of national identities than by economic considerations (e.g. Citrin and Sides 2004; Hooghe and Marks 2005). More recently, the economic concerns of the 2000s and the Great Recession have revived scholars' attention to economic factors but their conclusions are, again, contrasted. On the one hand, many studies observe no strong effect of macroeconomic factors on citizens' support for the EU. Analysing Eurobarometer data from 2007 to 2011, Armingeon and Ceka conclude that the effects of macroeconomic factors are weaker than those of the subjective evaluation of the national economy at the individual level and confirm the powerful role of political cues such as citizens' support for national government (Armingeon and Ceka 2014). Using the same dataset, Serricchio *et al.* conclude that when explaining variations in level of support for the EU '*the economic explanation has very limited analytical leverage. The crisis has not brought economics back in as the most important source of Euroscepticism*' (Serricchio *et al.* 2013: 61; see also Roth *et al.* 2014). Their results indicate that the crisis tends instead to reinforce the effect of national identity and national political cues on citizens' support.

On the other hand, however, other authors reaffirm the importance of macroeconomic factors on citizens' support for the EU. Balestrini *et al.* (2011) observe, over the 1990–2007 period, economic considerations (related to unemployment, but not to inflation, growth and the total tax burden) to have more explanatory power than considerations related to national identity (see also Balestrini *et al.* 2010 and Hobolt and Wratil 2015). Gomez underlines the role of high unemployment and interest rates in explaining the decline in citizens' support for the EU and claims the relationship is particularly strong for the young generations (2015). Braun and Tausendpfund (2014) perceive the effect of macro-economic factors on EU support to be limited during the global crisis (until the end of 2009) and much stronger since the beginning of the Eurozone crisis, which tend to prove that the EU is blamed for this second part of the crisis. Other authors acknowledge an effect, but analyse it as an indirect one. In particular, Garry and Tilley consider that the economic situation alters the magnitude of identity effects on citizen support. To say it otherwise, when the economy performs badly, people tend to refer more to their national identity when evaluating European integration than when the economy performs better (Garry and Tilley 2009). Their results echo former ones by Christin who showed that in Central and Eastern European countries, economic conditions shape the effect of individual attitudes towards economic and democratic reforms on EU support: they matter only when economic conditions are good, while bad national performance tends to nourish support for the EU, as it is expected to improve the situation (Christin 2005). Still other authors claim that the relationship between identity-related factors and economic factors is the opposite. In their view, economic factors at the aggregate level have a strong impact on EU support for people who identify strongly and exclusively with the nation. For other respondents, economic factors only play a role at the individual level, when people consider they will be personally affected by bad economic conditions (Levy and Phan 2014).

Faced with this contrasting evidence, two research perspectives seem particularly promising. First, the Great Recession that has brought economic problems back to the core of European politics since 2008 constitutes a critical moment which enables researcher to update previous findings and scrutinise the effects of dramatic deterioration of economic conditions on different dimensions of support: it is important to assess whether all of them, or only some of them, are affected, as well as to put these dynamics of EU support into perspective with respect to longer-term trends. Second, instead of seeking to assess whether economics matter for EU support, a challenging line of research consists in explaining *when and under which conditions* it matters. Several interesting hypotheses have been put forward in the literature, but they have not been tested over the recent period.

1 A first line of argumentation, anchored at the regional level of the EU, is particularly relevant to the present volume, which explores the links between economic crises and the institutionalisation of regional integrations. It suggests that the way in which the economic context shapes popular support for the EU may vary according to the level of **institutional density**[2] at the EU level, meaning the degree to which EU institutions and regulations constrain member states. Two contradictory hypotheses have been defended for this factor. Some authors argue that the effect of economic conditions on EU support is likely to fade, because they expect the EU to be less judged on economic performance as its competences are extended (Marsh 1999) or because in economic hard times, citizens may feel the need for closer EU cooperation or solidarity, and consider a deeply integrated EU as the relevant actor to tackle the origins and consequences of economic crises (Christin 2005; see Kuhn and Stoeckel, 2014: 619, for a similar argumentation). In contrast, other scholars expect citizens' support to be increasingly determined by economic performance as the EU becomes institutionally denser over time, as more and more competences are delegated to the EU, and citizens are likely to attribute it more

responsibility for economic outcomes (Gabel and Whitten 1997; Hobolt and Tilley 2014). It seems, in particular, plausible that citizens attribute partial responsibility to the EU for the economic concerns deriving from the crisis, as this crisis has been primarily tackled at the European level, with direct interventions from European institutions in domestic reforms and politics (Armingeon and Baccaro, 2012).

2 Other factors relate to the European integration background of individual member states. The impact of macro-economic conditions on EU support may be conditioned, or at least shaped, by the **length of membership**[3] and the socialisation effect membership produces. Following a spill-over logic, as member states' citizens become socialised into the European community and aware of the related benefits, and become exposed to the pro-European discourse of their elite, they may develop a belief in the virtue of the project, a feeling of belonging, and even affective, attachment to it and support European integration more independently from economic performance. Already Inglehart and Rabier (1978) noticed support to be more affected in the three countries which joined the EC in 1973 than in the older members, which made them conclude that support was better anchored and attitudes towards European integration more structured in older member states than in newer members. Numerous analyses indeed find a marked distinction between newer member states, in which economic performance seems to have more effect than in older member states (Anderson and Reichert 1995; Bosch and Newton 1995; Anderson and Kaltenthaler 1996).

3 Further explanations have been considered and need to be tested systematically in order to account for variations in the effect of economic considerations on EU support, in particular country-specific factors. Roth *et al.* (2014) for instance argue that high rates of unemployment exert a negative influence on trust in the ECB only in what they call the '**peripheral countries**', Spain, Portugal, Greece and Ireland (Roth *et al.* 2014). Furthermore, Rohrschneider and Loveless (2010) contend that citizens assess the macro-economic performance of the EU against the background of the **most pressing issues in a nation**, as well as their individual country's performance: economic factors matter to EU support when the country performs badly, while political factors matter more to citizens living in well-functioning democracies. In this perspective, citizens' support appears to depend on both economic and political performance. They analyse that, as older member states are all quite affluent, economic effects tended to decrease at the beginning of the years 2000, but with the membership of the former East European States, mostly poorer states, its effects have reappeared at the EU level.

In this paper, we take a step towards understanding when macro-economic conditions, in particular economic crises, matter for public support for the EU. This study is the first one to systematically explore the effect of all common indicators of macro-economic performance – inflation, unemployment, growth and public debt – on EU support over forty years. In a second stage, we explore how far their influence varies according to the country's length of membership and the overall degree of regional integration of the European community. It would be interesting and relevant to test for further variables, including the peripheral character of nations, but in this preliminary analysis, we have favoured a long period of study over the inclusion of numerous explanatory variables.

Citizen support through the recent economic crisis

The economic crisis that started at the end of the years 2000 is a critical case, which allows us to study the impact of economic factors on support for the EU with particular clarity. According to the literature, we might expect support to go down during that period [H1]. Following Easton's seminal work on political support (Easton 1965; 1975) we propose to distinguish different kinds of supports. Easton identified two kinds of support for a political system, output and input support. The former is based on evaluation of policy performance: when the system performs well, support is high; when it performs badly support is weak. The latter is based on an attachment to the norms and values backed up by the political system. Such an attachment is a strong legitimising source for a political system as it produces support even when the system produces unpopular outputs (see also Scharpf 1999: 10–12 for a definition of the 'output-oriented legitimation'). Considering that economic conditions are seen, at least partly, as an output of European politics we would predict that the economic crisis produces more impact on output support than on input support [H2].

To measure support for the EU political system, we use trend indicators from Eurobarometer data. We first examine data covering the months of the crisis, from Autumn 2007 to Spring 2013. Perceived economic performance is traditionally measured, at the European level, through the 'country benefit' indicator.[4] Unfortunately, this question has not been asked anymore since Spring 2011. We therefore added another indicator on respondents' judgement of the situation of the European economy.[5] When considering input support, Easton distinguished three 'recipients' of support: the political regime, the political authorities and the political community. Satisfaction with the way the democracy works at the European level[6] would have been a good indicator to measure support for the political regime but the question was asked for the last time in Autumn 2009. Similarly, measuring support for the political community appears difficult as the question concerning identification with Europe was asked only very sporadically between 2007 and 2014.[7] When considering support for authorities, Easton thought in particular of support for incumbent political elites – a dimension unfortunately not covered by the Eurobarometers. However they do offer the possibility to evaluate support for all EU institutions.[8] We have thus considered the indicators of trust in the Commission, in the European Parliament, in the Council of the EU and in the European Central Bank as proxies to measure both trust in the authorities and trust in the regime. Moreover, an indicator relative to the image of the EU offers us a general measure of EU support.[9]

Looking at Figure 5.1, our first hypothesis is confirmed: both general EU support and all the different measures of output and input support decline between 2007 and 2014. The economic crisis seems to have altered EU support. We can identify two periods: from the subprime crisis in March 2007 to Spring 2011, the decline in support remains very limited, we even observe a small return of support at the end of 2009, when the new Pasok Greek government acknowledged that its predecessor had been underreporting Greek budget deficits. In a second period though, from Spring 2011 to Autumn 2014, support decreases a little more but less than might have been expected. It even tends to grow at the end of the period, except in cases of judgements about the European economy.

It is likely that, during the first period, national citizens mainly blame governments for bad economic results, with the EU even appearing as a possible

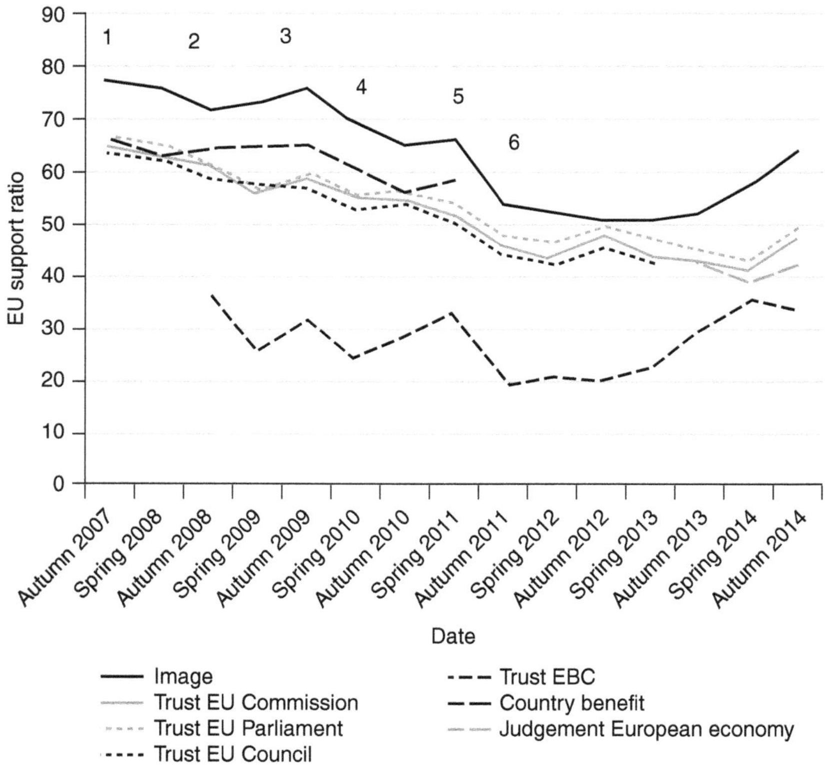

Figure 5.1 Ratio[10] of EU support (2007–2014/EU).

Notes
1 = beginning of the subprime crisis.
2 = beginning of the Eurozone crisis.
3 = beginning of the Greek crisis.
4 = beginning of the sovereign debt crisis.
5 = Creation of the European Stability Mechanism.
6 = Fiscal Compact.

rescuer of failing governments such as Greece. Conversely, in the second period, citizens develop distrust in the EU as a reaction to Greece's bailout and to the negotiations relative to the European Stability Mechanism. Whereas H1 is thus confirmed, this is not the case with our second hypothesis. Indeed, input support appears more affected by the economic crisis than output support. Support for the EU on the evaluation of economic performance decreases only marginally compared with support for EU institutions and above all EU image. These results are puzzling and would require further investigations. At this stage, it is sufficient to underline that opinions of the European economy are already quite negative at the beginning of the period due to the stagnation of growth since the adoption of the euro, which could explain why specific economic support decreases less than other kinds of support, as if it had reached a threshold. Thus the crisis did not significantly alter judgements about the EU's economic performance, but about its ability to resolve its problems, as shown by the decline in the EU's image throughout the period.

Citizens' support: a long-term perspective

We could suspect that part of our puzzling results derive from the fact that we observe change in EU support in too short-term perspective and at an EU aggregated level. Obviously, studying all indicators of support in the long run in each member state would be beyond the scope of this chapter, and would be complicated by numerous interruptions in data series. We thus propose to observe generalised support, as measured by the membership indicator,[11] from 1973 onwards for all nine countries that were members of the European Community at that time. This allows us to bring out both general trends and country specific features.

In the six older member states [Figure 5.2], three periods can be distinguished. In the first one, from 1973 to the early 1990s, support is high in all countries and variations of support are relatively low, even if some dramatic drops in support occasionally occur for very short periods of time in some countries (Germany in 1976, Luxembourg in 1979, Belgium in 1982). Support then fell at the beginning of the second period, from the Maastricht treaty to 1996, in all countries and then 'stabilised' from 1996 to the mid 2000s. Countries differ however as far as the size of the fall is concerned, with support stabilising at still very high scores in the Netherlands, Luxembourg and Italy and at a lower but still relatively high level in France and Germany. Belgium's support oscillated between the two, affected both by the most dramatic fall and the most spectacular rise. A third period opened up recently with a new drop in support in all countries in the second half of the years 2000.[12]

If we focus on support in the three countries that joined the EC in 1973 [Figure 5.3], four periods are noticeable. During the first period, from 1973 to 1983, support stabilised in the three countries at different levels, rather high in Ireland; rather low and affected by a small decrease in Britain, while Denmark presented an intermediary pattern. From 1983 to the adoption of the Maastricht

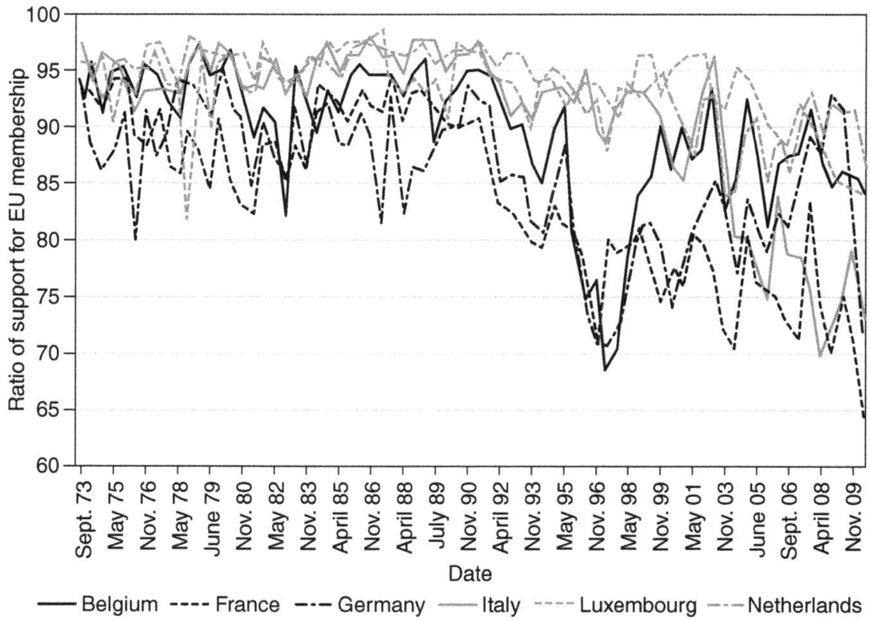

Figure 5.2 Ratio of membership support in older member states (1973–2011).

treaty, support tended to grow significantly in all three countries. From the years 1992–1993 to very recent times, trends in support diverged across the countries. While it stabilised at a very high level in Ireland throughout the period, it decreased in Britain during all the 1990s and tended to stabilise at the end of the period at a low level. In Denmark, support decreased from the Maastricht Treaty to 1996 and then grew regularly till the end of the years 2000. In all three countries a fall in support occurred recently, which seemed to open up a fourth period in EU support.

On the whole, what do we learn when observing variations of support by country from 1973 to nowadays? In hindsight, the drop in support in the 1970s does not appear as remarkable as was noticed at the time. The two biggest declines in support occurred first in the aftermath of the Maastricht treaty and second more recently in the context of the economic and debt crisis. Although the level of support at the member-state level and the trend over time sometimes diverge dramatically from the general pattern, we observe an impressive drop in EU-support during the economic crisis triggered in 2008, which tends to affect all countries. The wide time span covered allows us to confirm that this development is not part of a long-term trend, but that it coincides with the crisis, suggesting that the deterioration in economic conditions are key to understanding the crisis of support. This impression is reinforced by the observation that previous episodes of fading growth and rising unemployment have coincided

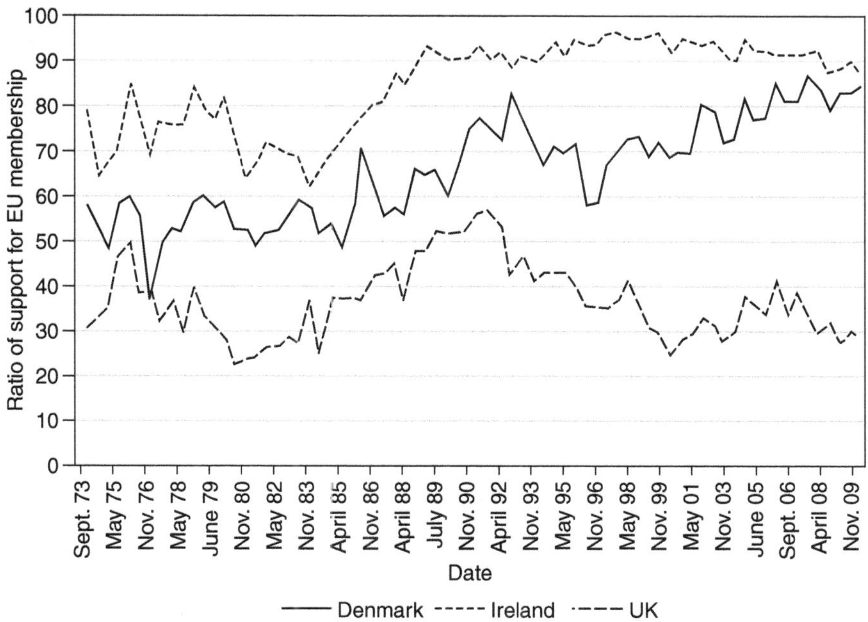

Figure 5.3 Ratio of membership support in member states which joined in 1973 (1973–2011).

with decreasing EU support, in particular in 1980 and in 1991–1993, while periods of prosperity often see a rise in support, as was the case in the second half of the 1980s. While several authors cited above hypothesise that the impact of macro-economic performance on public support for European integration tends to fade over time, our observations incite us to replicate the analyses, which have mostly been focused on the period up to the 2000s, in order to cover the most recent years marked by growing Europeanisation of macro-economic policy and high salience of economic considerations.

The real impact of the economy

In order to test for the impact of the economy on EU support, we have collected the available data on the aggregate-level of EU support in each member state, as measured by the question of whether membership in the EU is a 'good thing', 'neither good nor bad', or a 'bad thing', and we have calculated the ratio of support described earlier for all EU-15 member states from 1973 to 2011.[13] We have also collected yearly data on economic growth, inflation, unemployment and public debt, which are the most common proxies for the economic situation. This database allows us to test for how support for EU membership varies according to the economic context. While available studies provide mixed evidence as to their influence on EU support, depending on the dimension of economic performance examined and the timeframe and countries covered in the analysis, we analyse all four common indicators of macro-economic performance in 15 countries, over a period of almost 40 years.

Given the nested-structure of the data, the theoretical model suggests we should estimate a multilevel model in order to explain variations in our dependent variable (public support for the EU at a given point in time), while controlling for country-related specificities. As we expected the mean level of support to vary across countries, we use a random intercept.[14]

Our model can be summarised as follows:

$$Y_{ct}=\beta_0+\beta_1X_{1ct}+\beta_2X_{2ct}+\beta_3X_{3ct}+\beta_4T_n+\ldots+\delta_nT_n+u_{it}$$

where:
Y_{ct}: level of public support for the EU
β_0: intercept of the dependent variable in country c
$\beta_1, \beta_2, \beta_3, \beta_4$: slope of the relationship between resp. X_{1ct}, X_{2ct}, X_{3ct}, T_t and the dependent variable in country c
Y_{ct}: ratio of support for EU membership
X_{1ct}: yearly growth in country c
X_{2ct}: yearly unemployment in country c
X_{3ct}: yearly inflation in country c
T_t: number of years expired since 1973
u_{it}: error term

Table 5.1 presents the basic results of the models estimated. Model 1 reports the coefficient estimates for the empty model and provides information on the variance explained by country and individual (single data points over time) levels; put differently, this provides information on how far EU support is explained by differences within (over time) or across EU member states. The intra-class correlation coefficient (ICC = 71.3 per cent) shows that over 70 per cent of the variance occurs at the country-level. This confirms the point of a multilevel analysis, as country variations are of considerable amplitude.

Model 2 includes our dependent variables. We can see that they contribute to enhancing the explanatory power of the model, as indicated by the lower values of the AIC and BIC criteria. The coefficients presented in Table 5.1 clearly indicate that growth, inflation and public debt all significantly affect public support for the EU.[15] An increase in economic growth of 1 per cent appears to be associated with an average increase in EU support of 0.41 per cent, while a decrease of 1 per cent in inflation and public debt respectively lead to an average increase in EU support of 0.77 per cent and 0.20 per cent. In contrast, and in line with several studies discussed in the first section, we observe no significant effect of unemployment; this may reflect the more limited Europeanisation of this policy in comparison to inflation and debt, to which European institutions have been delegated considerable powers.

Table 5.1 Impact of economic conditions on support for EU membership (1973–2011)

	Model 1 (empty)	*Model 2*
Yearly nominal growth rate		0.413*** (0.109)
Yearly unemployment rate		–0.003 (0.123)
Yearly inflation rate		–0.772*** (0.092)
Debt		–0.195*** (0.019)
Time (number of years expired since 1973)		–0.147*** (0.041)
Intercept	79.18*** (3.30)	97.76*** (4.17)
Country-level variance	12.752 (2.348)	14.384 (2.649)
Individual-level residual variances	8.094 (0.190)	7.129 (0.172)
N (individual-level)	921	871
N (country-level)	15	15
Intraclass correlation	71%	80%
AIC	6,546	5,990
BIC	6,560	6,029

Notes
Statistically significant * $p < 0.05$; ** $p < 0.01$; *** $p < 0.001$. SE in parentheses.

Overall, our findings indicate that citizens tend to attribute the responsibility for economic performance, at least partly, to the EU – blaming it when the economy does bad, rewarding it in times of growth, low inflation and debt. These effects are highly significant, but seem relatively modest, which partly reflects the relative stability of support for EU membership when compared to the high fluctuations of economic indicators. However, it is also likely that these effects are underestimated because of the inclusion of a control variable for time, which partly overlaps with differences in economic situation.

These findings contradict the numerous studies that observe or speculate about an irrelevance, or a fading importance, of economic considerations when it comes to explaining citizen support for European integration. As we have used similar indicators to those studies, this diverging conclusion can only be explained with respect to our longer time span, which does not corroborate the idea of a fading influence of the economic context. The final section deals more systematically with this trend, based on an analysis of the mediating effect of the institutional density of the EU and of country's length of membership on how economics shape public support for EU membership.

The moderating effect of institutional density

We have established that EU citizens tend to blame the EU for bad economic performance, and thus to consider their country's EU membership more critically during economic crises. However, membership and European integration cannot be reduced to macro-economic policy, and we have hypothesised that as the institutional density of the EU increases and as member states become more integrated into it, citizens will less easily question EU membership. This hypothesis is often referred to by authors assuming a decreasing relevance of economic factors for explaining EU support, but it has never been tested.

We have filled this gap by estimating how far residuals (the u_{it} term in the equation above) can be explained by both the level of institutional integration of each individual country, and of the institutional density of the EC/EU as a whole.[16] In other words, we have analysed how far the model's capacity to approximate EU support based on macro-economic indicators relates to the degree of institutional density. A positive effect indicates that integration goes hand in hand with high residuals – or, put differently, with a lower effect of economic considerations on support – while a negative effect reflects that stronger integration is associated with a stronger effect of these considerations.

The country's degree of integration, or anchorage, in the European community, is approximated by a variable pertaining to the number of years the country has been a member. The overall level of institutional density of the EC/EU has been estimated using a variable regarding the number of policy domains covered over time by European treaties (see Biesenbender 2011 for a detailed presentation of how this variable has been computed), as well as a dummy distinguishing members of the Eurozone from other countries. If institutional density matters, we should observe a different pattern of influence according to the number of policies integrated at a point in time and to whether the country is a member of the Eurozone.

The results of our regression testing for these three variables' joint impact on how growth shapes EU support are presented in Table 5.2. The results are surprising, at first sight, because the degree of EU institutional density seems to condition the impact of economic conditions on mass support for the EU in two reverse ways. The effect of economic conditions on support for EU membership appears to decrease (and residuals in Model 1 to increase) the older the membership of the EC: this is congruent with the idea that citizens of EU member states become socialised into the European community over time. At a certain point in time, the more time has gone by since joining, the less

Table 5.2 How the length of membership and the degree of EU institutionalisation shape the relationship between economic conditions and support for EU membership (EU-15, 1973–2011)

	Model 3
Length of membership	0.070*** (0.010)
EU institutional density	–0.096* (0.036)
Eurozone	–0.766* (0.356)
Intercept	79.53*** (0.698)
N	886
Adj. R^2	5.75%

Notes
OLS regression.
Statistically significant * $p < 0.05$; ** $p < 0.01$; *** $p < 0.001$. SE in parentheses.

prompt citizens are to call the principle of EU membership into question in times of economic crisis.

However, this observation is based on an analysis all things being equal and long-term trends in EU support are also shaped by another effect with contradictory implications. The more integrated policies are at the European level, that is the more EU institutional density there is, the more EU citizens tend to adjust their support for EU membership according to the economic context – a relationship that probably reflects the growing attribution of responsibility to the EU, as it becomes more institutionalised and acquires more competences. This effect is also observed when looking specifically at monetary policy: the effect of macro-economic conditions on public support for the EU is substantially stronger in Eurozone members than in countries outside the Eurozone, which corroborates the idea that institutional density matters.

At this time, in a weakly integrated European political system, bad economic performance altered European support but only up to a certain point. Economic prosperity was already the main objective of European integration, and citizens thus blamed European institutions when prosperity declined, but they did not consider them as the only factor responsible for bad economic performance. In the course of the integration process and of the delegation of growing powers to European institutions, in particular macro-economic competences, the link between economic performance and support has tightened: in a more integrated European political system, and especially within the Eurozone, the EU is considered as increasingly responsible for economic performance, and is blamed in economic hard times. The length of membership only moderates this trend: at a given point in time characterised by a certain degree of institutionalisation, the climate of opinion is less sensitive to economic conditions in 'older' member states than in 'newer' ones.

Conclusions

The current crisis being 'the most difficult set of economic and financial circumstances for over half a century' (Buti and Carnot 2012: 910), it offers an extreme case with which to evaluate the effect of macro-economic performance on citizens' EU support. Contrary to what the literature of the 1990s and 2000s proposed, our findings suggest that economic considerations are not fading as determinants of EU support but, on the contrary, that they have become increasingly relevant. It could have been assumed that the impact of economic conditions was diluted over time because of the interference of further relevant policies that have been delegated to the EU. However given the overall limited public knowledge of the Europeanisation of public policies and given the increasing weight of the EU in economic policy, it is after all not so surprising that economic considerations tend to matter more over time. Yet, the time-honoured observation of a citizens' socialisation effect leading them to develop an affective support for European integration as time goes by: they are less prompt to call their support for integration into question in economic hard times, the more time has expired.

However, this result holds only all things being equal, and it does therefore not imply growing support over time: though, at a point in time, public support is less conditioned on economic performance in older member states, the latter nevertheless tend to hold the EU more responsible for this performance over time, as it becomes more institutionalised and is delegated a growing number of powers. In other words, our results suggest that *when the economy deteriorates, citizens tend to blame the EU more than in the past, as they assign the responsibility of economic condition to the EU.*

Our results also imply that despite the high degree of institutionalisation achieved, in times of crisis, bad economic performance not only affects support for specific policies and for incumbent representatives, as would be the case in a national political system, but alters input support as well, as trust for EU institutions decreases. It therefore jeopardises the legitimacy of the European political system as a whole. Why is there such a difference between national political system and a regional political system such as the EU? As claimed by Hobolt and Tilley (2014: 136) distrust results from the lack of an accountability mechanism at the regional level:

> every time the system fails to deliver, the result is declining levels of trust and a crisis of confidence in the regime as a whole, because voters lack the opportunity to 'throw the rascals out' and elect a new government.

As such accountability mechanisms are not easy to set up at the regional integration level,[17] notably because of the lack of a European public sphere, the discrepancy between the growing assignment of responsibility to the EU and its lack of accountability is destined to play an important role in citizens' support for European integration in the years to come.

At the institutional level, the effect of the economic crisis is double-sided: it weakens the system as it puts it under great pressure to react adequately, yet it appeals for more concerted responses at the European level. Whether it reactivates the intergovernmental vision of the European integration process or constitutes a new step in the neofunctionalist spill-over is still a matter of interpretation. At the citizens' level, our results show that the economic crisis, as it reveals that citizens hold the EU more and more responsible for bad economic performance without being able to punish it for these bad results, undermines public support not only for policy outputs in the economic field but also for the European political system as a whole.

How much will this affect European regional integration in the following years? A common prediction is that Eurosceptic political leaders will use this decrease in support to claim a spill-back of European regional integration. However their success would depend on their ability to make citizens believe they can still be held responsible for economic conditions in a globalised economic system. That this decrease of support will be used both by member states and by European institutions when bargaining for more power or changing rules in the EU political system does appear certain.

The neofunctionalist 'old regionalism' theory predicted that as regional integration increased due to the spill-over effect from the elites to the 'masses', citizens' support for the European project would grow and push forward more integration (Haas 1958; Lindberg 1963). The Danish 'no' vote to the Maastricht Treaty and the ensuing growing ambivalence in citizens' opinions put an end to such expectations and invited scholars to invoke citizens not as 'necessary ghosts' (Smith 1995) of the European democratic political system but as true EU political actors. Reinventing European citizens' role and boosting citizens' support in the aftermath of the European crisis to answer the legitimacy crisis shall be on top of political elites' agendas for the years to come.

Appendix: correlation matrix between the independent variables (Pearson's R)

Table 5.3

	Growth	*Unemployment*	*Inflation*
Growth	1		
Unemployment	–0.05	1	
Inflation	–0.04	–0.09	1

Notes

1 The authors would like to thank Frédéric Gonthier and Raul Magni-Berton for their precious help in defining and implementing the regression models. Comments from participants in the ECSA-C Montreal in May 2014 were also very useful.
2 See introduction for a more detailed definition of institutional density.
3 This country-specific factor has to be distinguished from the more general variable of institutional density of the EU. For example, Austria in 1995 and Ireland in 1973 may not be comparable, although both were in their first year of membership, because the overall degree of institutionalisation of the European community was very different.
4 'Taking everything into consideration, would you say that (your country) has on balance benefited or not from being a member of the European Community (Common Market)? Benefited/not benefited'.
5 'How would you judge the situation of the European economy? Very good/rather good/rather bad/very bad'
6 'On the whole, are you very satisfied, fairly satisfied, not very satisfied, not satisfied at all by the way democracy works in the European Union?'
7 The question 'In the near future do you see yourself as (national) only, (national) and European, European and (national), European only?' was asked only in 2010 and 2013.
8 'For each of the following institutions, tell me if you tend to trust it or tend not to trust it: the European Commission, the European Parliament, the Council of the EU and the European Central Bank'.
9 'In general, does the European Union conjure up for you a very positive, fairly positive, neutral, fairly negative or very negative image?'
10 Ratio = Positive opinions divided by the sum of positive + negative opinions, multiplied by 100.

11 'Generally speaking, do you think that [your country's] membership of the European Community [Common Market] is a good thing, a bad thing, neither good nor bad?'
12 It started even earlier in Italy.
13 As this item has often been included more than once a year in Eurobarometer surveys, this allows us to have between 30 and 75 data points for each country – depending on the country's date of joining. The panel is thus unbalanced.
14 The random intercept accounts for the two-level (country and EB wave) nature of the data, and corrects for the dependence of observations within countries (intra-class correlation). Modelled in this way, the intercept takes into account time-invariant national idiosyncrasies, or specific events affecting all individuals in a given year, which may alter the baseline values for the citizens of a particular country or during a particular year. Such national or temporal effects may include the type of events described by Çiftçi (2005), and contrasts linked to the country's position in the international system, national context, culture and memory (Diez-Medrano 2003) and to the timing and circumstances of the country's membership of the EU (Anderson and Kaltenthaler 1996).
15 As illustrated by the correlation matrix in the appendix, these indicators are not correlated in a way that could foster suspicions of multicollinearity and they can thus be treated in a single analysis.
16 It is important to distinguish between the two dimensions of general institutional density of the EU as a whole and individual member states' level of integration into the EU: some countries are, at some point, recent members, but in an already strongly integrated EU. This is in particular the case of Austria, Finland and Sweden in 1995. By contrast, founding members had already been members for several decades in 1973, but the EU was far less integrated at that time. The institutional density of the EU and the length of membership may even have contradictory effects. For instance, the cross-national convergence in public support for integration observed by Eichenberg and Dalton (2007) could indicate that the national differences linked to different timing of joining the EU decrease when the institutional density of the EU increases (Anderson and Kaltenthaler 1996; Balestrini *et al.* 2010).
17 Different solutions are proposed to tackle this lack of accountability such as the direct election of the European Commission's president, the emergence of European political parties which will compete both at European Parliament elections and the European Commission's President's election or the transfer of more and more executive power to the European Parliament (Follesdal and Hix 2006; Hix 2008).

References

Anderson, Christopher (1995). Economic Uncertainty and European Solidarity Revisited: Trends in Public Support for European Integration. In Rhodes, Carolyn and Mazey, Sonia (eds.). *The State of the European Union.* Vol. 3. Boulder: Lynne Rienner, 111–133.

Anderson, Christopher and Kaltenthaler, Karl (1996). The Dynamics of Public Opinion toward European Integration, 1973–93. *European Journal of International Relations, 2*(2), 175–199.

Anderson, Christopher and Reichert, Shawn (1995). Economic Benefits and Support for Membership in the EU: A Cross-National Analysis, *Journal of Public Policy, 15*(3), 231–249.

Armingeon, Klaus and Baccaro, Lucio (2012). The Sorrows of Young Euro. Policy Responses to the Sovereign Debt Crisis. In Bermeo, Nancy and Pontusson, Jonas (eds.). *Coping with Crisis. Government Reactions to the Great Recession.* New York: Russell Sage, 162–197.

Armingeon, Klaus and Ceka, Besir (2014). The loss of trust in the European Union during the great recession since 2007: The role of heuristics from the national political system. *European Union Politics*, *15*(1), 82–117.

Balestrini, Pierre P., Flood, Christopher and Flockton, Christopher (2010). National Public Opinion and the EU in the Post-Maastricht Era: Is the Socialisation Theory Actually Dead? *Journal of Contemporary European Studies*, *18*(3), 377–400.

Balestrini, Pierre P., Flood, Christopher and Flockton, Christopher (2011). How Identity Interacts with Economic and Societal Rationality to Drive Public Opinion on the European Union. The Role of Crime, Unemployment and Immigration, *Perspectives on European Politics and Society*, *12*(2), 121–138.

Biesenbender, Jan (2011). The Dynamics of Treaty Change: Measuring the Distribution of Power in the European Union? *European Integration Online Papers*, vol. 15, art. 5.

Bosch, Agusti and Newton, Kenneth (1995). Economic Calculus or Familiarity Breeds Content? In Niedermayer, Oskar and Sinnott. Richard (eds.). *Public Opinion and Internationalized Governance*. Oxford: Oxford University Press.

Braun, Daniela and Tausendpfund, Markus (2014). The Impact of the Euro Crisis on Citizens' Support for the European Union. *Journal of European Integration*, *36*(3), 231–245.

Buti, Marco and Carnot, Nicolas (2012). The EMU Debt Crisis: Early Lessons and Reforms, *Journal of Common Market Studies*, *50*(6), 899–911.

Christin, Thomas (2005). Economic and Political Basis of Attitudes towards the EU in Central and East European Countries in the 1990s. *European Union Politics*, *6*(1), 29–57.

Çiftçi, Sabri (2005). Treaties, Collective Responses and the Determinants of Aggregate Support for European Integration. *European Union Politics*, *6*(4), 469–492.

Citrin, Jack and Sides, John (2004). More than nationals: How identity choice matters in the new Europe. In Herrmann, Richard K., Risse, Thomas and Brewer, Marilynn B. (eds.). *Transnational Identities: Becoming European in the EU*, Lanham, MD: Rowman & Littlefield, 161–185.

Diez Medrano, Juan (2003). *Framing Europe. Attitudes to European Integration in Germany, Spain and the United Kingdom*. Oxford: Oxford University Press.

Easton, David (1965). *A Systems Analysis of Political Life*. New York: John Wiley and Sons.

Easton, David (1975). A Re-assessment of the Concept of Political Support, *British Journal of Political Science*, 5, 435–457.

Eichenberg, Richard and Dalton, Russell (1993). European and the European Community: the dynamics of public support for European integration, *International Organization*, *47*(4), 507–534.

Eichenberg, Richard and Dalton, Russell (2007). Post-Maastricht Blues: The Transformation of Citizen Support for European Integration, 1973–2004. *Acta Politica*, 42, 128–152.

Follesdal, Andreas and Hix, Simon (2006). Why There is a Democratic Deficit in the EU: a Response to Majone and Moravcsik. *Journal of Common Market Studies*, *44*(3), 533–562.

Gabel, Matthew (1998). *Interests and Integration: Market Liberalization, Public Opinion and European Union*. Ann Arbor: University of Michigan Press.

Gabel, Matthew and Whitten, Guy (1997). Economic conditions, economic perceptions, and public support for European integration. *Political Behavior*, *19*(1), 81–96.

Gamble, Andrew (1995). Economic Recession and Disenchantment with Europe. *West European Politics*, *8*(3), 158–174.

Garry, John and Tilley, James (2009). The Macroeconomic Factors Conditioning the Impact of Identity on Attitudes towards the EU. *European Union Politics*, *10*(3), 361–379.

Gomez, Raul (2015). The Economy Strikes Back: Support for the EU during the Great Recession. *Journal of Common Market Studies*, *53*(3), 577–592.

Haas, Ernst (1958). *The Uniting of Europe: political, social and economic forces – 1950–1957*. Stanford: Stanford University Press.

Hix, Simon (2008). *What's Wrong With the European Union and How to Fix It*. Cambridge: Polity Press.

Hobolt, Sara B. and Tilley, James (2014). Who is Responsible? In Hobolt, Sara B. and Tilley, James. *Blaming Europe? Responsibility without Accountability in the European Union*. Oxford: Oxford University Press, 8–28.

Hobolt, Sara B. and Wratil, Christopher (2015). Public opinion and the crisis: the dynamics of support for the euro. *Journal of European Public Policy*, *22*(2), 238–256.

Hooghe, Liesbet and Marks, Gary (2005). Calculation, Community and Cues. Public Opinion on European Integration. *European Union Politics*, *6*(4), 419–443.

Inglehart, Ronald and Rabier, Jacques-René (1978). Economic uncertainty and European solidarity: Public opinion trends. *Annals of the American Academy of Political and Social Science*, (440), 66–87.

Kuhn, Theresa and Stoeckel, Florian (2014). When European integration becomes costly: the euro crisis and public support for European economic governance. *Journal of European Public Policy*, *21*(4), 624–641.

Levy, Naomi and Phan, Bonnie (2014). The Utility of Identity: Explaining Support for the EU after the Crash. *Polity*, *46*(4), 562–590.

Lindberg, Leon (1963). *The Political Dynamics of Economic European Integration*. Stanford: Stanford University Press, 1963.

Mahler, Vincent A., Taylor, Bruce J. and Wozniak, Jennifer R. (2000). Economics and Public Support for the European Union: An Analysis at the National, Regional, and Individual Levels. *Polity*, *32*(3), 429–453.

Marsh, Michael (1999). Policy Performance. In Hermann Schmitt and Jacques Thomassen, *Political Representation and Legitimacy in the European Union*. Oxford: Oxford University Press, 91–106.

Rohrschneider, Robert and Loveless, Matthew (2010). Macro Salience: How Economic and Political Contexts Mediate Popular Evaluation of the Democracy Deficit in the European Union. *Journal of Politics*, *72*(4), 1029–1045.

Roth, Felix, Gros, Daniel and Nowak-Lehmann, Felicitas (2014). Crisis and Citizens' Trust in the European Central Bank – Panel Data Evidence for the Euro Area, 1999–2012. *Journal of European Integration*, *36*(3), 303–320.

Scharpf, Fritz (1999). *Governing in Europe: Effective and Democratic?* Oxford: Oxford University Press.

Serricchio, Fabio, Tsakatika, Myrto and Quaglia, Lucia (2013). Euroscepticism and the Global Financial Crisis. *Journal of Common Market Studies*, *51*(1), 51–64.

Smith, Andy (1995). Going beyond the Democratic Deficit: The European Union and Rural Development in Networked Societies. *Regional and Federal Studies*, *5*(1), 45–66.

Smith, Dale L. and Wanke, Jürgen (1993). Completing the Single European Market: An Analysis of the Impact on the Member States. *American Journal of Political Science*, *37*(2), 529–554.

Part II

Latin American regional integration

6 Economic crisis and regionalism in Central America

A path dependent logic of failure

Kevin Parthenay

On 15 September, five Central American nations (Costa Rica, El Salvador, Guatemala, Honduras and Nicaragua) celebrate their independence. In 1821, the Congress of Central American Countries declared its independence from Spain and ended the Captaincy General of Guatemala. Consequently, 15 September marks the emergence of a new era after five centuries of Hispanic domination. A hazardous coincidence made that 187 years later, another major event was to happen that would shake the Central American isthmus.

On the 15 September 2008, Lehman Brothers declared bankruptcy. The largest bankruptcy in US history that brought the beginning of an economic and financial crisis. The vicious circle of the crisis is clearly detailed in a World Bank analysis:

> the bankruptcy of a US investment bank, Lehman Brothers, in 2008 turned a severe credit crunch … resulting in an unprecedented dislocation in financial markets and damaging stability and confidence in many advanced financial systems. The unprecedented pouring of financial support from national governments and monetary authorities … also caused a rapid deterioration in many countries' fiscal balances, reducing the fiscal room and governments' ability to further support weak economic activity. As economic activity further weakened and a massive number of jobs were lost around the world, unemployment rates climbed to unprecedented levels. Countries with weak institutional capacity and limited fiscal room have been particularly hurt.
>
> (Otker-Robe and Podpiera 2013)

Why did this crisis, which expanded globally, have such an impact on the Central American countries? First, the Central American economic structure is highly dependent on external trade. The United States of America is the region's main trade partner. Exports to the US represent between 20 per cent (Panama) and 47 per cent (El Salvador) of total country exports. On average 48 per cent of all Central American exports are directed to the US (Aráuz 2009). Imports to the US represent between 19 per cent (Nicaragua) and 50 per cent (Costa Rica) (CIA Factbook 2014). Thus, the United States of America remains the main external actor and geopolitical reference in the isthmus (Caldentey and Rojas 2013). With the exception of Panama, the Central American economies are sparsely diversified which makes them highly vulnerable to international market hazards.

In economic and geographic terms, the Central American States can be ranked as 'small states'. With 44 million inhabitants spread over an area of 522,000 kms^2, the regional consumer market is small and produces predominantly raw materials and agricultural commodities. The global economic and financial crisis in addition to a general curbing of inflation (CEPAL 2009) had a negative impact on those small markets. Economies decelerated and the weakest members of society – already affected by development delays – became even more vulnerable. With the 2008 crisis, Central America paid a hefty price for its dependency on the US and its vulnerability to external events and which reinforced its status of 'peripheral region'.

What is the concrete impact of the crisis? Economically, the growth rate and exports slowed drastically as well as foreign direct investments, remittances and tourism (Aráuz 2009). Socially, the crisis increased food and hydrocarbon prices, as well as unemployment. It has shaken both urban and rural areas and raised the poverty rate.

Facing this international crisis, the Central American ministers oriented their actions primarily towards a regional macro-economic stability and fiscal responsibility. To protect Central America and mitigate crisis' impacts, ministers asked for an extension of the external financial cooperation (AFP 2009). Among regional organisations and political leaders, economic flexibility and openness as well as regional integration were immediate anti-crisis solutions. A month after Lehman Brothers' bankruptcy, Central American Presidents gathered in Tegucigalpa (Honduras) and called for an increase in intra-regional trade, via the implementation of several emergency measures and the consolidation of interregionalism (Official Statement, 4 October 2010). Since 2008, domestic policies against the crisis are formulated to work in synergy with regional plans, despite the differentiating impact of the crisis across countries. For instance, the percentages of remittances in the national GDPs greatly vary from a country to another. As a consequence, these variations meant each country had a differing exposure to the international crisis. Hence, a regional plan quickly became a priority to combat the economic and financial crisis of 2008–2009.

Considering that a financial and economic crisis threatens job security and welfare benefits of citizens and thus undermines the trust in the economic system and that it implies a sense of urgency, as underlined in the introductory chapter of this collective volume, my chapter offers a unique insight on how regional organisations in Central America responded to a historical crisis. The Central American region is such a neglected case study that not a single survey has been produced since 2008 on how the crisis has been influential to regional integration. As crises are critical junctures, which introduce periods of uncertainty in longer periods of stability or so-called 'punctuated equilibria' (Baumgartner and Jones 1993), the chapter will offer insightful perspectives to draw regional comparisons.

As claimed by the authors in the introduction, it is paramount to wonder, through a new institutionalist approach based on an actor-centred research design, if the regional institutions change in periods of economic and financial crises and to explain why they change to different degrees and in different directions. The main question of this chapter is then, has the economic crisis deepened Central American integration or conversely, did it lead to progressively weaker regional integration?

As proposed in the introduction of this book, to address those questions, I mainly focus on the power relations and the impact of institutional density. As far as the Central American case study is concerned, the issue of changing citizens' attitude may easily be dismissed, given the sharp disconnection between the Central American population and its regional institutions. However, given the unstable political systems, it makes sense to consider how member states' engagement or positions can evolve in periods of crisis. Moreover, it then becomes particularly relevant to put into question the impact of institutional density on structural change in a system that has been constantly under reforms and that encounters a systematic problem of compliance (Parthenay 2013). In that in-depth study of the Central American regional integration, the actors' behaviour will be observed based on their motivation and strategy to increase influence as well as legitimacy. Later on, the institutional density will be studied according to the levels of influence exercised by the specific regional integration through the existing formal and informal rules.

The chapter will be organised as follows: First, I propose a general overview of the regional setting in order to present the different actors at stake and an analysis of the organisational setting of the regional economic sector. Second, I will offer an empirical examination of the regional actors' behaviour and the institutional density's impact on regional integration during the period of economic and financial crisis of 2008. At the end of the chapter, I will finally explain to what extent the conservative approach – that is to say the stability of a pre-existing institutional essence – is more appropriate for our Central American case study to understand the regional organisations' response to the economic and financial crises, rather than a reformist approach.

The Central American economic institutionalism

In this first section, I offer a general overview of the Central American economic institutionalism. Added to the descriptive and historical value of the section, this overview will be necessary to better understand – in the second section – if the institutional density matters in times of crisis.

Regional economic integration backgrounds

The Central American economic institutionalism is dense and old. On 13 December 1960, Guatemala, El Salvador, Honduras and Nicaragua signed the first regional economic legal agreement: the General Treaty of Central American Economic Integration.[1] This treaty is the baseline of all regional economic and trade policies. It created the Central American Common Market (CACM) which aimed at promoting trade exchanges; reducing trade barriers; implementing GATT principles; and fostering free circulation of goods and persons.

At that time, the creation of the Central American Common Market was a tool to develop the region, economically and socially, and to promote its internationalisation. CEPAL's doctrine advised to substitute agro-exporting economies with industrial economies supported by regional cooperation. Economic regional integration was then a substitute to a failing economic model, enabling Central America to increase its production and trade to create growth. In a way, the very beginnings of Central American regional integration managed to avoid a general crisis. Interdependence and the creation of the background conditions for closer relationships were the main objectives. As Philippe Schmitter declared

> the General Treaty was not simply a once-and-for-all agreement to eliminate barriers on mutual trade or to distribute benefits according to some pre-established formula but a rather ingeniously contrived set of continuous obligations to meet recurrently in the elaboration of a number of interrelated endeavours.
>
> (Schmitter 1970: 5)

This general agreement had a great effect on liberalising trade and generating a spill-over effect. Consecutively, three bodies were created: Central American Economic Council (ministerial body), the Executive Council (countries' representatives), and a Permanent Secretariat (SIECA) (Schmitter 1970: 6). Rapidly, the institutional setting of regional economic integration intensified. A Central American Bank for Economic Integration (CABEI) was established in 1960 and received massive external support. As well as other institutions emanating from the General Treaty, the regional Bank remained mainly disconnected – since its creation – from other regional institutions. As a consequence, it cannot provide the expected results that motivated its creation. In a limpid formula, Schmitter said that CABEI 'has not functioned as a integral part of a coordinated integrationist strategy aimed at exploiting growing interdependence' (Schmitter 1970: 10). This remark goes far beyond the historical context, as similar phenomena have occurred regularly since.

Contemporary regional integration

After the 'lost decade' of the 1980s, Central America entered a new era. The domestic conflicts (mainly in El Salvador, Nicaragua and Guatemala[2]) progressively ended and a new international economic order was created. In June 1990, an Economic Action Plan for Central America (PAECA) intended to create a new legal framework and a new tariff structure (CEPAL 2009: 6). Thus, a new institutional configuration appeared with the Tegucigalpa Protocol that gave birth to SICA (*Sistema de la Integración Centroamericana*) in 1991. The Guatemala Protocol was established immediately following Tegucigalpa and contemplated economic regional activities. It created a subsystem of SICA that had no binding power over states. Once again, and as Schmitter explained for the 1970s, the economic subsystem lacked of general coordination with the overall regional integration system.

More recently, the complex coordination between institutions has been accentuated by states discrepancies over regional integration perspectives. Indeed, in Central America, the issue of 'differentiated integration' (Dabène 2009, Leuffen *et al.* 2013, Parthenay 2013) is at stake. Different subgroups emerged within the Central American Common Market since the early 1990s. El Salvador, Guatemala and Honduras signed a large number of trilateral agreements in order to accelerate regional integration (CEPAL 2009: 6). This so-called 'Northern Triangle' group is sometimes joined by Nicaragua and becomes the 'C4 Group'. Since 2009, El Salvador and Guatemala agreed to complementary bilateral agreements to further deepen the liberalisation of goods and people. Honduras joined these agreements in May 2009. Finally, El Salvador and Guatemala regularly announce the creation of a custom union, an initiative that has never came to fruition despite numerous attempts. Recently, Panama has also joined the Guatemala Protocol and the General Treaty (CACM) in order to ratify the free trade agreement with the European Union (Acuerdo de Asociación). Despite major economic asymmetries between Panama and the other Central American countries, the bi-regional initiative added a new member into the Central American economic institutionalism.

Differentiated integration

Like in the 1970s, the current economic institutionalism stays mainly disconnected from the SICA. The economic integration success story has led to a semi-autonomous functioning of the regional economic bodies and a strong competition between political and economic integration. This differentiated integration explains the conflictual nature of institutional relations (Parthenay 2013). This competition has not only legal and organisational but also sociological evidences.

The Tegucigalpa Protocol offers an institutional supremacy to political organs. As the main subsystem, intuitively we should consider that it benefits from a stronger legal apparatus. However, the reality of the differentiated integration is that it largely favours the economic subsystem and disrupts the harmony and equilibrium of the regional institutional order. In terms of legal instruments, the economic system has 42 instruments, with 13, seven and six, respectively across the political, social and environmental subsystems. The economic subsystem is much more developed and institutionalised than any other subsystem in the Central American regional integration. We can number 67 legal instruments (2,372 norms[3]) against 49 for the political subsystem (1,010 norms), 40 for the social subsystem (1,111 norms) and 15 for the environmental subsystem (336 norms).

The organisational perspective constitutes another evidence of the differentiated integration that will then help to understand the consequences of the crisis on Central American integration. The Economic Secretariat (SIECA) is the only one to survive the regional crisis of the 1980s. As a consequence, the Secretariat has beneficiated from a longer institutionalisation dynamics with more human resources. In 1991, 61 officials were working at the SIECA while seven were recruited to start the General Secretariat's activities. In 2011, an important difference is still exists between the economic sector and all the other sectors. Today, 35 officials are working permanently in the General Secretariat while more than 100 officials are represented at the SIECA. Despite this human resources asymmetry, this regional economic organisation faces a lack of administrative regulation in terms of professional relations and organisational management (Price Waterhouse Coopers 2008). In organisational terms, the economic secretariat is deeply specialised and no major change is observable in terms of internal structure. Since its creation in 1993, SIECA is composed of several programmes: intra-regional trade, extra-regional trade, Central American cooperation, physical integration and infrastructure, economic and social investigation. From 1993, the dynamics of change is characterised by a deep vertical specialisation. For instance, the Economic and Trade Direction is composed with 'units' for integration, transport and physical infrastructure and a Technical Unit that gathers a large variety of activities (custom areas, administrative records, taxes). The SIECA still receives the major financial contribution among regional organisations. Each Economic minister provides an annual allocation of $500,000 ($3,500,000 with seven countries). Despite such a diagnostic, the SIECA has constantly faced internal crises. The General Secretary changed several times in a short period of time. The Economic Ministers elected at SIECA's head Ernesto Torres Chico in January 2011, in replacement of Yolanda Mayora de Gavidia who headed the institution for only two years. After another two years in function, an institutional controversy generated the replacement of Torres Chico. In July 2013, the Council of Economic Minister elected for the first time a woman and a Panamanian at SIECA's head, Carmen Gisela Vergara. As a consequence, institutional instability is also a constant in the development of SIECA.

In spite of this instability, an important number of regional organisations in the economic subsystem have been created since the beginning of the decade 2000. Those organisations are listed below.

Table 6.1 Regional economic organisations in Central America

SICA	*Organisations*
Sectorial Councils	SE-COSERN, SE-CONPLAN, CCT, SE-CAC, COMIECO, COMITRAN, SE-CMC, SE-COSEFIN.[4]
Comities, commissions, institutions, specialised organisms	COCATRAM, COCESNA, BCIE, CENPROMYPE, CONCADECO, CRICAP, ACNA, ACSA, REPICA, ROCRAM, COCAVIAL, CODITRANS.[5]

Source: author's elaboration.

To conclude this general overview of economic regional institutionalism, we note that the Central American integration has developed in a differentiated pace. Compared to other subsystems, the economic subsystem is much more institutionalised. Moreover, the regional economic regulation is also a competence of high political authorities such the presidential Summits and the Councils of Foreign Affairs Ministers. The landscape of regional economic institutions seems to have bettered the countries' capacity to respond to a major crisis. However, there is a necessity to go through an empirical examination. Has the institutional density of the Central American integration system – in particular the economic subsystem – been an efficient shield against the crisis? The empirical examination that follows in the second section of the chapter will enable to offer a clear answer to the authors' second hypothesis (see introduction): in period of crisis, does the institutional density structure help to push integration forward or does it foster path dependence logic?

Facing the crisis: the 'failed regional tilt'

In 2009, an economic report from the ICEFI (Central American Institute for Fiscal Studies) asserts that 'in response to the deepest economic crisis for decades, managers that dictate public policies in advanced and emerging economies adopted monetary and fiscal countercyclical measures, intending to support economic activities and, in turn, to protect the population' and wonders if 'a same recipe in Central America would be necessary and how it would be funded?' (Baroni 2009: 68). Unfortunately, the Central America States have not been able to act like more advanced economies.

Reactions against the economic crisis: agenda

On 29 May 2008, the very first impacts of the crisis were observed. In reaction, the Central American Presidents called an Extraordinary Summit[6] to discuss the increase of oil prices, and its negative impact on food prices. During this summit of San Salvador (El Salvador), the Presidents called for a decrease in oil prices and offered to explore – in partnership with Brazil – alternative sources of energy. Moreover, they asked the board of the Central American Bank for Economic Integration (CABEI) to meet and take initiatives to support food production and the labour market. The intergovernmental SICA was then calling for the support of a supranational body.

On 26 June 2008, a second presidential summit dealt with the economic instability. This presidential meeting ended with several proposals: an emergency plan for food production created by the Central American Agricultural Council (CAC), a food security programme with the Central American Bank for Economic Integration, measures to strengthen intra-regional trade, ministerial coordination to integrate Panama to the regional integration framework, a convergence of free trade agreements to open new opportunities in the international market, a support to Central American economic integration in order to face the crisis. Rapidly, a diagnostic was made regarding the positive outcomes of regional complementarity and institutional coordination at national and regional levels. For the first time, during the San Salvador Summit (26 June 2008), the Central American Presidents underlined the necessity to face the economic and financial crisis through regional and collective initiatives. At that time, the support of several regional actors had already been asked, among them the Central American Agricultural Council (CAC) and the Central American Bank for Economic Integration (CABEI).

On 4 October 2008, the Central American Presidents finally made an official statement over the economic crisis. They stressed at Tegucigalpa, during another summit, the crisis' gravity and called for emergency actions to mitigate social impacts. The Presidents asked the COMIECO (Council of Economic Ministers) and the SIECA to elaborate immediate measures to consolidate and strengthen intra-regional trade; they asked the CABEI to extend credit lines, CABEI and CAC to implement a Food Security Program under 30 days; the General Secretariat of the SICA to strengthen relations with Latin American regional integration initiatives; the national ministers to increase food production; and the Foreign Relations Ministers Council to foster and tighten strategic and financial alliances with southern countries. Unanimously, the Central American Presidents clearly bet on regional initiatives to protect Central American countries from the crisis, like they already did in 1998 after the natural disaster provoked by Hurricane Mitch. Indeed, at the end of the following summit, the Presidents finally declared that the crisis was an opportunity to consolidate the regional integration system.[7]

The Presidents insisted heavily on regional and multilateral cooperation in the following summit's official statements (5 December 2008). They asked the SGSICA to get closer from the CARICOM (Caribbean Common Market), the UNASUR (Southern Nations' Union), and the United Nations. A year later, on 25 March 2009, the Presidents assured that this unity was the best way to offer solutions to Central American problems, one of them being the economic and financial crisis.[8] Similarly, on 23 February 2009, the Council of Finance Ministers met and decided to unify the region in order to address collectively against the crisis. From the presidential summits to the ministerial councils, all the Central American authorities agreed on regionalism as the right tool to mitigate crisis impacts over the isthmus.

As the regional discourses have been slow to be operationalised, the Central American governments also implemented a series of measures at a domestic level. Despite the regional tilt described above, each country elaborated its own plan in order to fight against the crisis effects: 'Plan Escudo' in Costa Rica, 'Plan Global contra la crisis' in El Salvador, 'Plan de defensa de la producción, crecimiento y empleo' in Nicaragua. Moreover, all governments planned tax reforms to mitigate the effects of the crisis. In Guatemala, the Colom government planned a complete tax reform in 2008. However, the reform was rejected by the Congress, lacked of support from the executive and faced conflict with the private sector. A similar discussion started in 2009 in El Salvador. Except for the creation of a Tax Commission, the Congress approved no reform and a new reform proposal is still in progress within the Finance Ministry. In Honduras, political turmoil blocked any tax reform process. Indeed, on 28 June 2009, a coup d'état ended Manuel Zelaya's presidency and blocked all political and economic reforms. Meanwhile, the International Monetary Fund (IMF) compensated the absence of political stability with external financial support. Nicaragua is the only country that technically succeeded in passing a tax reform in 2009 ('Ley de Concertacion Tributaria'). However, its efficiency has been debated and a new proposal is still under consideration by the executive. Finally, in Costa Rica and Panama, opposition from both the political left wing and the private sector prevented any reform (ICEFI 2011). As a consequence, at a domestic level, political authorities did not manage to pass the required reforms to face the economic and financial crisis. Tax reforms are very emblematic of that incapacity to offer political answers to turbulent economic circumstances. In many countries, private sectors and political cleavages in the Congresses impeded the reforms. However, the main outcome is that national authorities appeared to be unprepared and unable to promote the adequate answers to a critical context. As a conclusion, Central America has suffered not only from its national authorities' inability to respond to the crisis but also from the incapacity of regional institutionalism to implement concrete measures. The Central Americans had then to face a regulation vacuum. In that perspective and as organisational sociologists would say, in the absence of formal response to the crisis, some actors might take advantage of what appears to be an 'opportunity zone' (Crozier and Friedberg 1971) in order to strengthen their power and autonomy.

Reaction against the economic crisis: actors

In such a turbulent economic context, is there a continued engagement towards regional integration or a progressive disillusionment and decline? Facing the economic and financial crisis, Central American entrepreneurs pushed for regionalism. Saying that, we still have to define: what kind of entrepreneurship and what kind of entrepreneurs? Indeed, entrepreneurs may promote regional integration positively (regional policies) or negatively (contestation and social mobilisations) (Scharpf 1999). Both categories of political entrepreneurs took part to the public debate while the region was hit by the crisis.

Entrepreneurs who were supportive of an alternative regional integration appeared as the Central American Free Trade Agreement (CAFTA) was ratified with the United States of America and implemented in 2009. In fact, this trade agreement was simultaneous to the beginning of the crisis. Many anti-neoliberal forces mobilised to contest, on the one hand, an asymmetrical agreement and, on the other hand, the incarnation of a neoliberal economic model. In that sense, the crisis fuelled the claims. They promoted alternative regional integration projects based on solidarity and common goods rather than inter and intra-regional trades. Some governments of the region also supported these initiatives. As a reaction against neoliberalism, Nicaragua, Honduras and later El Salvador (2009), joined the ALBA (Alternativa bolivariana para las Américas), a Venezuelan initiative launched by Hugo Chavez in December 2001. Its main mechanism of cooperation and influence, called Petrocaribe, is a programme of Venezuelan oil supply at a preferential price. As the energy demand of all Central American States is solely relies on imported resources, they suffered deeply from the rising of oil prices – which peaked in 2008 – and agreed to be part of this Venezuelan initiative. As mentioned by Martin Mowforth for the case of Honduras,

> Zelaya signed up for cheap petrol with Petrocaribe after a brief visit to Venezuela, thereby giving rise to conspiracies amongst the rightists. It didn't seem to occur to anyone that the decision would be any less ideological than a defence of the economy against a barrel of oil at 150 dollars.
>
> (Mowforth 2014: 73)

In 2009, it stopped with a coup d'état against Mel Zelaya. This 'alternative' had the double effect of presenting an alternative model of regionalism, grounded on solidarity, complementarity and justice, and one opposed to CEPAL 'open regionalism' model (CEPAL 1994). The best indicator of the positive economic effect generated by the ALBA is that many countries joined Petrocaribe without showing or wishing to forge a political-ideological alliance with Chavez's regime (Caldentey and Rojas 2013: 332). Guatemala joined Petrocaribe on the 13 July 2008. El Salvador is only starting to negotiate its adhesion to Petrocaribe (La Prensa Grafica 2014) but has created a mixed company 'ALBA Petroleos El Salvador' in 2006. Since then, many companies spread across all economic sectors were created, for instance Alba Gas, Alba Alimentos y Alba Medicamentos (Ferraro and Rastrollo 2013). Not only does this new model of regional cooperation – hence the use 'regionalism' rather than 'regional integration' – offer an ideological alternative to neoliberalism but it also offers a solution to compensate one of the major concrete effects of the crisis in Central America (energy price growth). The death of President Hugo Chavez raised many questions over the future of ALBA as well as the post-crisis recovery. Indeed, Guatemala already decided to leave Petrocaribe in November 2013.

Another pro-integration political entrepreneurship appeared as the Salvadorian government, and particularly the Foreign Affairs Minister Hugo Martinez, tried to push Central American integration forward through SICA's reform plan. Historically, El Salvador has always sought to act as a regional leader. A small market and geopolitical vulnerability explain this national strategy. The promotion of regional integration – in an extensive supranational dimension – is part of the diplomatic stand of the country (Sanchez 2009). Indeed, the regional activism is even formalised in the article 89 of the Constitution of 1983. The Salvadoran government assumed a leadership in three aspects at least.[9] The first dimension is that the country fosters the production of regional public goods through the promotion of regional political stability (Honduran crisis in 2009), the mitigation of environmental vulnerability (E-12 tropical storm), and the promotion of regional security. Second, the Salvadoran government assumed a leadership as an agenda-setter. It promoted a sectorial extension of the regional intervention capacities, particularly regarding social, environmental and security matters. Third, the Funes' government managed to support and promote the institutionalisation process of SICA. On 20 July 2010, it called for an Extraordinary Summit in order to lead a modernisation and rationalisation of the regional institutionalism. It acted in favour of an agenda focused on five pillars and rationalisation of administrative process (Parthenay 2013). It was not an immediate reaction to the economic crisis but an attitude forged by the crisis's experience.

As a consequence, from governments to civil society, a large spectrum of actors made the promotion of regional integration. However, we observe an important distinction on the type of integration promoted. Some defend an 'alternative' type of regional integration (alternative regionalism) while others promote a more traditional and classical form of regionalism promoting a reformist path (institutionalisation). As a consequence, it seems that a positive answer can be addressed to one of the authors' hypothesis (see introduction: 12). Indeed, we have observed there is a large spectrum of existing institutions, at both regional and national level, able to help face the economic crisis. We observed as well that many entrepreneurs were pushing integration forward, even if sometimes it is in different directions. The Central American experience seems to confirm that in period of crisis, the density of institutional structure produces a continued engagement with regional integration.

However, we must assess this empirical validation. Indeed, in the Central American case, the crisis did not actually 'push forward' regional integration but rather 'push for another type of regional integration'. In that perspective, it is quite obvious that the entrepreneurs that promoted 'alternative regionalism' belong to the later category. Notwithstanding, it is less obvious regarding the Salvadorian entrepreneurship. First, the whole strategy of the Salvadoran government is not oriented towards the consolidation of regional integration in order to fight against the economic crisis but towards a general modernisation of the Central American integration. In that sense, it is not the crisis but the institutional inertia that led the Salvadoran government to push forward regional integration. Subsequently, the SICA reform of 2010 has less to do with the economic crisis than it has with a general necessity to reactivate the regional political cooperation in different sectors, particularly security. As a consequence, the measures that were meant to directly avert the effects of the economic crisis suffered from this regional inertia. It appears that a better explains the lack of efficient response towards the economic crisis in Central America. Why the Central American regional integration remains rooted to a path dependent logic of inertia and inefficiency? The following part is fully dedicated to that question.

The path to Central American integration: the institutional stalemates

In order to explain the prominence of the path dependent dynamic, I now submit two major explaining variables. Those variables are the heavy legacy of a progressive disjunction between norms or legality and institutional practices. Then, we explore different aspects of that disjunction and observe how they operated during the economic and financial crisis of 2008. All the phenomena that happened during the crisis affected heavily Central America and explained the incapacity to reach an efficient resolution of the crisis.

The summit diplomacy

The Central American Presidents and Heads of States have lost the institutional control of the Central American Integration System (Parthenay 2015). The crisis of the presidential diplomacy generated a series of negative externalities and among these: a lack of trust and procedural stability, a misunderstanding of the integrationist rationality, a scattered and asymmetric institutional design, a low operationalisation of the ordinary agenda, an inefficiency of regular summits to contain the integration agenda, a strengthening of divergent diplomatic positions and finally a differentiated pace of regional integration.

One of the major contemporary critics towards SICA regards the inefficiency of the Presidential summits and particularly their outputs: the presidential mandates. Political legitimacy lies in the capability to foster change over society and economy. These presidential mandates are the main tools to promote change over the region. Indeed, to face the economic and financial crisis, two types of agenda have been set, national ones and a regional one. The national plans were elaborated soon after the bankruptcy of Lehman Brothers and as the first effects of the crisis appeared. In parallel, the regional agenda was set between the Presidents who called an exceptional summit but has hardly been implemented. On the 5 December 2008, the Central American Presidents approved a document called 'Plan of emergency measures to face in the region the international financial crisis' (Plan de Medidas Urgentes para Atender en la Region el Impacto de la Crisis Financiera Internacional) at the end of an Ordinary Summit (thirty-third Regional Summit). This plan elaborated in San Pedro Sula as the result of the summit diplomacy never came to fruition. In fact, on the 25 March 2009, the Presidents gathered in an Extraordinary Summit, organised in Managua (Nicaragua), and asked the SGSICA to elaborate regional proposals to face the crisis that hit the isthmus. The statement begins with a reminder that 'it is important to develop mechanisms to fight against the consequences of the different crisis that affect equally the countries of the region, in particular the financial crisis'.[10] These official statements never reached concrete application and the initial 41 measures of the emergency plan were mostly left unapplied.

As for many other issues, summit diplomacy failed to produce outputs to fight efficiently against the crisis. The Honduran political crisis that led to the coup d'état of July 2009 impeded even more the collective capacity to face the crisis with unity. This is because the SICA intergovernmental decision-making process is based on consensus and unanimity. Each state is fully sovereign and may veto the creation of norms and institutions. The political turmoil that extends to January 2010 prevents any regional intervention. The emergency had turned towards defending regional political stability defence.

The variable geometry

The regional institutional setting is pretty uncertain and differentiated. This may be conceptualised as 'variable geometry' or 'differentiated integration' (Leuffen *et al.* 2013). The uncertainty is the result of a high variability of legal instruments ratification. This is particularly significant for fundamental legal instruments. Among the seven fundamental pillars of SICA, only four instruments are fully ratified by all the member states. Some have been ratified only recently (2010) such as the social treaty in Honduras. Some others are still partially ratified like the Tegucigalpa Protocol (Dominican Republic unratified) or the Guatemala Protocol and the Social Treaty (Belize and Dominican Republic). Finally, the Security and Democratic Treaty as well as the Court of Justice Convention are still waiting respectively for three and four ratifications (Costa Rica, Panama and Dominican Republic; Belize, Costa Rica, Panama and Dominican Republic).

As a consequence, one cannot speak about a unique regional integration but a variety of Central American integrations. In 2009, what was variable geometry in the economic sector about? In 2008–2009, Panama, one of the major economic countries of the isthmus was not a member of the old economic integration system. Considering this data, it becomes difficult to understand how an opening strategy towards southern countries of Latin America (MERCOSUR) or Asia can be made possible without associating Panama, given it is one of the most economically open country of the world (thanks to the Panama Canal). When the crisis emerged, one of the main strategies was to diversify the trade partnerships and benefit from the advanced negotiations on a free trade agreement (Acuerdo de Asociación) with the European Union. The Panamanian ratification of the economic integration treaty (Guatemala Protocol) came on the 21 June 2013, at the edge of the final ratification of the interregional agreement. In 2008, this variable geometry affected once again the regional unity required to fight efficiently and strongly against the economic and financial crisis.

Conclusion

As a peripheral region, the 2008 economic and financial crisis underlined exposed the Central American countries' extreme vulnerability.

Considering the structural absence of mighty States in Central America, we have effectively seen that no actors had been able to sufficiently promote a regional reform in response to the crisis. Moreover, the harsh economic asymmetries between Costa Rica/Panama and their neighbours increase even more the complexity of a coherent and unified regional reaction to the crisis. In that perspective, the institutionalism has been an obstacle to necessary actions.

As a consequence, the empirical examination showed that institutional density in situation of crisis has lead to a continued engagement of institutions and member states towards regional integration in a path dependent dynamic. In that sense, the Central American integration system appeared to be mainly resilient to the crisis. Despite a regional relevance, national attempts to fight the crisis finally prevailed. The mistrust towards regional institutionalism was the main reason for this failure. The institutionalisation of Central American integration has been mainly ineffective in its response to the crisis when, paradoxically, all the authorities agreed on the necessity of a regional regulation. In the end, neither economic nor political regional resources have been engaged sufficiently to respond to the economic crisis.

The main explanation for this a paradoxical phenomenon is the presence of external interventions that compensated for the executive authorities' inaction and overcame national discrepancies. This led to aforementioned specific and isolated attempts to respond to the crisis where a regional dynamic would have been a more relevant option. The lesson is that Central America kept looking outside to address inner difficulties, as it occurred so many times across modern and contemporary regional history.

As a conclusion, the Central American case study tends to validate the authors' intuition that within a peripheral region, power relations and institutional density are weakly operative, the main explanatory lever still being external. When in 1970 Central America was told as a 'paradox of success' (Wynia 1970), we could say that nowadays Central America suffers a path dependent logic of failure.

Notes

1 Costa Rica ratified the treaty two years later, in 1963.
2 El Salvador 1992, Nicaragua 1990, Guatemala 1996.
3 Taking into account articles.
4 CONPLAN: Consejo de Ministros de Planificación de Centroamérica; CCT: Consejo Centroamericano de Turismo; CAC: Consejo Agropecuario Centroamericano; COMIECO: Consejo de Ministros de Economía de Centroamérica; COMITRAN: Consejo Sectorial de Ministros de Transporte de Centroamérica; CMC: Consejo Monetario Centroamericano; COSEFIN: Consejo de Ministros de Hacienda o Finanzas de Centroamérica.
5 COCATRAM: Comisión *Centroamericana* de Transporte Marítimo; COCESNA: Corporacion *Centroamericana* de Servicios de Navegación Aerea; BCIE: Banco Centroamericano de Integracion Economica; CENPROMYPE: Centro para la Promoción de la Micro y Pequeña Empresa en *Centroamérica; CONCADECO:* Consejo *Centroamericano* y de República Dominicana de Protección al Consumidor; CRICAP: Consejo Registral Inmobiliario de *Centro América*, Panamá y República Dominicana; ACNA: Agencia *Centroamericana* de Navegación Aérea; ACSA: Agencia *Centroamericana* de Seguridad Aeronáutica; REPICA: Reunión Portuaria del Istmo *Centroamericano; ROCRAM:* Red Operativa de Cooperación Regional de Autoridades Marítimas de *Centroamérica* y República Dominicana; COCAVIAL: Comité *Centroamericano* de Fondos Viales; CODITRANS: Comité Técnico Regional Permanente de Transporte.
6 Ordinary summit occurs one time per semester. However, a SICA member state may propose and organise an extraordinary summit on a specific issue.
7 Presidential Official Statement, twenty-third Meeting of SICA's Heads of State and Government, San Pedro Sula, Honduras, 5 December 2008: '*Que el impacto de la crisis financiera internacional es preocupación de nuestros países, por lo que debemos tomar medidas urgentes para enfrentarla y hacer de la misma una oportunidad para consolidar nuestro Sistema de Integración*'.

8 Extraordinary Meeting of SICA's Heads of State and Government, Managua, Nicaragua, 25 March 2009.

9 Mauricio Funes assumed the presidential function in 2009 after an historical election that brought for the first time the leftist party (FMLN) to power since the civil war (that ended 16 January 1992). This successful conquest of power has been impacted however by the economic and financial crisis and the private sector's fears to see the left assuming the power. Many difficulties impacted the government and the regional integration became one of the government's priorities.

10 Original statement: 'es importante desarrollar mecanismos para enfrentar las consecuencias de las distintas crisis que nos afectan por igual, en especial la financiera'.

References

AFP (2009). Consejo de Ministros CA pide mas apoyo al FMI para la crisis», Guatemala, 27 April.

Aráuz, A. (2009). El impacto de la crisis en América Central, *Nueva Sociedad* n°220.

Baroni, B. (2009). Centroamérica y la crisis económica: ¿cuál es el rol de las políticas contracíclicas?, Guatemala: Instituto Centroamericano de Estudios Fiscales.

Baumgartner, F. and Jones, B. (1993). *Agendas and Instability in American Politics*. Chicago: University of Chicago Press, American Politics and Political Economy Series.

Caldentey, P. and Rojas, F. (2013). Central America's Relations with Latin America. In Sanchez Ancochea, Daniel and Marti I Puig, Salvador (eds.). *Handbook of Central American Governance*. London: Routledge.

CEPAL (1994). *Open regionalism in Latin America and the Caribbean. Economic Integration as a Contribution to Changing Productions Pattern with Social Equity*. Santiago de Chile, Chile: CEPAL.

CEPAL (2009). La reacción de los Gobiernos de las Américas frente a la crisis internacional: una presentación sintética de las medidas de política anunciadas hasta el 31 de mayo de 2009. Santiago de Chile, Chile: CEPAL.

CIA Factbook (2014). Central America and Caribbean.

Crozier, M. and Friedberg, E. (1971). *L'acteur et le système*. Paris: Seuil.

Dabène, O. (2009). *The Politics of Latin American Integration*. New York: Macmillan.

Ferraro, A. and Rastrollo, J. J. (2013). Informe de consultoria: ¿Clientelismo político en El Salvador? Estudio de caso de Alba Petróleos y sus empresas relacionadas, Salamanca University/FUSADES.

ICEFI (2011). Reformas tributarias recientes en América Central: respondiendo a la crisis mundial, *Boletín de Estudios Fiscales No. 14*, San Salvador.

La Prensa Grafica (2014). El Salvador inicia negociacion acuerdo energia Petrocaribe, 5 July.

Leuffen, D., Rittberger, B. and Schimmelfennig, F. (2013). *Differentiated Integration: Explaining Variation in the European Union*. Basingstoke: Palgrave Macmillan.

Mowforth, M. (2014). *The Violence of Development. Resource Depletion, Environmental Crises and Human Rights Abuses in Central America*. New York: Pluto Press.

Otker-Robe, I. and Podpiera, A. M. (2013). The social impact of financial crises: evidence from the global financial crisis. *Policy Research Working Paper 6703*, World Bank, Washington.

Parthenay, K. (2013). *L'intégration régionale en Amérique centrale. Une sociologie politique du changement*. Thèse de doctorat, Institut d'Etudes Politiques de Paris.

Parthenay, K. (2015). Presidential Summitry in Central America: A Predictable Failure? In Mace, Gordon, Thérien, Jean-Philippe, Dabène, Olivier and Tussie, Diana (eds.). *Summits & Regional Governance. The Americas in Comparative Perspective*, Global Institutions Series. London: Routledge.

Price Waterhouse Coopers (PWC) (2008). *Informe final. Diagnostico institucional de la Secretaria de la Integración Económica Centroamericana (SIECA)*, Guatemala Ciudad, Guatemala, June.

Sanchez, R. (2009). *The Politics of Central American Integration.* New York: Routledge.

Scharpf, F. (1999). *Governing in Europe: Effective and Democratic?* Oxford: Oxford University Press.

Schmitter, P. (1970). A Revised Theory of Regional Integration. *International Organization, 24*(4), Autumn.

Wynia, G. (1970). Central American Integration: The Paradox of Success. *International Organization, 24*(2), (Spring 1970), 319–334.

7 Crisis-induced agenda setting in the Union of South American Nations (UNASUR)[1]

Olivier Dabène

UNASUR was born in 2008 out of a series of crises, but none of them had much to do with the financial crisis evoked in this volume. Hence, at first sight, UNASUR does not easily fit in the framework sketched in the introduction. There is, prior to 2008, a dynamics of summits, with a dominant player, Brazil, who takes the lead when the region has to cope with a crisis situation. In a way, hypothesis 1 presented in the introduction can be considered validated by UNASUR. The second and third ones are much more difficult to test, considering that UNASUR is a nascent integration process when the financial crisis erupted in 2008.

On a more general standpoint, however, Latin America does offer a very fertile ground to think of the relation between integration and crisis.

Contrary to Europe, where a single process of regional integration has experienced several waves of enlargement, Latin America is characterised by a succession of waves that saw the signing of several agreements launching or reactivating several distinct integration processes. Since the 1950s, Latin America has gone through four waves of regional integration, weaving a complex patchwork quilt (Dabène 2012a). Each wave has been the product of a paradigm shift intersection with a disruptive event. Each entails a change in agendas and policies and some institutional adjustments.

The first wave (1950s–1960s) was the product of the Economic Commission for Latin America's structuralist doctrine offering an alternative to the theory of comparative advantage at a time when export-led growth was deadlocked.[2] The second wave (1970s) was brought on by an economic crisis without a paradigm shift. Hence, it was a 'revisionist' wave (Rosenthal 1991).[3] When the paradigm shift finally occurred at the end of the Cold War, it triggered the third wave of open regionalism.[4] A decade later, the economic crisis and the continent's turn to the left paved the way for a new wave of regional integration.[5] This fourth wave of integration has been shaped by a series of responses to crisis situations.

This chapter examines this latest wave, focusing on the Union of South American Nations (UNASUR). It considers UNASUR's peculiar 'post-trade' agenda largely as a product of emergency presidential summits convoked to address crises.[6]

The summit process began in 2000 in the midst of the worst economic crisis since the first half of the 1980s. Then the region recovered and benefited from an amazing commodity export boom. Politically, the period was marked by political instability and the election of many leftist presidents. On the international front, the region has been affected by a U.S.-fed Cold War in the Andean region followed by a rapid reconciliation, while Brazil and Venezuela were competing for regional hegemony.

A quick look at the three defining summits of 2000 (first South American summit), 2004 (first summit of the Community of South American Nations, CSN) and 2008 (first summit of the Union of South American nations, UNASUR), evidences that the scope of issue areas included in the agenda has widened substantially (Table 7.1).

This chapter suggests that this enlarged agenda is context-driven. It focuses on three issues: one that was left out of UNASUR's agenda (trade), on that was added (defence) and one that has always been there (democracy) since 2000. It shows that trade has been excluded from the agenda mainly because the negotiations for the Free Trade Agreement of the Americas (FTAA) have failed. Defence, by contrast, has been included because the U.S. has extended its war on terror to Latin America. Even if Brazil planned to address the issue, the Colombian crisis spill-over in 2008–2009 has affected the timing and the content of the project. Finally, democracy was part of the initial priority of the South American summits. Yet, two crises, in Bolivia (2008) and Ecuador (2010), precipitated the adoption of a democratic clause and shaped its substance.

The methodology used in this chapter combines process tracing and counterfactual arguments. The former highlights the prominence of timing and sequences, showing that 'different temporal orderings of the same events or processes will produce different outcomes' (Pierson 2004: 68). The latter unveils the importance of a series of unexpected and sometimes very pressing events (Tetlock and Belkin 1996). As Capoccia and Kelemen (2007: 368) put it,

> only by taking counterfactual analysis seriously can contingency be studied. The reconstruction of plausible counterfactual scenarios, based on theoretically informed expectations and narrative reconstruction of the decision-making process supported by empirical evidence, is therefore the key in this kind of analysis.

In Fearon's words (1991: 176),

> support for a causal hypothesis in the counterfactual strategy comes from *arguments* about what would have happened. These arguments are made credible (1) by invoking general principles; and (2) by drawing on knowledge of historical facts relevant to counterfactual scenario.

Accordingly, in the remainder of the chapter, I proceed to trace the process of UNASUR's agenda setting, looking at contexts of crisis and using counterfactuals.

Table 7.1 Issue areas put at the agenda of three defining summits[7]

Agenda	*2000*	*2004*	*2008*	*UNASUR Councils*
Democracy	*X*	*X*	*X*	*Electoral council (CE, 2012)*
Trade	*X*	*X*		
Infrastructure	X	X	X	Infrastructure and Planning (COSIPLAN, 2009)
Drugs	X		X	Council on the world problem of drugs (CSPMD, 2010)
Science	X	X	X	Education, Science, Technology and Innovation (COCECCTI, 2009) Divided in 2012 in 3 councils: Education (CSE), Culture (CSC) Science, Technology and Innovation (CSCTI)
Energy		X	X	Energy (CES, 2007)
Social development			X	Social Development (CSDS, 2009)
Economy/Finance			X	Economy and Finance (CESF, 2010)
Defence			*X*	*Defence (CDS, 2008)*
Health			X	Health (CSS, 2008)

Source: author's elaboration based on summits' final declarations and action plans.

Note
ital.: case studies.

I develop the three case studies on trade, defence and democracy. In the next three sections, I start with a simple 'had it been different if' question, and examine the validity of the counterfactual speculation. Then I try to assess the importance of crises with the case narrative.

Trade

Counterfactual speculation

Had trade been removed from UNASUR's agenda, if the FTAA negotiations had succeeded? There is empirical evidence showing that (1) U.S. President George Bush took an aggressive attitude towards Latin America before 9/11 (Vanderbush 2009), and after 9/11 he tried to impose his war on terror to Latin America (Emerson 2010; Leogrande 2007; Prevost and Campos 2007); and (2) the 2002 U.S. Farm Bill and Trade Act were inacceptable for Latin America. These policy choices affected the U.S.-Latin America relations. They reinforced the anti-American stance in Latin America and undermined the pursuit of mutually beneficial negotiations. Both policy options were highly contingent. The war on terror was a response to U.S. domestic political pressures, and both the Farm bill and the Trade act were voted by a slim margin.

For the sake of the demonstration, there is actually no need to speculate about a successful negotiation, but simply about an ongoing negotiation, with a will to compromise on sensitive issues. The way the negotiations unfold between 1998 and 2001 showed that the U.S. administration could not impose its views (because it lacked the 'fast track' authority). However, 9/11 disrupted this course of events.

Case narrative

Trade has always been a key issue of both CAN and MERCOSUR's agendas. Despite disappointment regarding the outcomes (low level of intra-regional trade), the aim of forming a customs union has been reaffirmed quite regularly in sub-regional summits. Additionally, there was a strong political will to make the different sub-regional agreements converge, and ALADI consistently worked on it. However, during the 1980s, ALADI only made sure it registered the different agreements signed in the region, without managing to have them merge.

During the 1990s, the convergence issue got more complex, because a new regional agreement emerged: MERCOSUR. From its inception, MERCOSUR aimed at building a South American block, and as early as 1996 it welcomed Bolivia and Chile as associate members.

Yet, no progress was made towards convergence, although during the 1990s, it was a 'magic word' often referred to (SELA 1995). The end of the Cold War signalled a renewed optimism regarding the convergence of interests and values in the region. Yet, it did not translate into a Latin American Free Trade agreement (Dabène 1998).

A change would eventually come as a result of external pressures. The U.S. proposals, first of a Western Hemisphere open market (Bush's 1990 Enterprise for the Americas Initiative) and in 1994 of a Free Trade Area of the Americas (FTAA), had the Latin Americans getting closer together to prepare for a U.S.-Latin America negotiation (Feinberg 1997). In parallel, the European Union offered an interregional partnership that compelled the sub-regional groupings to tentatively agree on a common external tariff.

Brazilian president Itamar Franco first evoked a South American Free Trade Area (SAFTA) in 1993. But it was not until the years 1996–2000, when some progress was mades toward SAFTA through a series of negotiations. MERCOSUR signed trade agreements with Chile and Bolivia in 1996 and two years later a framework agreement was signed between MERCOSUR and CAN launching negotiations. On 12 August 1999, Brazil signed a separate free trade agreement with the Andean countries. Argentina did the same on 22 June 2000.

Campaigning in Florida, George Bush Jr. declared on 29 August 2000 that Latin America would be a top priority of his administration, and that if elected he would attend the April 2001 Quebec Summit of the Americas with a 'fast track' authority from Congress to boost the FTAA negotiations. In response, when Cardoso convened the first South American Summit on 31 August–1 September 2000 in Brasilia, he had in mind speeding up the creation of SAFTA.[8]

Bush attended the Québec Summit without the trade promotion authority (TPA) but he promised he would have it before the end of the year. Meanwhile Brazilian negotiators also made clear they had serious claims regarding U.S. anti-dumping provisions and high tariffs on agricultural products.

In 2002, the trade issue had to accommodate to changing circumstances. The second South American summit (Guayaquil, Ecuador, 26–27 July 2002) took place exactly when the U.S. Congress was passing the TPA legislation, after two years of a fierce battle that would delegitimise this instrument (Tucker and Wallach 2009). The South Americans had reasons to be displeased by the content of this 2002 Trade Act, since it explicitly set limits to the U.S. administration's ability to modify tariffs on import-sensitive products. South American countries such as Brazil or Argentina willing to gain access to U.S. beef, sugar, citrus and vegetable markets were understandably frustrated. Moreover, the U.S. Farm bill had been passed on 13 May 2002, setting the level of subsidies to an unprecedented high.

However, on the domestic political front, in July 2002 South America was not ripe for a collective reaction. Cardoso was an outgoing president and Brazil was in the midst of an electoral campaign. Venezuelan president H. Chavez was in the aftermath of a coup that ousted him for two days. E. Duhalde in Argentina had been elected president on 1 January 2002 to complete F. De la Rua's term. Only A. Toledo, the new Peruvian President, proved to be enthusiastic over integration issues.

The Guayaquil summit was dominated by criticism of protectionist trade policies pursued by the U.S. and the E.U. Cardoso criticised a 'world ruled by a global directorate' and all the participants agreed to close the CAN-MERCOSUR deal.[9] Before the end of the year, the U.S. signed a free trade agreement with Chile, signalling a trend to extent NAFTA model through bilateral agreements.

Then came 2003, a year of intense Brazilian diplomatic activities. The new president Lula travelled a lot, meeting Bush at the White House (20 June) and visiting five African countries (2–10 November). Trade issues were clearly given full attention. Lula was instrumental in putting together a coalition of developing countries (G22 group) that managed to derail the WTO negotiations in Cancun (10 September) because the U.S. and the E.U. would not offer progress on agricultural subsidies. Lula also planed a bi-regional meeting with the Arab world, pointing out 'the overall strategy is to go and seek markets instead of waiting for them to discover us'.[10] In South America, Lula wanted to further develop infrastructure linkages, claiming 'it is up to us [The Brazilians] to take the initiative to open up roads for trade to improve, between the countries of Latin America – and those of Africa'.[11] On 16 December 2003, an agreement was finally signed between CAN (Ecuador, Colombia and Venezuela) and MERCOSUR, opening up new perspectives.[12]

The next year started with a languish Special Summit of the Americas (Monterrey, 12–13 January 2004), which included in its final declaration a vague reference to the 'framework and calendar' for concluding FTAA negotiations reached at the Miami Ministerial in November 2003. During the first months of 2004, the FTAA negotiations ran paralysed.

In the backdrop of this complex regional setting, the U.S. opened bilateral trade negotiations with Ecuador, Colombia and Peru on May 2004, a few months after the U.S.-Chile FTA entered into force. In a way, this U.S. strategy shift made South American trade talks all the more urgent, but also more complicated, as the South American free-trade defenders were offered an alternative option. Gaining possible access to the much more attractive U.S. market, they would lose motivation for a South American deal.

The year 2004 closed with the third South American summit, held in Cusco, Peru (8–9 December). Trade was still a top priority in the Cusco's Declaration. The aim was 'the deepening of the convergence between MERCOSUR, the Andean Community and Chile through the perfecting of the free trade area'.

During their next meeting (Brasilia, 29–30 September 2005), the South American heads of State issued a 'Declaration on the convergence of integration processes in South America'. All the participants committed themselves to open a South American free trade area. Chile even pressed for a fixed deadline but Brazil opposed it. Later on 4–5 November 2005, the Mar del Plata (Argentina) IV Summit of the Americas witnessed a clash between MERCOSUR countries and the rest of the continent over the opportunity to reactivate FTAA negotiations. It became obvious that the FTAA project would be discarded for quite a while.

In December, a Strategic Reflection Commission (SRC) was set up. This Commission issued a document that triggered a paradigm shift, endorsed during the next South American Summit held in Cochabamba (Bolivia) on 8–9 December 2006.

SRC's final report, titled 'A new model of South America's regional integration. Towards a Union of South American Nations', claimed that the 'new model of integration cannot be based solely on trade relations'. It added,

> in the view of building a balanced integration and of consolidating an agenda of social and productive integration, South American countries, putting the emphasis on trade convergence, ought to look for a broader economic and productive articulation, and forms of cultural, social and political cooperation.

Trade was no longer an end but an instrument to achieve higher goals, a change I described as a politicisation (Dabène 2012b). Yet, the paradigm shift was only partial, as the document did include the objective of a free trade area, building on the existing groupings and addressing asymmetries. Trade for the people was the new conception defended by Venezuela in the framework of ALBA.

In 2006, some regional realignment took place. Venezuela left CAN to join MERCOSUR and Chile was reincorporated to CAN as associate member. On the political front, H. Chavez and Lula were easily re-elected. A. García in Peru defeated the Chavez-backed candidate O. Humala and in Ecuador the leftist candidate R. Correa was victorious. That did not work in favour of CAN-MERCOSUR convergence, as the region was growing more polarised. During the April 2007 Energy Summit in Margarita (Venezuela), it became obvious that trade liberalisation in South America was no longer a priority. The Peruvian president A. García, who did not attend the Margarita meeting, suggested in September to create a 'Pacific Arch', in order to promote trade with the Asia-Pacific region.

The year 2008 witnessed a climate of Cold War in the Andean region. Brazilian diplomacy put up a lot of efforts to convince the rest of South America to sign a new treaty giving birth to UNASUR on 23 May, amidst much scepticism. Other than the May Summit, the year was very busy, with no less than three informal presidential meetings to deal with crises.

Regarding trade, UNASUR's treaty only mentioned in its article 3.1 a vague objective of

> economic and commercial cooperation to achieve progress and consolidation of an innovative, dynamic, transparent, equitable and balanced process focused on an effective access, promoting economic growth and development to overcome existing asymmetries by means of the complementarities of the economies of the countries of South America, as well as the promotion of the wellbeing of all sectors of the population and the reduction of poverty.

There is no mention of SAFTA, a fact that has been presented as a proof of a new 'post-trade' orientation.

What lessons can be drawn from this narrative?

Trade was removed from South America's priority list when it became clear that the FTAA negotiations had failed. It occurred in 2005–2006. Had the negotiations been prolonged in a pacified climate, the South Americans would have been compelled to cement their unity.

As indicated, the negotiations failed because of policy shifts introduced by the Bush administration (Trade Act, Farm Bill). Without them, Latin America would have kept on negotiating the FTAA. Although some countries were resisting, a consensus would probably have been reached on some kind of 'light FTAA'. I further claim that this ongoing FTAA negotiation would have been accompanied by substantial progress towards a SAFTA. The UNASUR treaty would probably have included a reference to SAFTA. Without the FTAA incentive, and with alternative coalitions (FTA, Arc of the Pacific), SAFTA, entailing a complicated negotiation on its own, could be postponed for better times. Hence, UNASUR is post-trade by default, as a consequence of an evolving context. I argue that this simple causal claim, resting on process tracing and counterfactuals, is self-sufficient. Nonetheless, it is compatible with other types of explanations, be they ideational or interest-centred.

Tracing back the origins of UNASUR's post-trade agenda, we found that the key context evolution occurred in 2002 with policy changes in the U.S. By 2006, the South Americans were taking full advantage of the export boom and could remove SAFTA from their priority list.

Defence

Counterfactual speculation

Would defence have been placed on UNASUR's agenda, if the U.S. had not tried to export its war on terror to Latin America? As previously mentioned, President G. Bush took an aggressive attitude towards Latin America even before 9/11, appointing Cold-War inspired officials to key positions in his administration (Otto Reich, Roger Noriega…) (Vanderbush 2009; Emerson 2010). President B. Clinton before him endorsed the Plan Colombia, in the name of the war on drugs, translating into a sharp increased militarisation of the Colombian crisis. G. Bush then reframed the Colombian crisis as a war on terror.

The election of a far-right President in the U.S. was not meant to be. His policy options were controversial and contingent on the will to meet specific constituencies' demands that could secure his re-election. Moreover, 9/11 was a highly unexpected and disruptive event. And finally, Latin America has never been the theatre of any 'fundamentalist' or terrorist activities.

Case narrative

Unlike trade, defence and security have never been on Latin American regional groupings' agendas. True, the region has never been plagued with many deadly wars. Yet it is characterised by a violent peace (Mares 2001), with many border disputes and militarised interstate incidents that could have been addressed by regional organisations. In addition, the very processes of economic integration can also foster insecurity (Hurrell 1998).

Instead, the defence issues were dealt with in the framework of the 1947 Rio Treaty, as part of the inter-American system and under the strict control of the United States, which left no room for the Latin Americans to have an organisation of their own. There are exceptions, though. Following the Cuban Missile crisis, the Latin Americans committed themselves to ban nuclear weapons. The 1967 Tlatelolco Treaty declared Latin America a denuclearised zone of peace. During the 1990s, Central America adopted a Treaty on democratic security (1995), and MERCOSUR issued on 24 July 1999 a political declaration, together with associate members Bolivia and Chile, making the region a zone of peace.[13] On 17 June 2002, the Andean Community adopted an Andean Charter for peace and security, also called Lima compromise, setting limits and controls to the military expenditures. Ten days later, the South American foreign ministers agreed on a Declaration on South America as a peace zone.

With the exception of Central America, those formal declarations never entailed effective military cooperation to address regional security problems. Except during the 1970s, for political repression purposes (Condor Plan), the Latin American armies never collaborated. They only had the chance to work together within the recent peace mission in Haiti (MINUSTAH), under a UN mandate.[14]

The disruptive event that triggered a change is the Plan Colombia and the U.S. backing it in the name of the war on drugs. U.S. involvement was hardly a surprise, as President Bush launched in 1989 a National Drug Control Strategy appropriating $65 Millions in military supply to Colombian armed forces. At that time, 'there was a strategic shift from viewing drugs solely as a domestic issue to collectively viewing drugs, cartels and the effects of trafficking in Latin America as threats to U.S. national security interests' (Oehme 2010: 225). Plan Colombia went a step further, providing a link between drugs, guerrillas and paramilitaries. The U.S. moved from supporting counter-narcotics police units to assist counterinsurgency military operations.

After months of debates, President Clinton signed the Plan Colombia law on 22 August 2000, approving a $1.3 billion package, mostly military aid (Díaz Rivillas 2002). He then travelled to Cartagena (Colombia) on 30 August in a display of commitment to Plan Colombia. As a result, the 31 August–1 September 2000 first South American summit, programmed to discuss economic integration, was dominated by concerns regarding the U.S. military assistance to Colombia resulting in further militarisation and possible spill-overs.

After 9/11, G. Bush reframed his Latin American policy to fit his war on terror. Colombia became an outpost for combatting terrorism in South America. In February 2002, President Bush sent to Congress a budget request that, for the first time, included military assistance for Colombia not linked to counter-narcotics operations. Then, on 23–24 March 2002, he travelled to Lima to meet with the presidents of Peru, Bolivia, Colombia and the vice-president of Ecuador, in preparation for the renewal of the Andean Trade Promotion and Drug Eradication Act (ATPDEA).

The war on drugs caused unease in the region. When the U.S. refrained from condemning the 12 April 2002 coup against Chavez in Venezuela, it made things worse. A perception of threat grew in South America. Venezuela was persuaded that Bush wanted to destabilise its revolutionary regime and Brazil suspected the U.S. to use Colombia and the Manta base in Ecuador to expand its control capacity over the Amazon forest. As a reaction, on 26–27 July 2002, the second South American summit declared South America a zone of peace.

In January 2003, G. Bush's State of the Union Address did not include a single reference to Latin America, and his initial reaction to Lula's inauguration was lukewarm. The U.S. president did make an effort though, receiving his new Brazilian colleague at the White House on 20 June. On 29 October 2003, the first Conference on Hemispheric Security (OAS) in Mexico issued a Declaration on security in the Americas, but failed to address the much-awaited issue of the Rio Treaty's reform.

In this context, during his first year in office, Lula installed a Strategic council that started in 2004 to unveil important documents regarding short, medium and long-term defence objectives. The purpose was for the Brazilian civilians to regain control over defence matters, a task initiated by Cardoso with the creation of a Defence ministry in 1999. Yet the prospective reflection had a potential regional impact, as it explicitly envisioned a possible collective defence capacity to cope with new security threats in the region.[15]

In parallel, in June 2004, Brazil deployed troops in a UN stabilising mission in Haiti (MINUSTAH), as a strategy to give credit to its bid for a permanent seat at the UN Security Council (Malamud 2011). Later that year, two important meetings took place. One in the MERCOSUR gathered the defence ministers to study the creation of a permanent secretary for military affairs. The other, in the OAS framework (Inter-American Defense Board), saw the U.S. clashing with Brazil over the issue of expanding the focus of the Board to security issues.

On 13 July 2006, the Amazon Cooperation Treaty Organization[16] convened its first meeting of Defense ministers to examine a wide range of security threats affecting the Amazon region. The discussions dealt with transnational organised crime, monitoring systems and plant and animal trafficking. The countries showed concern about possible sovereignty threats. Brazil offered the benefice of its Amazon monitoring system to the other countries.

During 2007, as part of a much more assertive security policy during Lula's second term (Villa and Trindade 2010), Brazil went a step further, evoking the idea of a South American Defense council. The Colombian bombing of a FARC camp in Ecuadorean territory, on 1 March 2008, gave the project a particular salience. On 22 March 2008, Brazilian Defense minister Nelson Jobim made a presentation at the Inter-American Defense Board, receiving full support. Then, in April-May 2008, Jobim toured South America, presenting a more elaborate project. Only Colombia proved reticent, asking the rest of South America to acknowledge that FARC was a terrorist group. On 28 May 2008, when signing the UNASUR treaty, the Presidents decided to create a working group to elaborate a project of a South American Defense Council (CDS). The same day, Obama pronounced his first campaign speech about Latin America, showing support to Colombia's fight against the FARC. Retrospectively, it made Colombia's attack appear much like the kind of 'preventive strike' Bush claimed legitimate to use on the war on terror. It was all the more preoccupying that on 24 April 2008, the U.S. had decided to re-establish its fourth fleet, with a mission to operate around South and Central America, provide 'humanitarian assistance' and help fight drug trafficking. This move sparkled swift reactions in the region, with Argentina and Brazil demanding explanations, and Venezuela preparing naval exercises with Russia in the Caribbean. With some differences in the tone used, all South American countries suspected the U.S. to have a view on their natural resources.

Without a doubt, the redeployment of the fourth fleet strengthened the will of the region to get a defence council. Yet, the debate regarding its purpose grew further polarised, with an anti-American option opposing a more conciliatory tone. During the 7 hours UNASUR Summit in Santiago (15 September 2008), convoked to deal with the Bolivian crisis, Chávez and Cristina Kirchner tried to shift the blame of Eastern Bolivia's separatist claims to the U.S. intervention in the region. Lula reframed the discussion, asking if Bolivian President E. Morales would accept a UNASUR-sponsored mediation mission. The final declaration left the U.S. out of the picture.

The South American Defense Council (CDS) was finally created during the 11 December 2008 UNASUR meeting with the ambition of consolidating South America as a zone of peace, creating a South American identity in defence issues and generating consensus to strengthen regional cooperation for defence issues. More precisely, the Action plan adopted on 10 March 2009 included four lines: defence policies, military cooperation, humanitarian assistance and peacekeeping operations, defence industry and technology, and education and training.

Then, as if CDS was to be tested right at its inception, press reports mentioned a military agreement between Colombia and the U.S., whereby the former would grant the latter the access to seven military bases. Colombian President A. Uribe, under fierce pressure, announced he would not attend the 10 August UNASUR Summit and embarked on a tour of seven South American countries to explain the defence agreement with the U.S. It did not prove enough to calm down even the more moderate governments of Chile and Brazil, while Venezuela and its ALBA allies were infuriated.

On 28 August, an extraordinary summit addressed the U.S./Colombia military agreement. In order to have Uribe in, the agenda of talks included all military acquisitions, framed by a policy of transparency. The summit witnessed a clash between A. Uribe and H. Chavez. Brazil proved unable to rally support to its idea of a meeting with U.S. President B. Obama, and failed to have UNASUR advanced on military or other issues. However, the final declaration did

> reaffirm that the presence of foreign military forces cannot, with its means and resources linked to its own goals, threaten the sovereignty and integrity of any South American nation and as a consequence, the peace and security of the region.

It also instructed the CDS to 'analyze the text of the "South American Strategy. White paper, air mobility command"' that Chavez displayed during the summit as a proof of U.S. intentions to use the bases to plan military operations in the whole region.

On 27 November 2009, an extraordinary meeting of UNASUR's Foreign and Defense ministers agreed on a series of much needed confidence building measures. One of them was that

> Cooperation agreements on defense concluded by the Member States of UNASUR will include an express clause to ensure respect for the principles of sovereign equality of States, territorial integrity and inviolability and non-intervention in internal affairs of other States.

Regarding the U.S./Colombia agreement, the meeting could not reach a consensus.

In August 2010, the Colombian constitutional Court declared the agreement unconstitutional. The new Colombian President J. M. Santos buried the project. As a result, the CDS lost its momentum and, in the last years, it has not made progress towards building a new doctrine or implementing the confidence building measures.

What lessons can be drawn from this narrative?

Right from the start, there was clearly a Brazilian ambition to engage its neighbours with some military cooperation in order to cope with perceived regional security threats and assert leadership. In a way, it prolonged the initiatives launched by the military regime with the La Plata Basin Treaty (1969) and the Amazon cooperation treaty (1978). Ironically, it also benefited from the 1990s reinvigoration of the OAS and the new relationships established between Latin American defence ministers within the Committee on Hemispheric Security, created in 1995 in the framework of the continental summitry process (Franko 2006).

Considering the diplomatic ambitions of the Lula administration and its determination to build a regional leadership to project power at the global level, there is no doubt that a defence treaty would have been signed, one way or another, in South America. Nonetheless, the context, namely the U.S. supporting Plan Colombia and imposing its post-9/11 war on terror, did play an important role. It affected both the timing of the sequence and the content of the project.

In 2008–2009, UNASUR's agenda setting regarding defence and security overlapped with a crisis-resolution effort. Such coincidence turned out to accelerate the negotiations. It also compelled the actors to reach a consensus on a modified agenda, with issues such as military expenditures and military agreements getting at the forefront.

This causal claim is compatible with Battaglino's account of UNASUR's defence agenda, stressing both material changes (militarisation of the security policy of the United States towards the region, revival of territorial and ideological disputes and emergence of Brazil as a regional power) and ideational changes (new regional consensuses regarding how to deal with development and defence) (Battaglino 2012). As this author puts it,

> the increasing U.S. military presence and the arrival of one of the most dangerous features of the 'war on terror' to the region (preventive strike) prompted the emergence of the SADC. Its emergence, however, would not have been possible without the existence of an emergent identity in defense matters, which recognizes that the maintenance of the national defense in this new scenario demands more interstate cooperation, that is, a regional approach.
>
> (Ibid.: 88)

This argument can be pushed a step further, identifying the context as a key variable shaping the agenda on defence matters.

Democracy

Counterfactual speculation

Had democracy been on UNASUR's agenda, if it were not for two crises undermining democracy in 2008 in Bolivia and 2010 in Ecuador? In post-transition Latin America, there are no cases of successful military coups, nor installation of long-lasting authoritarian regimes. Peru under A. Fujimori during the 1990s is the only exception.

Instead of classical coups, Latin America in the 2000s has suffered from political instability (Pérez-Liñán 2010) and downgraded quality of democracy. Some authors have evoked electoral authoritarianism (Schedler 2006) or illiberal democracy (Smith and Ziegler 2008).

Although there are patterns of instability explored by the literature, each of the cases mentioned in the narrative below was highly contingent on crisis factors related to particular events and domestic trajectories.

Case narrative

In the mid 1980s, democracy was the initial preoccupation that drove Argentina and Brazil to initiate bilateral talks and later launch an integration process (Dabène 2009, Gardini 2010). Democracy was not included in the 1991 MERCOSUR treaty, but the issue eventually resurfaced after the 1996 coup attempt in Paraguay. MERCOSUR then adopted a democratic clause in 1998, and so did the Andean Community the same year.

In the months preceding the first South-American Summit, some political events in the region were motives of concern regarding the quality and stability of democracy. On 21 January 2000, J. Mahuad was ousted in Ecuador. Then in neighbouring Peru, A. Fujimori won a fraudulent third consecutive election (9 April–28 May). He would eventually step down on 18 September. In Bolivia, a state of emergency was declared on April, to cope with social unrest. On 28 May, there was an attempted coup in Paraguay against president L. G. Macchi. Finally, for some conservative sectors in Latin America, H. Chavez's re-election in Venezuela on 30 July was a clear sign of authoritarian drift.

The only 'good news' came from Mexico, where an alternance occurred on 2 July after more than 70 years of a dominant-party (PRI) regime.

The defence of democracy was on the agenda of the 2000 Summit convoked by Cardoso. The countries agreed to limit the invitations to future summits to democratic governments. Together with trade and infrastructure, the extension of MERCOSUR's democratic clause to South America was the priority of the Brazilian diplomats.[17] Regarding Peru, Brazil wanted South America to deal with the crisis, while the U.S. called for sanctions and wanted the OAS to make the decision. Democracy was the first issue mentioned in the final declaration, with point 23 referring to consultations in case of democratic breakdown.

In 2001, Argentina was hit by a devastating economic crisis that translated into violent street protests and riots. On 21 December, President F. de la Rua resigned. In a few days, Argentina saw a succession of three presidents. E. Duhalde would eventually finish de la Rua's term in office, until the election of N. Kirchner on 25 May 2003.

On 12 April 2002, a coup against H. Chavez in Venezuela fuelled preoccupation in the region, not only over Venezuela's political situation, but also regarding a possible U.S. Cold-War style anti-left crusade. The coup failed but as a result, the second South-American summit in 2002 put a strong emphasis on democracy. Peruvian new president A. Toledo took the lead and suggested a solidarity fund to defend democracy and governability in the region, in the face of serious global financial instability (point 2 of the final declaration). In 2004, the third South-American summit also referred to democracy and the 2001 Inter-American democratic charter. It did not include a democratic clause, though. Ecuador was again the centre of attention on 20 April 2005, when president L. Gutiérrez was forced out of office by massive street protests. However, on 29–30 September, a South American meeting of heads of state in Brasilia did not include the defence of democracy on its action plan.

In 2006, Bolivia hosted a South American summit amidst a serious crisis situation with Santa Cruz soya growers resisting government agrarian policies. Santa Cruz governor Rubén Costas sprayed a hunger strike, opposing the voting procedure in the constitutional assembly. The 'new model of integration for the XXIst century' referred to in the declaration included democracy as one of its core principle (*principio rector*). However, it did not include the defence of democracy in its list of objectives. The next year, the energy summit did not address democracy either, and the 2008 UNASUR treaty included in its article 2 a very brief mention to the objective of strengthening democracy.

A few months later, the context forced UNASUR to take action on matters related to the defence of democracy. The Chilean President convoked an emergency summit to deal with the degradation of the Bolivian crisis that resulted in violent incidents leading to many casualties on 11 September. In its 15 September 'Moneda Declaration', UNASUR's members 'energetically reject and do not recognize any situation that implies an intent of civil coup d'état, the rupture of institutional order, or that compromises the territorial integrity of the Republic of Bolivia'.

Then after a year 2009 busy addressing the defence issues, UNASUR was again forced to react when a crisis erupted in Ecuador on 30 September 2010. R. Correa accused the police to plot a coup to overthrow him, and an emergency summit was convened on 1 October in Buenos Aires. Lula was absent from the meeting because he was campaigning, with three days to go before the election. His foreign minister Amorin was in Haiti, coordinating humanitarian assistance. Brazil was nonetheless active. In an interview,[18] Amorin said that UNASUR had to react swiftly in order to avoid a Honduras-type of situation (where the reaction was too slow and the ousting of M. Zelaya irreversible). Understandably, Ecuador was also instrumental as R. Correa was at that time holding UNASUR's pro-tempore presidency. In the Declaration of Buenos Aires, UNASUR members issued a strong condemn of the coup attempt and warned potential coup candidates that UNASUR would not hesitate to apply economic or political sanctions.

During the next UNASUR summit, held in Georgetown on 27 November 2010, an 'Additional protocol to the constitutive treaty of UNASUR on commitment to democracy' was adopted. Interestingly, its content went far beyond MERCOSUR or CAN's democratic clauses, regarding both the scope of application and the type of reaction. Its article 1 mentions

> This Protocol shall apply in the event of a breach or threat of breach against the democratic order, a violation of the constitutional order or any situation that jeopardizes the legitimate exercising of power and the application of the values and principles of democracy.

The measures to be applied are mentioned in the Article 4. They include the 'suspension of the right to participate in the various bodies and branches of UNASUR', and the 'partial or complete closure of land borders, including the suspension and/or limitation of trade, air and maritime traffic, communications and provision of energy, services and supplies'.

The scope of application of this protocol is potentially very wide, as the notion of 'threat of breach' is opened to interpretation, and the sanctions are potentially very severe. Less than two years after the Georgetown summit, UNASUR's new democratic clause would be tested when the Paraguayan congress impeached the leftist president F. Lugo on 16 June 2012. Although the new president F. Franco claimed the constitutional dispositions had been respected, the move was highly controversial and both MERCOSUR and UNASUR were quick to react. Both blocs decided to suspend Paraguay but without applying sanctions. Ironically, the fact that Lugo signed the protocol was one of the motives evoked by the Paraguayan congress to justify the accusation of 'poor performance of his duties' and ensure its demise.

What lessons can be drawn from this narrative?

Although the defence of democracy was a key priority of the initial south-American summits, it lost salience during the 2005–2006 summits. The issue re-emerged after the dramatic events in Bolivia (2008) and Ecuador (2010), showing once again that UNASUR's agenda formation is partly driven by crisis resolution efforts. UNASUR adopting a democratic clause is hardly surprising, though. MERCOSUR and CAN and many other regional organisations have become clubs of democracies with risks of suspension for renegade members.

As for the defence issue, I claim that the turbulent political context of the years 2008–2010 has affected the timing of the democratic clause's adoption and, more importantly, has shaped its content. The fact that democracy has been jeopardised in two countries exercising the presidency pro-tempore (Ecuador 2010, Paraguay 2012) has added saliency to the issue. The scope of applicability ('any situation that jeopardizes the legitimate exercising of power and the application of the values and principles of democracy') and the severity of the sanctions can only be explained paradoxically looking at the political polarisation of the continent. If all UNASUR members share the same preoccupation regarding the stability and quality of democracy in the region, they are not likely to agree on a set of criteria to be used to assess the threats to the 'values and principles of democracy'. However, there was a strategic convergence of interests between conservative sectors thinking that they might try to apply such a democratic clause to, say, Chavez-led Venezuela, and the leftist sectors keen to shield the region from U.S.-led destabilising attempts. In Chile, for instance, the leader of the Senate's foreign affairs Commission, the rightist Hernán Larraín, said in an interview on 9 August 2010 that he would only ratify UNASUR's treaty if it included a democratic clause to defend freedom in the region.[19] Two years later, he enthusiastically endorsed the additional protocol. His colleague Eugenio Tuma, the new president of the Commission, lamented that the clause did not extend its applicability to human rights violations, but he also voted the ratification.[20] Meanwhile, leftist Bolivia was proud to announce that it was the first country to ratify the protocol.[21]

These overlapping but nonetheless competing conceptions of the threats to democracy have facilitated the adoption of the Additional protocol in times of crisis, but they will hinder its enforcement. The reaction to the Paraguayan coup, suspension without sanctions, can set a precedent.

Conclusion

The objective of this chapter was to highlight the importance of crisis context in UNASUR's agenda-setting process. Table 7.2 summarises the main findings.

Table 7.2 Impact of crisis context on UNASUR's agenda

Issue area	*Context*	*Effect*
Trade	FTAA failure	Trade not on UNASUR's agenda
Defence	War on terror Colombia 2008	Affects the timing of UNASUR Defence council's creation and shapes its content
Democracy	Bolivia 2008 Ecuador 2010	Affects the timing of UNASUR Democratic clause's adoption and shapes its content

Source: author's elaboration.

The context only had a direct impact on trade, explaining its removal from the agenda. Defence and democracy would have been on UNASUR's agenda even in a different scenario. However, the timing and content of the policy choices regarding these two issues have been deeply affected by the sequence of events described in the above sections.

UNASUR clearly provides a validation of this volume's core hypothesis regarding the impact of crises on regional integration. The onset of the series of summits paving the way for the creation of UNASUR was linked to the 1999–2001 economic crisis. Then several crises hit the incipient regional arrangement in 2008–2010 and forced it to adjust its agenda and institutions.

Regarding the institutional density hypothesis, the future will show whether UNASUR's institutional arrangement will be affected by crises. Based on previous Latin American experiences, we can speculate it will not. UNASUR's treaty only mentioned four organs: a Council of heads of State, a Council of foreign ministers, a Council of delegates and a Secretariat. However, over the years, UNASUR has formed 12 sectoral councils, and each of them has created numerous committees, working groups or even full institutions, such as the South American institute of government in health or the Center for Strategic Defense Studies. Despite a will to avoid duplications with existing MERCOSUR or CAN's agencies, this increasing institutional complexity is putting UNASUR on a familiar path. Older groupings in Central America, the Andean region or MERCOSUR have all been characterised by mushrooming organs that proved to be resilient, even when facing severe crises. There are good reasons to think that UNASUR will not depart from this trend.

Notes

1 This chapter draws on a paper written while the author was visiting OxPo fellow at Oxford University (Dabène 2012a). A preliminary version was delivered during the ECPR seventh general conference (Bordeaux, 5 September 2013).

2 Wave 1 includes the Latin American Free Trade Agreement (LAFTA 1960), the Central American Common Market (CACM 1960) and the Andean Group (GRAN 1969).

3 Wave 2 includes the transformation of LAFTA into a more flexible Latin American Integration Association (LAIA) and the creation of the Caribbean Community (CARICOM 1973).

4 Wave 3 includes the reactivation of CACM and GRAN and the creation of the Common Market of the South (MERCOSUR 1991).
5 Wave 4 includes the Bolivarian Alliance of the Americas (ALBA 2004), the Union of South American Nations (UNASUR 2008), the Latin American and Caribbean Community (CELAC 2011) and the Pacific Alliance (PA 2012).
6 Between 2000 and 2012, out of a total of 22 presidential summits held in South America, 11 were 'extraordinary meetings'.
7 UNASUR in 2008 covered an even wider range of issues. However, only the ones that are addressed in a Council are mentioned.
8 *Folha de S. Paulo*, 30 August 2000.
9 *Latin American Weekly Report*, 30 July 2002.
10 *Latin American Weekly Report*, 16 September 2003.
11 *Latin American Weekly Report*, 16 September 2003.
12 Registered by ALADI as Economic Complementation Agreement (ECA) 59.
13 In addition, many countries signed bilateral agreements. The most emblematic is the 1991 Argentina/Brazil agreement for the peaceful-only use of nuclear energy.
14 Nine countries took part: Argentina, Bolivia, Brazil, Chile, Ecuador, Guatemala, Paraguay, Peru and Uruguay.
15 Núcleo de Assuntos Estratégicos (NAE), *Projeto Brasil 3 tempos, 50 temas estratégicos*, 2008.
16 Treaty signed in 1978 by Bolivia, Brazil, Colombia, Ecuador, Guyana, Peru, Suriname and Venezuela. The organisation was founded in 1995, and was originally dedicated to the preservation of the Amazonian environment and natural resources.
17 *Folha de S. Paulo*, 30 August 2000.
18 *Folha de S. Paulo*, 1 October 2010.
19 http://globovision.com/articulo/senadores-chilenos-pidieron-que-unasur-no-debilite-a-oea.
20 www.senado.cl/suscriben-protocolo-de-unasur-sobre-compromiso-con-la-democracia-y-los-derechos-humanos/prontus_senado/2011–12–01/134432.html.
21 www.lostiempos.com/diario/actualidad/nacional/20110608/bolivia-ratifica-protocolo adicional-al-tratado-constitutivo-unasur-sobre_129089_260654.html.

References

Battaglino, Jorge (2012). Defense in a Post-Hegemonic Regional Agenda. The Case of the South American Defense Council. In Riggirozzi, Pia and Tussie, Diana (eds.). *The Rise of Post-Hegemonic Regionalism, The Case of Latin America*. London: Springer, 81–100.

Capoccia, Giovanni and Kelemen, Daniel (2007). The Study of Critical Junctures: Theory, Narrative, and Counterfactuals in Historical Institutionalism. *World Politics*, *59*(3), 341–369.

Dabène, Olivier (1998). Intégration Régionale en Amérique Latine: Economie Politique de la Convergence. *Etudes du CERI* 45.

Dabène, Olivier (2009). *The Politics of Regional Integration in Latin America. Theoretical and Comparative Explorations*. New York: Palgrave Macmillan.

Dabène, Olivier (2012a). *Explaining Latin America's fourth wave of regionalism. Regional integration of a third kind*, Paper delivered at the 2012 LASA Congress, San Francisco, 25 May.

Dabène, Olivier (2012b). Consistency and Resilience Through Cycles of Repoliticization. In Pia Riggirozzi and Diana Tussie (eds.). *The Rise of Post-Hegemonic Regionalism, The Case of Latin America*. London: Springer, 41–64.

Díaz Rivillas, Borja (2002). Política Exterior de los EE.UU Hacia Colombia: el Paquete de Ayuda de 1300 Millones de Dólares de Apoyo al Plan Colombia y la Región Andina. *América latina hoy* 31, 145–186.

Emerson, Guy (2010). Radical Neglect? The 'War on Terror' and Latin America. *Latin American Politics and Society*, *52*(1), 33–62.

Fearon, James (1991). Counterfactuals and Hypothesis Testing in Political Science. *World Politics*, *43*(2), 169–195.

Feinberg, Richard (1997). *Summitry in the Americas*. Washington, DC: Institute for International Economics.

Franko, Patrice (2006). *Toward a New Security Architecture in the Americas. The Strategic Implication of the FTAA*. Washington, DC: CSIS issues series.

Gardini, Gian Luca (2010). *The Origins of MERCOSUR. Democracy and Regionalization in South America*. New York: Palgrave Macmillan.

Hurrell, Andrew (1998). Security in Latin America. *International Affairs*, *74*(3), 529–546.

Leogrande, William (2007). A Poverty of Imagination: George W. Bush's Policy in Latin America. *Journal of Latin American Studies*, *39*(2), 355–385.

Malamud, Andrés (2011). A Leader Without Followers? The Growing Divergence Between the Regional and Global Performance of Brazilian Foreign Policy. *Latin American Politics and Society*, *53*(3), 1–24.

Mares, David (2001). *Violent Peace. Militarized Inter-State Bargaining in Latin America*. New York: Columbia University Press.

Mittelman, James (1996). Rethinking the 'New Regionalism' in the Context of Globalization. *Global Governance*, 2, 189–213.

Oehme, Chester (2010). Plan Colombia: Reassessing the Strategic Framework. *Democracy and Security*, *6*(3), 221–236.

Pérez-Liñán, Anibal (2010). *Presidential Impeachments and the New Political Instability in Latin America*. Cambridge: Cambridge University Press.

Pierson, Paul (2004). *Politics in Time. History, Institutions and Social Analysis*. Princeton: Princeton University Press.

Prevost, Gary and Campos, Carlos (2007). *The Bush Doctrine and Latin America*. New York: Palgrave Macmillan.

Rosenthal, Gert (1991). Un Informe Crítico a 30 años de Integración en América Latina. *Nueva Sociedad*, 113, Mayo–Junio, 60–65.

Schedler, Andreas (ed.) (2006). *Electoral Authoritarianism. The Dynamics of Unfree Competition*. Boulder: Lynne Rienner.

SELA (1995). Convergencia: la Palabra Mágica de la Integración. *Capítulos de SELA*, 42, 119–125.

Smith, Peter and Ziegler, Melissa (2008). Liberal and Illiberal Democracy in Latin America. *Latin American Politics and Society*, *50*(1), 31–57.

Tetlock, Philip and Belkin, Aaron (eds.) (1996). *Counterfactual Thought Experiments in World Politics*. Princeton: Princeton University Press.

Tucker, Todd and Wallach, Lori (2009). *The Rise and Fall of Fast Track Authorities*. Washington, DC: Public Citizen.

Vanderbush, Walt (2009). The Bush Administration Record in Latin America: Sins of Omission and Commission. *New Political Sciences*, *31*(3), 337–359.

Villa, Rafael Antonio Duarte and Viana, Manuel Trindade (2010). Security Issues During Lula's Administration: From the Reactive to the Assertive Approach. *Revista Brasileira de Política Internacional*, 53, 91–114.

8 Reinforcing or ignoring the supranational level during crises?

Brazilian parties' views on regionalism[1]

Clarissa Dri

The history of regional integration after the 1950s shows that moments of difficulty can sometimes trigger union in a more effective way than periods of stability. This seems to be precisely the case of Mercosur, founded by Argentina, Brazil, Paraguay and Uruguay in 1991 and including Venezuela since 2012. In the 1950s, Juan Perón and Getúlio Vargas, heads of state of Argentina and Brazil, respectively, seriously considered enhanced political cooperation in a moment of industrial retraction after an increase in exports during World War II. In the late 1960s, an agreement was reached on the hydroelectric usage of the Rio de la Plata Basin, in a period when South American countries realised they could not rely solely on the United States to achieve economic development. In the 1980s, the debt crisis motivated a larger and more permanent regional dialogue, which led to structured cooperation between Argentina and Brazil and subsequently to the creation of Mercosur (section 1).

Additionally, the 1997–1999 Asian economic crisis had a considerable political impact on Mercosur, especially after the Argentinean breakdown of 2001. Commercial exchange was at its peak and the crisis had had a devastating effect on member states' economy. This crisis led Mercosur governments to take measures to reinforce integration, such as creating an international secretariat and reforming the dispute settlement system. Ultimately, it also influenced the creation of a directly-elected parliament. This process was therefore twofold, with each phase corresponding to different political forces driving the countries. In both cases, citizens' general attitudes towards integration were far from negative after the crisis (section 2). Nevertheless, a similar impact was not seen in the 2008 world financial crisis. This time, responses to the crisis were mostly national and no important regional political mechanisms were introduced as a result of the process (section 3). How can this situation be explained? The economic effects of the crisis on developing countries were less important this time, but is it enough to justify the marginal place of regional discussions?

This chapter argues that the views and attitudes on regionalism across time of two important Brazilian political parties can account for this difference. The Brazilian Social-Democracy Party (PSDB, Portuguese acronym) and Workers' Party (PT, Portuguese acronym) have been in power in Brazil since 1994 and represent the traditional left-right divide. Whilst the 2001 crisis contributed to a punctual change in the PSDB's sceptical behaviour towards Mercosur, the 2008 crisis consolidated the position of a nationalist-left sector within the PT. The objective here is to analyse to what extent the last two major economic crises affected Mercosur and what was the role of specific social actors – Brazilian political parties – in these cases. This chapter thus proposes a twofold analysis, focused on how crises affected partisan views on regional integration and, most importantly, on how these positions affected the way Mercosur dealt with critical economic moments. By doing so, this chapter tests the third hypothesis guiding the book, referring to the impact of civil society organisations – political parties – on member states' and institutional responses to crises. The partisan influence is not negligible especially in the Latin American case, where the low level of institutional integration allows national actors to treat issues in an ad hoc and informal manner.

On one side, the choice of Brazilian political parties is based upon the assumption that Brazil's relative economic power does provide a special place for the preferences of national actors. Especially after the 2001 Argentinean breakdown, Brazil was perceived by some political actors within Argentina as a central source of economic vitality. This leads to the first hypothesis of the book, concerning member states' positions in periods of crisis, also to be addressed in this chapter. On the other side, parties can reflect how civil society influences and is influenced by regional integration in times of crisis. If parties are understood as a means of political expression that integrates proposals of social groups regarding state actions, the analysis of right and left parties' positions can account for the representation of perspectives within civil society. Considering foreign policy is a recent topic of social discussion, parties' positions on regionalism are in general older and structured than in other social groups. The chapter will analyse crisis events by interpreting official documents, press declarations and semi-structured interviews conducted with members of the two mentioned parties. The main elements that contributed to the political result are highlighted so that the causal chains can be reconstructed, in light of the process tracing methodology (George and Bennett 2005).

1 The 'lost decade' triggering regional dialogue in Latin America

The beginning of the 1980s witnessed the Latin American debt crisis. After borrowing money for industrialisation and infrastructure investments during the 1970s, most Latin American countries saw their external debt vis-à-vis international financial institutions increase exponentially. In 1982, the debt reached more than half of the gross domestic product of the region, and thrice surpassed Latin American annual exports (Portela Filho 1994). On one hand, this economic scenario contributed to increases in poverty, as public investments were restricted and inflation and unemployment rose to high levels. On the other, it triggered a structured regional dialogue among governments, launching a new pattern of interaction after years of dictatorships and military conflicts.

Protectionist and nationalist Latin American countries were obliged to manage collectively a way out of the crisis, which eventually led to a movement towards economic integration.

Latin American essays for integration during the twentieth century have been minimal until the creation of the United Nations' Economic Commission for Latin America (CEPAL) in 1948. In the 1910s, Argentina, Brazil and Chile signed an agreement known as the ABC Pact, intended to assure consultation and non-aggression among the neighbours. Brazilian Minister of Foreign Affairs, Barão de Rio Branco, had a leading role in this negotiation, which he considered essential to Brazil's international autonomy (Conduru 1998). Although Argentina never ratified the document, its president Juan Perón made efforts to relaunch the Pact in the 1950s as a means of limiting the influence of the United States of America (US) in the region (Cisneros and Piñeiro 2002: 333). Although political cleavages in Brazil related to the origins of the Cold War did not allow the implementation of the treaty at this time, CEPAL economic proposals led to the creation of the Latin American Free Trade Association (ALALC) in 1960. At the time, CEPAL was led by Raul Prebicsh, Celso Furtado and other economists maintaining that states should have a central role in economic development and should implement strategies conceived nationally (Bresser-Pereira 2010: 22). ALALC aimed to promote import substitution industrialisation and trade liberalisation within the whole of Latin America, but its aims were jeopardised by industrial capability gaps and military coups in several countries (Medeiros 2000: 104).

The 1980s, following the petroleum shocks, brought new challenges for the region. ALALC was replaced by the Latin American Integration Association (LAIA), with less ambitious economic and institutional goals. Its efforts to foster development policies and commercial agreements among Latin American states were enhanced by the political rapprochement during the external debt crisis. Collective negotiations were organised in order to increase debtors' bargaining power vis-à-vis international creditors, with the direct participation of heads of state and ministers. A first meeting was held in Quito in January 1984, when a presidential declaration mentioned the will to launch regional institutions in order to provide better coordination of positions. In June, the Cartagena meeting established a consensus based on the principle of co-responsibility between creditors and debtors and the consequent political character of negotiations (Mallmann 2008: 91). Periodic meetings were held afterwards and a committee was created in 1987 to follow and deliberate on presented proposals. Economically, the pressure resulted in small concessions related to flexible deadlines, amortisation amounts and interest rates. Politically, nevertheless, the Cartagena Consensus contributed to create an innovative dynamics of systematic communication and compliance around common concerns in Latin America.

This was reflected, for instance, in the gradual establishment of the Argentinean-Brazilian axis. The decline of the bipolar world and the beginning of globalisation impacted both countries' perceptions of their national capacities and of the mutual gains of enhanced cooperation. The decline of authoritarian governments in the Southern Cone allowed a democratic turn which called for deeper multilateral dialogue, as had already happened in the 1960s (Dabène 2009: 61). In this sense, regionalism brings continuity to the collective political waves that have marked Latin America since the colonial period (Dabène 2003). By this time, regional objectives were guided mostly by political needs. Consolidating the newly established democratic regimes and reorienting national policies in order to be recognised by the international system were the main goals of the efforts to further unify the region (Seitenfus 1989: 116; Gardini 2007: 808). Members of executive and legislative powers participating in negotiations were interested in international legitimacy that would enhance their internal mandates. In 1988, after presidential meetings and declarations, Argentina and Brazil signed the Treaty of Integration, Cooperation and Development, which defined the terms for commercial and technological cooperation in 12 sectors and created the basis for the Mercosur treaty.

The beginning of the 1990s witnessed an economic revival of regional movements in Latin America. Regional organisations created after World War II following the UN's recommendations were reformed in light of economic globalisation. In 1991, the Central-American Integration System (SICA) replaced the Organization of Central-American States of 1951; the Caribbean Community (CARICOM) was reformed in 1992, superseding the Caribbean Free Trade Association of 1965; the Andean Community (CAN) was revitalised in 1996 with the intention of avoiding a repetition of the failures of the Andean Pact of 1969. The launching of Mercosur in 1991 and the North American Free Trade Agreements (NAFTA) in 1994 are also part of this same wave of open regionalism. Financial global actors have imposed market rationale to the protectionist regionalism of the 1960s (Spindler 2002: 25), leading to a multidimensional process of economic opening articulated to the strongest tendencies of globalisation (Hettne and Inotai 1994: 69). The internationalisation of capital and the creation of transnational companies required not only free trade areas, but also common markets with an external tariff that would assure liberalisation (Gardini 2005: 416).

Guided by neoliberal principles, regionalism became an intrinsic part of Latin American states' foreign policies in the 1990s. Commercial relations with traditional and new partners were framed by neighbouring agreements, which called the European Union's attention. By this time, Europe was searching to affirm its unity and vitality in a world that had moved past bipolarisation and saw, in its example projected overseas, an opportunity to increase external trade and international legitimisation. A new era was thus inaugurated in relations between Europe and Latin America: the interregional approach had replaced the timid development aid of the 1960s and the commercial agreements of the 1970s. The main difference was the political perspective that underlined the EU's pacific and democratic values and principles, and its intention to foster an international system built on horizontal regions rather than on coercive powers (Telò 2006: 51). The growing economic and cultural influence of the United States in Latin America furthered European interests. George Bush launched the Initiative for the Americas in 1990, consisting of a continental plan to liberalise trade, increase investments and consolidate 'political freedom'. Europe and the United States have thus engaged in an explicit competition for Latin American markets and for exporting norms to structure Latin American economies. In this sense, interregionalism can be understood as a product of the perspective according to which globalisation is the dominant ideology for economics management (Santander 2005: 290).

The interregional approach was translated into a consistent European programme to politically and economically support Latin American regional organisations. The main strategy implemented by the European Commission consisted in offering economic aid and trade agreements that would foster integration over cooperation. During the 1990s, it was common for Latin American partisans of the regional approach, such as political authorities or academics, to associate cooperation with the past or with an incomplete stage of regionalism, in which collective projects could be sectorial and rely on the unstable will of governments. European integration thus became an imperative model for the building of truly integrated blocs through pooling of sovereignty and binding rules. EU actions of support to Mercosur, for instance, usually combined financial aid with transfer of know-how. Since 1992, agreements established information exchange, staff training in Montevideo and Brussels, technical assistance to the Secretariat, and other measures intended to enhance the institutionalisation process, along with an increase in development aid to Mercosur countries. Members of the European Parliament, mainly from Italy, Germany, and later on, Portugal and Spain, were also interested in increasing connections with Latin America through joint parliamentary meetings (Costa and Dri 2014). In 1994, a framework agreement formalised all these axes and established negotiations for trade liberalisation, which are not yet concluded.

In spite of European efforts, during the 1990s, Mercosur as well as other organisations, kept its minimal institutional framework and the requirement of unanimity for every decision, which made explicit the preference of members' governments and ministries of foreign affairs by its intergovernmental character (Ventura 2003: 103). The three decisional bodies are composed exclusively by members of the Executive powers and the Secretariat was responsible only by administrative tasks until 2004. Regional rules have to be internalised in national juridical systems before becoming enforceable and conflicts among member states are arbitrated by ad hoc judges in a dispute settlement system close to the World Trade Organization (WTO). The parliamentary committee nearly failed to be included in the foundational treaty, showing the marginal place accorded to Legislative representatives – the few that even timidly have dared to challenge sovereignty taboos of diplomacy (Dri 2014: 101). Nevertheless, the lack of more robust institutions did not prevent a high increase in trade exchanges among Mercosur members, which went from U$10,201 million in 1991 to U$41,074 million in 1997 (Hoffmann *et al.* 2008: 106).

This landscape of commercial vitality combined with low political integration corresponded exactly to the aims of neoliberal political forces in power in all Mercosur member nations during the 1990s. Different from the nationalist groups of the 1980s that articulated integration as a way out of the crisis and a step towards protected internationalisation, this time regionalism was reduced to just trade negotiations. The rhythm of commercial increase was only interrupted by the devaluation of the Brazilian currency in 1999, following the Asian economic crisis. This event slightly changed the way the PSDB was dealing with regionalism, as Brazil needed Mercosur in order to share the economic costs of helping Argentina and prevent new drawbacks.

2 Relaunching and revitalising Mercosur after the 1999 crisis

Monetary crises starting in Southeast Asia in 1997 and in Russia in 1998 led the Brazilian government to depreciate its currency in order to maintain exports. This fact, along with the negative global economic situation, severely affected Argentinean international trade, as its national economy was structured at that time around the parity dollar-peso. This policy was part of the neoliberal reforms implemented since the beginning of the 1990s, such as privatisation, market deregulation, and commercial and financial opening. They implied in a transformation of the Argentinean economic structure and of its links with international players, culminating in an unprecedented crisis in 2001 (Felder 2009). Brazilian governments, representing right-wing and later on left-wing political forces, chose to enhance integration in order to help Argentina. This was the first way in which the 1999 crisis affected regionalism. The second was the questioning of neoliberal solutions, which delayed the negotiations for the FTAA. Mercosur was seen as a concrete alternative to the agreement with the United States. Either way, this crisis brought closer the perspectives of different parties on regionalism, which tried to compensate for the negative economic effects of the crisis with political measures.

The 1999 Argentinean presidential elections, marked by a context of recession and GDP decline, brought to power the opposition candidate Fernándo de la Rúa, reassembling centre-right political forces against the Justicialist Party. The new government tried to implement fiscal austerity measures and reduce public investments in order to face the crisis, but its sole effects were increasing popular dissatisfaction and eroding government's political support. The Brazilian right-wing government at the time decided, not after some hesitation, to help its long-time partner through a relaunching of Mercosur institutions and economic integration in 2000. The PSDB has always been a partisan of a minimal Mercosur, ideally centred on free-trade. A PSDB member of the Mercosur Parliament believes that 'we should take the root of a more economic Mercosur'.[2] The former candidate of the PSDB for presidential elections in Brazil in 2002 and 2010 states he was 'opposed to Mercosur when we were in the Collor government (1990–92), when it was launched. I wrote a ten-page article against it, because it was non-sense. It was like renouncing sovereignty'.[3]

Nevertheless, the risk of an Argentinean breakdown motivated new measures that could avoid negative consequences for the Brazilian economy. The Brazilian Minister of Foreign Affairs, also from the PSDB, stated in 1999 that

> in Argentina, numbers are worrying, for they indicate a drop in economic activity, especially in industry, and growing unemployment. The Brazilian government is sensitive to this reality and bets on Argentina's recovery, which is our common interest.[4]

Looking for the economic improvement of the region in order to surpass the most difficult crisis of Mercosur since its creation, governments proposed several policies stimulating trade liberalisation, juridical efficiency of regional norms and institutional reinforcement.[5] The Brazilian president at the time affirmed that 'Argentina needs support from international organs. If the country does not get this support, it will never leave this situation. Someone will have to make a tenacious decision and propose a heroic solution to Argentina'.[6] The PSDB board did not change its dominant view opposed to a supranational regional institution, but members of government did agree that neighbours could not simply neglect Argentina and that the regional level was the best option for Brazil to deal with the crisis. Macro-economic regulation therefore replaced neoliberalism principles, which left important lessons to Mercosur representatives while negotiating the FTAA.

Institutionally, the main reforms within the Mercosur relaunching programme were the creation, in 2002, of the Technical Assistance Sector (SAT, Spanish acronym) of the Mercosur Secretariat and the approval of the Olivos Protocol, which should facilitate dispute settlement among member states. The decision of creating the SAT was motivated, according to its presidents, by a decision to 'advance the process of institutional reinforcement of Mercosur', considering it as 'an essential tool to handle the increasing challenges presented by the international system ... that should enhance growth and development'.[7] The SAT was composed of four experts – two lawyers and two economists – recruited by international public selection, for the first time in Mercosur. Representing the region and not their state of origin, they were intended to follow and evaluate the evolution of integration, besides elaborating studies and monitoring the juridical quality of norms adopted by decision organs.[8] Professionals chosen at the time showed a high academic profile and a solid formation on Mercosur, which made them legitimate choices to represent supranational interests and challenge diplomatic routines (Dabène 2009: 99).

The Olivos Protocol replaced the dispute settlement system established by the Brasilia Protocol in 1991. Both treaties proposed an arbitration framework to solve queries among states, in which a mediator, not a judge, is called to decide. Intending to 'strengthen juridical security within Mercosur',[9] the Olivos Protocol instituted a Permanent Review Tribunal. The Tribunal has its headquarters in Asunción and is formed by five arbitrators selected by national governments, who can review ad hoc decisions or act as the first step in arbitration, after the failure of direct negotiations or the mediation by the Common Market Group. The Tribunal can also provide advisory opinions when demanded by national jurisdictions, which should harmonise the interpretation of the Mercosur law (see Perotti 2009). However, in spite of its innovations and the prominent jurists indicated to compose the Tribunal (see Arnold and Rittberger 2013), the Protocol did not change the most common procedure of solving problems among Mercosur states: presidential dialogue.

If the changes proposed by the Olivos Protocol did not have a substantial impact in the Mercosur normative system, the SAT did bring important critics to the political procedures. SAT experts initiated a structured dialogue with regional organisations, political parties, research centres and international foundations interested in Mercosur. This led to the formation of a new epistemic community that advocated for stronger institutions that could implement Mercosur goals and for enhanced transparency of regional decision-making. The contents of Mercosur meetings were rarely accessible to the public and often classified as 'confidential' (Peña 2003: 30). They defended the end of the 'ministries monopole' and the interaction with social, political and economic actors in order to increase democratic legitimacy of regional norms (Ventura 2003: 590). These demands were organised later on around the conception of the Mercosur Parliament, which could at the same time deepen institutional framework and regional accountability, assuring a political lead for the integration process. The perspective of this new group was not coincident with the PSDB's views on integration, but a consequence of the SAT's relative institutional autonomy and inertia, which confirms the unpredictable effects of a new institution once it is launched (Pierson 2004; Mahoney 2000).

Along with the Argentinean economic needs, another event related to the 1999 crisis had a considerable influence on Mercosur civil society. Negotiations for the establishment of a free trade area in the American continent were developing when the neoliberal model, representing the success of economic North American interests in Latin America, started to show its limits (Coll 1997: 51). Policies willing to reduce government expenses, stabilise reserves, privatise public companies, encourage foreign investment and reduce import taxes were considered responsible for difficulties in facing the crisis. Neoliberalism was therefore blamed for the period of economic adversity (Camargo 2002: 94), and social groups like workers' unions and political parties started to question the supposed benefits of the FTAA. In Brazil, an informal referendum was organised in 2002, in which 10 million people rejected the agreement. Liberal governments themselves, including the PSDB-run Brazil, began to question the consequences of a complete market opening with the United States. Other groups increased the pressure: on one hand, industrial sectors were reticent towards the economic benefits of the FTAA; on the other, ministries of foreign affairs were worried of losing autonomy after an exclusive geopolitical alignment with the United States (Dupas 1997: 40).

The election of left-wing forces to the presidency in Argentina and Brazil only reinforced the perception centred on the limits of the FTAA. In Argentina, Nestor Kirchner was elected in 2003 with the support of the former president Eduardo Duhalde – the main leader of the country's institutional and economic normalisation. Fernando de la Rúa had resigned in 2001, after the failure of his economic stabilisation plan. In the absence of a vice-president, the power then came back to the Justicialist Party after the resignation of a candidate elected by the Congress. Duhalde and Kirchner represented a branch of the Justicialist Party opposed to the neoliberal policies of the Menem government and advanced values such as social justice and national sovereignty (Stuart 2008: 26). A few months before Kirchner, Lula took office in Brazil after the first presidential victory of a left-wing party in the history of the country. The Workers' Party intended to build 'an alternative national development project' through income redistribution and regional integration.[10] In spite of the different groups coexisting within the parties, elites who won the elections represented general projects supporting the role of the state over the market. Their objective was reinforcing public management capabilities: internally, promoting social inclusion; externally, consolidating South-American relations and autonomy in regards to the United States (Ayerbe 2008: 9).

The PT's government programme highlighted the implementation of a 'new foreign policy', capable of protecting the country from the instabilities of world financial markets and of converging Brazilian interests with those of its neighbours. In order to do so, reforming Mercosur to be able to face globalisation challenges with political and juridical institutions was necessary.[11] The programme also referred to difficulties of the FTAA, which, if following conditions proposed by the United States, would not be 'a free trade agreement but a process of economic annexation of the continent with serious consequences for the productive structure of our country'.[12] By this point, Mercosur started to be seen as a project capable of facing the FTAA, in contrast to its original commercial conception.

> The FTAA allowed Mercosur to advance because it got the left-wing forces together, it compelled the left to strongly support Mercosur. Before that, the left was nationalist, they though Mercosur belonged only to businessman and multinational companies. With the FTAA, the left started to bring its support, to get to know Mercosur.[13]

In 2003, Lula stated that the intention was to 'gradually eliminate fragilities still present in Mercosur, and therefore be more prepared to negotiate with other countries and organizations … facing together challenges of agreements with the FTAA, WTO and European Union'.[14]

Historically, the PT was internally divided concerning Mercosur. Some groups considered it a neoliberal project from the 1990s that should be abandoned in favour of a larger political integration project encompassing all South American states. Other groups considered the possibility of reforming Mercosur and reinforcing its social, cultural and political dimensions. When the party arrived to power in 2003, the context and PT's board preferences supported the second option, which would be faster considering the evolution of the FTAA. Instead of getting rid of Mercosur, it would be wiser to agglutinate forces around the existent structure.

> The Mercosur that we inherit when we get to power ... is an institution with exclusive commercial goals. Political, institutional and strategic goals of integration come in second place. When we arrive, political forces in Latin America are not the same as today, it was a transition period. Therefore we try to adapt Mercosur, to use Mercosur not anymore as a way to the FTAA, but as a way, a springboard towards a project of integration.[15]

Marco Aurélio Garcia, the special councillor of the president for international affairs, personified this tendency within the government. An old PT militant, he supported the progressive increase of the political dimension within Mercosur so that the organisation could 'conceive a South American agenda'.[16] 'Brazil has understood that we cannot solve the problems of the construction of a united, fair and democratic South America only by the means of trade' (Garcia 2010: 161).

After the PT, reforms in Mercosur received the image of a revitalising project, more comprehensive than the PSDB relaunching, as it was thought to include social and political dimensions. The main institutional impacts of this phase are the creation of the Structural Convergence Fund (Focem) and the Mercosur Parliament (Parlasur), both in 2005. Even if their potential to actually account for stronger regional decisions is still limited, these innovations brought important changes in terms of reinforcing the transnational character of Mercosur institutions. Indeed, they carried a close-to-supranational perspective on regionalism as they were based on rules advancing political cleavages over nationality, legality over informality, cohesion over asymmetry, majority over consensus, citizenship over state representativeness. The progressive questioning of the neoliberal model from the 1999 financial crisis onwards and difficulties around negotiations for the FTAA therefore had a concrete influence on Mercosur. These events have destabilised the principles that anchored the integration for a decade, introducing possibilities of an alternative project. Nevertheless, this was only partially completed. The next section will show that the 2008 crisis did not find Mercosur as integrated as the PT's intentions had demonstrated a few years beforehand.

3 The national turn: the 'emerging power' approach to the 2008 crisis

The 2008 world financial crisis, considered the most critical one since the 1929 depression, started after the bankruptcy of Lehman Brothers, a North American financial firm with a global scale. This event followed the complex policies built around the bursting of the United States' housing bubble, which affected the level of confidence of investors and led ultimately to a crash in global stock markets. As a result, industry did not have enough credit to operate. Industrial production decreased significantly in developed countries and, in a less important way, even in the developing world. Latin American states suffered from exports reduction and tried to stimulate national markets to absorb products that were not sold internationally with measures such as income transfer programmes and salary increases (Singer 2009). Brazilian president Lula da Silva stated that the poor saved Brazil from the crisis when they bought industrial items and accounted for the maintenance of consumption rates.[17]

Left-wing forces were in power in all Mercosur countries by this time, and all of them criticised the faith in the market's ability to self-regulate. They suggested a reinforcement of the role of the state in economic decisions in order to prevent new severe crises. According to Lula in the 2008 G20 meeting, the crisis demonstrated the ruins of the neoliberal model and of 'the dogmatic faith in the principle of no state intervention in the economy'.[18] The presidential declaration of the December 2008 Mercosur summit affirmed 'the need of anticyclical economic and social policies that attenuate the effects of this crisis originated in developed countries. Social investments should assure universal access to education, health, employment and public goods'.[19] The declaration also mentions that member states should act 'harmonically' in order to surpass challenges for development and social equality and that the international financial architecture should be transformed in order to assure a better regulation of markets. Even if these are official government statements, the ideology of the PT and other political forces in power are clearly reflected in the emphasis put on the social consequences of the crisis and on the conditioning of economic recovery to social measures.

The document emphasises the commitment of Mercosur states to implement – nationally – social policies, but it does not mention concrete regional proposals to face the crisis. Timid responses came in CMC decisions on 12/2008 and 39/2008. The first instituted a Programme for Productive Integration, planned to stimulate economic complementarity and intra-sectorial specialisation among small and medium companies. Its implementation is nevertheless conditioned to initiatives of a web of national actors related to industry, which compromises the scale and effectiveness of the projects. Also, the norm creating an institution of credit for complementary industries was not yet ratified by member states.[20] The second decision established a committee of ministries responsible for social questions, which should conceive a Mercosur Plan for Social Action. The Plan was presented in 2010 and approved in 2011,[21] with support of the Mercosur Social Institute established in 2007, but it simply presented social directives to be coordinated at the national level. Unlike in decisions related to regional trade and institutional reinforcement made in 2000, in 2008, collective responses were based upon cooperation rather than integration mechanisms. These measures consolidated the national route that had already been paved mainly by Argentina and Brazil since mid-2000s.

Indeed, since the second term of the Lula government, Brazil adopted a different approach to Mercosur. The 2006 PT's Government Programme kept South America as the declared priority, but this time integration was mentioned in the context of the Brazilian 'sovereign insertion in the world'.[22] Whilst the 2002 Programme contained an item on 'foreign policy towards regional integration and global negotiation',[23] the 2006 document mentioned regionalism together with south-south cooperation, namely with Asia and Africa. Structural conditions and policy behaviour have been pointed out as reasons for the growing mismatch between the regional and global performance of Brazil's foreign policy (Malamud 2011). Brazil's larger economy and population in comparison to its neighbours may have led Brazilian elites to consider regional relations less enticing than other global opportunities. The participation in coalitions as BRICS and IBAS (Oliveira and Onuki 2010) and the signing of a strategic partnership with the European Union in 2007, for instance, confirm this tendency. According to a PT's member, 'the Brazilian government implemented a strategy of investing in Mercosur without limiting itself to Mercosur, always looking ahead'.[24] At the moment of the 2008 crisis, Brazilian foreign policy priorities were beyond Mercosur. The opposition did not criticise only the regional approach, but also the emphasis on south-south relations. To the PSDB, Brazil should largely concentrate on relations with developed regions such as North America and the European Union. The 2010 and 2014 PSDB's Government Programmes consider south-south cooperation to be 'ideological' and only marginally mention BRICS and IBAS. Even the search for more space in international decisions is criticised: 'it is essential to deeply evaluate the implications of the search for a bigger role than our international potential allows, for mistakes can jeopardize our real interests'.[25]

Regarding Brazil's reluctant regional policy, the question is to what extent the country will be able to keep its image and achieve its goals internationally without the proper support from its neighbours (Malamud 2011). The consensual hegemony as a strategy of soft power (Burges 2008) may reach its peak if it is not followed by a consistent regional policy that maintains shared perceptions and cooperation. In other words, the structural vision that the Brazil of the PT exported to some neighbours depends more on actions than on rhetoric to last. Values such as 'regionalism' and 'multilateralism' cannot build strong alliances if Brazil itself chose the unilateral way. This situation corresponds not only to the lack of collective reaction after the 2008 crisis, but also to the discontinuity of mechanisms implemented after the 2000 crisis. Some years after entering into force, national agents imposed tacit restrictions to the recent close-to-supranational measures, such as the moral harassment suffered by the first specialists working in the SAT, the use of presidential diplomacy rather than the new dispute settlement system, the low budget assigned to FOCEM and the lack of political efforts to approve Parlasur direct elections.

Therefore, the main explanation accounting for the different impacts of the 1999 and 2008 crises in Mercosur is not related to institutional density, for it did not change substantially from one period to the other. If these measures were properly followed and implemented, it is possible that the institutional reinforcement of Mercosur would have led agents to push integration forward in 2008 as hypothesis 2.1 sustains, but it was not the case here. Institutional design was simply kept constant in spite of discourse and restricted reform efforts. The almost nonexistent political consequences of the 2008 crisis in Mercosur, in comparison to the previous crises, is best explained first by the greater relative power of Brazil in comparison to Argentina, as indicated by hypothesis 1. Argentina has not yet completely recovered from the breakdown of 2001, and the feeling that the country should follow Brazil and other medium-income Latin

American countries is still shared by part of the political elite. From this basis, Brazil was in a stronger position to influence Mercosur responses in 2008.

Brazilian responses are nevertheless neither unitary nor neutral, and depend largely on the struggle among political and economic actors. The diversity of regional actions defended by Brazil during crisis periods came from different insights from the two main political parties. In 1999, the PSDB agreed to regionalise measures of economic assistance to Argentina and fostered trade liberalisation within Mercosur. The region was treated as a necessary level of negotiation if countries wanted to find a way out of the crisis, partially because of Mercosur's economic success during the 1990s. In 2008, after the diversification of Brazilian foreign policy promoted by the PT, the region was not perceived as central during the crisis. As economic integration had not been firmly and continually stimulated, nationalist measures were encouraged and dialogue at the regional level was limited. These developments confirm hypothesis 3.1, according to which the degree of support of civil society organisations is directly proportional to the degree of integration. In spite of political discourses, Mercosur was clearly weaker in 2008, which resulted in a weaker impact of the crisis on regional design.

Conclusion

This chapter has analysed three periods of economic crisis in Latin America – 1980, 1999 and 2008 – and their relations with actors' behaviour and parties' views on regional integration. The first one is among the main factors that led to the creation of Mercosur in 1991; due to the level of dialogue established in order to collectively surpass national debts. The 1999 crisis also had a positive impact on regional organisation, as economic integration was stimulated and new political institutions were inaugurated in Mercosur. Nevertheless, these mechanisms proved themselves insufficient to trigger regionalism some years later. The 2008 crisis arrived in this same context of reinforcement of national priorities but did not have a positive effect on regional schemes. This chapter has shown that the influence of right or left wing Brazilian parties in each period accounts for this difference. The impact of crises in reinforcing or eroding integration depends not only on institutional structures but also on beliefs and interests of political agents. The way political parties perceive the crisis according to their central ideological lines influences how they chose to deal with regionalism at each time. This implies that endogenous mechanisms are an important source of change in Mercosur and that Brazilian decisions regarding regionalism are crucial due to its high economic power, attesting hypothesis 1.

In the 1980s, leading actors were willing to open national markets and regionalism seemed to be the most careful and possible way. In 1999, the Brazilian PSDB was interested in regionalising the political and economic costs of helping Argentina. In 2008, the PT was investing in the construction of an 'emergent and solidary power' image for Brazil. Nevertheless, the results of the 1999 measures came in the mid-2000s, already showing the lack of interest of the PT in deep economic integration. When the country was considered autonomous enough, the regional way was no longer a priority. This confirms the hypothesis 3.1 of the book, according to which the more integrated a region, the greater is the support of civil society's organisations. The lack of integration in 2008 left a great space for nationalist currents of the PT to empty regional discussions on the crisis. Therefore, differently from the 1980s, the following economic crises were not able to trigger regionalism in an efficient and stable manner. The 1980s' regional effects were considerable but the intergovernmental structure was kept, which gave national actors space to manoeuvre in subsequent actions. In other words, regional institutions in Mercosur were never dense enough to reflect a continued engagement with integration, which connects the chapter marginally with hypothesis 2.

The 2008 crisis had two main impacts on the economic and political culture of Mercosur societies. The first one is associated with the need of diversifying trade relations and investing in commercial partners outside the traditional developed world. The second one is related to the negative economic results of the Eurozone, so that the financial crisis was interpreted by the large media as a regionalism crisis. Considering the three periods analysed, this is the first time in which crisis was linked to citizens' negative attitudes towards regionalism. Ultimately, the 2008 crisis contributed to the abandonment of the European model as the guide for Latin American regionalism and legitimated the rise of alternative practices identified with elastic regionalism (Wehner *et al.* 2013).

In terms of economic integration, Latin American integration may have peaked, having reached its high point during the 1990s (Malamud and Gardini 2012). Nevertheless, regionalism is still a compelling foreign policy as it brings international visibility, regional stability, regime legitimacy and popular support (Malamud and Gardini 2012: 130). Flexible forms to keep regionalism are thus arising, based more on sectorial cooperation than on supranational projects. Regional methods are being developed explicitly in order for states to deal with issues of common interest maintaining sovereignty: there are no supranational decisions but rather joint policies in some areas. This corresponds to the perspective of regional dialogue with autonomy defended by the PT in the last decade in Brazil and can be considered a result of this kind of foreign policy. These instruments include finding a place in deliberative instances for a diversity of interested states, multiple negotiating tables and several intersecting topics, forming a kind of modular regionalism (Gardini 2013). Considering this current status, future research will respond under which conditions cooperative projects may generate genuine shared practices in policy-making that were not developed under the 'integration' umbrella. If they are effective, future crises will have to deal with a new material of intervention.

Notes

1 The author thanks the editors and anonymous reviewers for comments that helped to improve the arguments, as well as Quentin Heilbroner for language editing.

2 Author's interview, Brasília, 16 April 2009.

3 José Serra, Folha de São Paulo, 19 October 2013. Available in www1.folha.uol.com.br/poder/2013/10/1354077-serra-chama-mercosul-de-bobagem-e-fala-em-fru-fru-do-pais-com-a-bolivia.shtml.
4 Luiz Felipe Lampreia, Folha de São Paulo, 15 August 1999. Available in www1.folha.uol.com.br/fsp/opiniao/fz15089908.htm.
5 Common Market Council Decisions 22–32/2000.
6 Fernando Henrique Cardoso, Folha de São Paulo, 17 November 2002. Available at www1.folha.uol.com.br/fsp/brasil/fc1711200208.htm.
7 Joint Declaration of Presidents of Mercosur Member States, Buenos Aires, 5 July 2002.
8 CMC Decision 30/2002.
9 Olivos Protocol for the Dispute Settlement in Mercosur, 2002.
10 Partido dos Trabalhadores, Programa de Governo 2002, São Paulo, 2002, p. 6.
11 Partido dos Trabalhadores, Programa de Governo 2002, São Paulo, 2002, p. 6.
12 Partido dos Trabalhadores, Programa de Governo 2002, São Paulo, 2002, p. 7.
13 Author's interview with a parliamentary assistant, Brasília, April 2009.
14 Lula e Kirchner criarão Parlamento do Mercosul, BBC Brasil, 11 June 2003. Available in www.bbc.co.uk/portuguese/economia/030611_mercosulbg.shtml.
15 Author's interview with a member of PT's Committee, Brasília, April 2009.
16 Interview with Alfredo Atanasof and Silvia Lospennato, Red Mercosur Parlamentario, Brasília, May 2006.
17 Quem salvou o país da crise foi o povo, diz Lula, O Estado de São Paulo, 13 November 2009. Available in http://economia.estadao.com.br/noticias/geral,quem-salvou-o-pais-da-crise-foi-o-povo-diz-lula,466088.
18 Lula cobra maior controle dos mercados financeiros internacionais, Zero Hora, 8 November 2011. Available in http://zh.clicrbs.com.br/rs/noticia/2008/11/lula-cobra-maior-controle-nos-mercados-financeiros-internacionais-2286918.html.
19 Declaración sobre medidas de promoción y protección en el área social en respuesta a la crisis financiera mundial, Salvador, 15 December 2008.
20 Decision CMC 48/08 – Mercosur Funds of Assurance to Micro, small and medium companies.
21 Available in http://ismercosur.org/doc/PEAS-Portugues-web.pdf.
22 Partido dos Trabalhadores, Programa de Governo 2006, São Paulo, 2006, p. 14.
23 Partido dos Trabalhadores, Programa de Governo 2002, São Paulo, 2002, p. 6.
24 Author's interview with a member of PT's Committee, Brasília, April 2009.
25 Em plano de governo, Aécio diz que política externa foi superdimensionada. Rede Brasil Atual, 1 October 2014. Available in www.redebrasilatual.com.br/eleicoes-2014/em-plano-de-governo-aecio-diz-que-politica-externa-do-brasil-foi-superdimensionada-987.html.

References

Arnold, Christian and Rittberger, Berthold (2013). The Legalization of Dispute Resolution in Mercosur. *Journal of Politics in Latin America*, *5*(3), 97–132.

Ayerbe, Luis Fernando (2008). Apresentação. In Ayerbe, Luis Fernando (org.). *Novas lideranças políticas e alternativas de governo na América do Sul.* São Paulo: Editora da UNESP.

Bresser-Pereira, Luiz Carlos (2010). As três interpretações da dependência. *Perspectivas*, São Paulo, 38, 17–48.

Burges, Sean (2008). Consensual hegemony: theorizing Brazilian foreign policy after the Cold War. *International Relations*, *22*(1), 65–84.

Camargo, Sonia de (2002). O canto da sereia: América Latina perante a ALCA. *São Paulo em Perspectiva*, *16*(1), 94–104.

Cisneros, Andrés and Piñero, Carlos (2002). *Del ABC al Mercosur: la integración latinoamericana en la doctrina y praxis del peronismo*. Buenos Aires: Nuevohacer.

Coll, Albert (1997). United States strategic interests in Latin America: an assessment. *Journal of Interamerican Studies and World Affairs*, *39*(1), 45–57.

Conduru, Guilherme (1998). O subsistema americano, Rio Branco e o ABC. *Revista Brasileira de Política Internacional*, *41*(2), 59–82.

Costa, Olivier and Dri, Clarissa (2014). How Does the European Parliament Contribute to the Construction of EU's Interregional Dialogue? In Baert, Francis, Scaramagli, Tiziana and Söderbaum, Fredrik (eds.). *Intersecting Interregionalism: regions, global governance and the EU*. London: Springer, 129–150.

Dabène, Olivier (2003). *América Latina no século XX*. Porto Alegre: EDIPUCRS.

Dabène, Olivier (2009). *The politics of regional integration in Latin America: theoretical and comparative explorations*. New York: Palgrave Macmillan.

Dri, Clarissa (2014). *La construction du Parlement du Mercosur: régionalisme et démocratie en Amérique du sud*. Luxembourg: Larcier.

Dupas, Gilberto (1997). *ALCA e os interesses do Mercosul*. São Paulo: Fundação Memorial da América Latina.

Felder, Ruth (2009). Reformas institucionales e integración global la intervención del Banco Mundial en Argentina durante los '90. *Revista Sociologia e Política*, *17*(33), 55–68.

Garcia, Marco Aurélio (2010). O lugar do Brasil no mundo: a política externa em um momento de transição. In Sader, Emir and Garcia, Marco Aurélio (org.). *Brasil: entre o passado e o futuro*. São Paulo: Boitempo, 153–176.

Gardini, Gian Luca (2005). Two Critical Passages on the Road to Mercosur. *Cambridge Review of International Affairs*, *18*(3), 405–420.

Gardini, Gian Luca (2007). Who Invented Mercosur? *Diplomacy & Statecraft*, *18*(4), 805–830.

Gardini, Gian Luca (2013). The added value of the Pacific Alliance and 'modular regionalism' in Latin America. *LSE Ideas*.

George, Alexander and Bennett, Andrew (2005). *Case studies and theory development in the social sciences*. Cambridge: MIT Press.

Hettne, Björn and Inotai, András (1994). *The new regionalisms: implications for global development and international security*. Forssan Kirjapaine Oy: ONU/WIDER.

Hoffmann, Andrea, Coutinho, Marcelo and Kfuri, Regina (2008). Indicadores e Análise Multidimensional do Processo de Integração do Cone Sul. *Revista Brasileira de Política Internacional*, *51*(2), 98–116.

Mahoney, James (2000). Path dependence in historical sociology. *Theory and Society*, 29, 507–548.

Malamud, Andrés (2011). A leader without followers? The growing divergence between regional and global performance of Brazilian foreign policy. *Latin American Politics and Society*, *53*(3), 1–24.

Malamud, Andrés and Gardini, Gian Luca (2012). Has Regionalism Peaked? The Latin American Quagmire and its Lessons. *The International Spectator*, *47*(1), 116–133.

Mallmann, Maria Izabel (2008). *Os ganhos da década perdida: democracia e diplomacia regional na América Latina*. Porto Alegre: EDIPUCRS.

Medeiros, Marcelo (2000). *La genèse du Mercosud*. Paris: L'Harmattan.

Oliveira, Amâncio and Onuki, Janina (2010). India, Brazil and South Africa: collective action, divergent positions. *New Global Studies*, *2*(2).

Peña, Félix (2003). *Concertación de intereses, efectividad de las reglas de juego y calidad institucional en el Mercosur*. Montevideo: Konrad Adenauer Stiftung.

Perotti, Alejandro (2009). El principio de primacía del derecho del Mercosur en las tres primeras Opiniones Consultivas del Tribunal Permanente de Revisión. In Ulate, Chacón (org.) *Derecho internacional, derecho comunitario y derechos humanos*. San José: UCR, 291–316.

Pierson, Paul (2004). *Politics in time: history, institutions and social analysis*. Oxfordshire: Princeton University Press.

Portella Filho, Petrônio (1994). O ajustamento na América Latina: crítica ao modelo de Washington. *Lua Nova: Revista de Cultura e Política*, 32, 101–132.

Santander, Sebastian (2005). The European partnership with Mercosur: a relationship based on strategic and neo-liberal principles. *Journal of European Integration*, v. *27*(3), 285–306.

Seitenfus, Ricardo (1989). A cooperação argentino-brasileira: significados e perspectivas. *Lua Nova: Revista de Cultura e Política*, 18, 107–126.

Singer, Paul (2009). A América Latina na crise mundial. *Estudos Avançados*, *23*(66), 91–102.

Spindler, Manuela (2002). New regionalism and the construction of global order. *Working Papers of the Centre for the Study of Globalisation and Regionalisation*, University of Warwick, 93.

Stuart, Ana Maria (2008). Novas lideranças na América do Sul: o caso Kirchner. In Ayerbe, Luis Fernando (org.). *Novas lideranças políticas e alternativas de governo na América do Sul*. São Paulo: Editora da UNESP, 15–35.

Telò, Mario (2006). *Europe: a civilian power? European Union, global governance and world order*. Hampshire: Palgrave Macmillan.

Ventura, Deisy (2003). *As assimetrias entre o Mercosul e a União Européia: os desafios de uma associação inter-regional*. Barueri: Manole.

Wehner, Leslie, Nolte, Detlef and Weiffen, Brigitte (2013). *The Regional Governance Architecture in Latin America: Between institutional elasticity and segmentation*. Paper prepared for the 7° Congreso de la Asociación Latinoamericana de Ciencia Política (ALACIP), Bogotá, 25–27 September.

Part III

Asian regional integration

9 Crisis and regional integration

Human rights and environmental governance in ASEAN[1]

Reuben Wong

Introduction

This chapter re-examines the dominant narratives concerning ASEAN's collective responses to the regional crises of 1997. It tests the hypothesis that powerful state actors (in this case, Indonesia) play an instrumental role in influencing institutional change in a situation of a crisis. This chapter will show that Indonesia's domestic political change and subsequent support for human rights – which responded to the Asian Financial Crisis of 1997 – was a critical ingredient in the advancement of a human rights regime in ASEAN. The AFC and the 1997–1998 environmental crisis strongly validate the hypothesis that key actors play an important role in influencing institutional change in a situation of crisis). But key actors can also be stumbling blocks. Indonesia was the most important limiting factor on a multilateral solution to an ongoing environmental crisis; the promulgation and implementation of the 2003 Transboundary Haze Agreement were stymied by the lack of Indonesian support.

While the hypothesis of state power is validated in ASEAN, the jury is still out on the hypothesis relating institutional density to the continued engagement of institutions and member states.

Institutional density in ASEAN could hardly be described as 'dense' in 1997; but member states (always the main actors) found ways to deepen institutional linkages and cooperation so that by 2002, they were committed to plans for greater community-building and even adopted an ASEAN Charter by 2008.

Institutional density was not high to begin with, but institutions were nonetheless developed for human rights and for environmental governance in the 2000s following the financial and environmental crises. The low institutional density in ASEAN was *not* an obstacle to the continued engagement of institutions and member states. The low level of institutional density turned out to be a blessing for human rights, as there was no set path to follow; NGOs and states in favour of human rights could act as policy entrepreneurs to introduce novel structures in the absence of entrenched norms or path dependence.

Backdrop: the 1997–1998 crises

Much has been written about the 1997 Asian Financial Crisis (AFC) and its important effects on the states, economics and politics of the Southeast Asian region. The AFC, which had started as a domestic currency crisis in Thailand had rapidly extended its reach to other neighbouring ASEAN states – Malaysia, Philippines, Indonesia, and had sparked off similar contagion effects in South Korea, China and Hong Kong (Baig and Goldfajn 1999; Giancarlo *et al.* 1999). The attendant fall of the authoritarian Suharto regime in Indonesia (ASEAN's largest member state), and its democratisation process set the stage for decisions taken not only by ASEAN states, but also ASEAN in concert with China, Japan and Korea, to launch several regional cooperative projects. For international political economists, the Chiang Mai Initiative Mechanism and the Bali II concord of 2003, which envisaged the creation of three communities in ASEAN (Economic, Socio-Cultural and Security) by 2015, seemed to suggest that economic integration was taking place.

Concurrent to the 1997 AFC, which had caused much volatility in ASEAN financial markets, ASEAN states had experienced a pressing environmental crisis that had threatened to adversely impact the environmental security of the region, and threaten bilateral relations between Indonesia and neighbouring ASEAN states. The onset of the 1997–1998 forest fires, which had been primarily caused by the slash-and-burn techniques of Indonesian farmers and plantation owners had not only blanketed Indonesia in thick haze but had also shrouded neighbouring countries Singapore, Malaysia and to a lesser extent Thailand, Brunei and the Philippines (Cotton 1999; Mayer 2006; Quah 2002).

With air quality levels reaching hazardous ranges in these states, schools and even some airports were shut down; these events were threatening to undermine the already vulnerable economies of most ASEAN states. ASEAN member states (led by Singapore and Malaysia) expressed grave concern and underscored the need to engage in constructive dialogue with their Indonesian counterparts on the establishment of a multilateral framework to enhance existing environmental safeguards. An extended period of negotiations had eventually culminated in a consensus on the creation of an early warning system – the Regional Haze Action Plan (RHAP) to prevent forest fires coupled with improved management policies and enforcements via Fire Danger Rating System (FDRS) (Jones 2006).

Against the backdrop of the twin crises (1997 AFC and 1997–1998 environmental crisis), the passage of the ASEAN Charter at the organisation's fortieth anniversary in 2007 and the subsequent setting up of a human rights commission set the stage for debates about whether or not ASEAN was starting on the path of institutionalisation, if not serious EU-style integration. Some scholars argued that post-crisis institutionalisation in ASEAN had been significant enough to be considered integration (functionalist or transactional) – a significant shift from the previous inter-governmental arrangements and outright rejection of the precepts of supranationalism by ASEAN member states. (Tan 2011; Jetschke and Murray 2012; Wong 2012; Christiansen *et al.* 2013; Wong 2015.)

This chapter focuses on the role of major states (chiefly Indonesia) on this new area of regional cooperation. It argues that Indonesia was the key actor; one that both promoted institutional development (in human rights) and hindered integration (in environmental governance) in ASEAN. The economic, political and environmental crises of 1997 represented a shock and threat to ASEAN's cosy organisational values of non-interference, the safeguarding of one's national sovereignty and inter-governmental cooperation.

Next, this chapter tests the first hypothesis outlined in Chapter 1: that the most powerful actor in ASEAN – in this case the state of Indonesia – influences the direction of institutional change in ASEAN and finds that this is true in the two case studies (the AFC and 1997–1998 environmental crisis). With regards to the AFC, exogenous shocks had placed severe politico-economic strain on Indonesia. Thailand's decision to devalue the baht had an immediate impact on the Indonesian rupiah; the baht's devaluation resulted in repeated falls in the value of the rupiah. In an attempt to quell speculative attacks and maintain export competitiveness, Indonesian policy-makers had abandoned the rupiah's trading band and allowed the rupiah to float freely. However, notwithstanding the best efforts of the Indonesian Federal Reserve to contain the currency crisis, intense pressure was placed on the Indonesian rupiah, causing daily fluctuations of the exchange rate. Continual market volatility coupled with domestic ills of the Indonesian economy (pervasive neopatrimonialism and bureaucratic inefficiency) had seen a quick succession of withdrawals of investments by international and domestic investors. With a total of US$9.6 billion and US$7.8 billion withdrawn in the last quarter of 1997 and the first quarter of 1998, Indonesia had little option but to request for a monetary loan package from the International Monetary Fund (IMF) to stem widespread panic and to sustain its fragile economy (Rosenberger 1997: 225; Soesastro and Basri 1998).

Nonetheless, despite the loan package by the IMF, problems had continued to plague Suharto's administration with the economy continually subject to speculative attacks and the population feeling the pain of structural reforms imposed by the IMF. Throughout 1997–1998, massive riots and demonstrations had broken out in Jakarta against Suharto and the ethnic Chinese community (a small minority which controlled much of the economy) were targeted as scapegoats for attack. By May 1998, Suharto had been displaced by General Wiranto as internal factionalism broke out in the Indonesian armed forces. Suharto's subsequent resignation had marked the end of an authoritarian regime and the beginning of political transition in Indonesia (Kammen and Chandra 1999). Importantly, the resignation of Suharto had removed the impasses on human rights institutions in ASEAN and marked a significant shift in human rights dialogue within ASEAN.

While Indonesia's democratisation process was nascent and had experienced several challenges during the political leadership of a quick succession of post-Suharto presidents (first B. J. Habibie, then Abdurrahman Wahid and Megawati Sukarnoputri) in the post-Suharto era, there had been a subtle shift within ASEAN, from an antipathy towards human rights discussions, towards the setting up of more institutionalised human rights mechanisms at the regional level (Chandra and Douglas 2002). Against this backdrop, I would posit that the Indonesian story supports the state power hypothesis, hence the higher the relative power of actors (cognitive, economic, political, military) before a crisis occurs, the higher the probability that these actors influence institutional change in a situation of crisis).

In contrast to the AFC, which had seen Indonesia play an instrumental role in shaping human rights dialogue within ASEAN, ASEAN's failure to deal with the 1997–1998 environmental crisis and subsequent annual air pollution, can largely be attributed to the ambivalent stance undertaken by the Indonesian government to mete out punishment to both errant farmers and plantation owners who had engaged in illegal slash-and-burn techniques to clear their plots of land. Numerous attempts by other key ASEAN member states (Singapore and Malaysia) to coax Indonesia to introduce stronger environmental safeguards and enact stricter legislative measures against repeat offenders had been met with resistance from Indonesian officials who had underscored that more time was needed for Indonesian farmers to adapt to new practices to preserve their livelihood, but also to protect the economic interests of giant and well-connected palm-oil companies.

Indeed, the 1997–1998 environmental crises had oftentimes led to a gridlock in negotiations with Indonesia adopting a nonchalant attitude towards adopting radical reform of its environmental policies. Further attempts to persuade Indonesia to be a more responsible actor in environmental governance had reared its ugly head during the last serious 'haze' (in June 2013) when Indonesia accused Singapore and Malaysia of being complicit in allowing large companies incorporated in Singapore and Kuala Lumpur to contribute to the haze in Indonesia. Diplomatic tensions had further escalated in 2013 when Indonesia's Minister for People's Welfare Agung Laksono accused Singapore of 'behaving like a child' with their continual complains about the haze (AFP 2013). With the annual environmental crisis unresolved and the existence of persistent concerns about the haze situation till the time of writing (2015), it is clearly evident that there has been little progress with Indonesia being the primary foot-dragger in environmental protection in the region. We now look in detail at the two very different institutional responses to the financial crisis and to the environmental crisis, and ask why they differed so much. But first, some clarifications about the concept of 'crisis' as applied to ASEAN, and research methodology.

Research methodology

When studying crises, it is imperative to distinguish existential crises from critical situations and not impose the label of crisis retrospectively (Elvert 2011: 51). The definition of crisis is thus fundamental to this study. According to Arjen Boin *et al.*, a crisis is ' … a serious threat to the basic structures or the fundamental values and norms of a system, which under time pressure and highly uncertain circumstances necessitates making vital decisions' (Boin 2005: 2–4) Utilising Boin *et al.*'s definition, this paper postulates that crises disrupt the punctuated equilibrium of institutional frameworks and discredit the status quo (Boin *et al.* 2008:3). Domestic reforms enacted at the national level by important state actors and, subsequently, at the regional level through inter-governmental agreement, have the potential to bring about greater regional integration Regarding regional integration, there are three possible outcomes of a crisis: 1) greater integration, 2) rolling back of integration or 3) the maintenance of the status quo. This chapter uses process-tracing to examine the effect of crises on regional integration (George and Bennett 2005: 209–210).

In the case of human rights institutionalisation in ASEAN, a severe economic crisis in 1997 discredited the authority of a regional authoritarian hegemon (Indonesia under Suharto, 1965–1998). Facing a crisis of legitimacy and with its minimum winning coalition under great strain, there was great societal unrest. Demonstrators demanded regime change. In the event of a successful toppling and replacement of the authoritarian regime with a reformist government, the new leader at the helm has greater latitude and agency (because of the clean slate and public support) to drive the process of democratic reform at home and abroad. During this reformist era, the politically active citizenry and Civil Society Organisations continue to reinforce and cement the institutionalisation process of these human rights reforms, while also forming an epistemic community with similar-minded groups in the region. Moreover, the new found democratic norms are also externalised by the new state in its foreign relations as it pushes for regional integration in the area of human rights so as to 'lock-in' domestic reforms. Throughout this process, the international community pressures and encourages the crisis-hit regimes and the region as a whole to move towards greater institutionalisation of human rights.

1997 crises in ASEAN

The word 'crisis' aptly encapsulates the year 1997 for the Association of Southeast Asian Nations (ASEAN). Ruminating shortly after the Asian Financial Crisis (AFC), Michael Leifer, the eminent scholar of Southeast Asia's international relations, observed (Leifer 2005: 165):

> ASEAN has now reached a turning point in the expansion of its collective role as a result of shortcomings exposed in the face of challenges to its institutional competence. An inability to cope with regional economic adversity, with regional environmental pollution with its source in Indonesia and also with the aftermath of a coup in Cambodia in July 1997, which provoked a postponement of its membership, have damaged the standing and credibility of the association. ASEAN's predicament has been compounded by the way in which economic crisis has overtaken Indonesia, in particular, which has been the pivotal state of the Association from the onset.

Almost 20 years after the critical juncture of the Asian Financial Crisis, the question worth considering is – whither ASEAN integration; if indeed the concept 'integration' can be applied to ASEAN's regional cooperation. Most scholarship on ASEAN integration implicitly subscribes to Karl Deutsch's ideal of a security community which possesses '…"a sense of community" and of institutions and practices strong enough and widespread enough to assure, for a "long" time, dependable expectations of "peaceful change" among its population' (Deutsch *et al.* 1957: 5). That said, scholars disagree about on the nature of ASEAN integration and whether it truly reflects this Deutschian ideal. On the one hand, ASEAN enthusiasts, like Estrella Solidum, laud the substantive level of institutionalisation which has allowed ASEAN to '…[remain] vibrant and relevant as the 21st century has begun' (Solidum 2003: 222). Similarly, from a constructivist perspective, Amitav Acharya adds that the organisation's achievements as a 'nascent security community' are by no means insignificant (Acharya 2014: 264; see also Ba 2009: 3; Eaton and Stubbs 2006). Sceptics, however, consider ASEAN as having more 'form' than 'substance'. David Jones and Michael Smith dismiss ASEAN as 'neither a security nor an economic community, either in being or in prospect … [but] an imitation community' (Jones and Smith 2001; Jones and Smith 2003: 108. Echoing their 'imitation community' assessment from a realist perspective, Nicholas Khoo also questions the influence of ASEAN norms in bringing about regional integration (Khoo 2004; Narine 2009).

This chapter focuses not on the nature of ASEAN's integration or on whether a security community is coming into existence but on the *institutional outcomes* of two contemporary but different crises. It accepts that whilst a significant degree of regional integration has taken place since 1997, this integration may not lead to the kind of 'security community' of shared values and identity as envisioned by Deutsch, or even by more recent scholarship such as those by Acharya, or Adler and Barnett. The complex realities of Southeast Asian regionalism are glossed over by extreme positions of adulation or cynicism. Such views do not do justice to the original intent, historical development and continuously evolving role of ASEAN. One should be careful about applying Eurocentric standards and theories to very different contexts in Asia (Acharya 2009: 495; Katzenstein 1996: 130). Tellingly, Rizal Sukma even rejects comparisons with the Deutschian ideal of a security community, arguing that ASEAN is 'merely a security regime' (Emmerson 2005: 178). It is therefore necessary to assess ASEAN on its own terms. In other words, instead of comparing ASEAN to the European Union (EU), the organisation of ASEAN should be analysed and evaluated based on the standards and objectives it set for itself.

All that said, amidst this meta-debate on ASEAN, scholars have not adequately considered the relationship between crisis and regional integration. Although Ludge Kühnhardt has – in the case of the EU – theorised that '[t]he outcome of past integration crises … has often strengthened the rationale for integration and the renewal of its form' (Kühnhardt 2011: 6; Gehler 2011; Elvert 2011) the research on 'crisis' (and its political/economic effects) and 'human rights institutionalisation' in ASEAN remain as two separate domains of inquiry. For the former, scholars such as Acharya astutely point to what was a clear deviation from the ASEAN norm of non-interference in the aftermath of the AFC as economic ministers proposed a regional framework that would allow '…"mutual surveillance" of each others' economic policies' (Acharya 1998). Although Acharya identifies the intra-regional pressures for advances in human rights and democratisation after the AFC, the causal link between crises and regional integration is not explored (Acharya 2003; Acharya 1999).

Following on the conceptual framework in Chapter 1, this chapter traces the causal chain of events in the development of the human rights framework in ASEAN. It starts off with a regional organisation in which institutional density is low to begin with in the issue-area of human rights; but which culminates in unexpected integration when crisis opens up windows of opportunity for new actors (human rights advocates and ordinary citizens) to introduce and institutionalise new norms and organisational structures for the region.

Bearing in mind that the domain of human rights encompasses both Civil and Political (CP) rights and environmental rights; this chapter contends that the AFC has contributed to greater regional integration in the area of CP rights as attested by the ASEAN Charter (2008) and AICHR (2009). We thus observe a higher institutional density, without initial institutional density.

The third and fourth sections of this chapter trace the effect (or lack thereof) of the AFC on civil and political rights, and the 1997–1998 environmental crisis on environmental rights. The next section shows how new actors (e.g. human rights NGOs, a liberalising Indonesia, and the Philippines and Thailand) were empowered and how old actors (regimes resistant to a regional human rights framework, such as Indonesia under Suharto, Singapore, Malaysia, but also new ASEAN members Myanmar, Vietnam, Laos and Cambodia) were persuaded to come on board. The final section shows how Indonesian political and economic interests resisted calls for greater intergovernmental or even supranational forms of environmental governance in Southeast Asia for over a decade, and how individual states resorted to unilateral rather than multilateral solutions.

Civil and political rights

In 1997, the AFC exposed not only the myth of the Asian economic miracle, but also the institutional fault lines within ASEAN itself. The financial crisis drove integration in two fundamental ways. First, the uncoordinated, abysmal response of ASEAN to the AFC damaged the organisation's standing and led to the Chiang Mai Initiatives (CMI 2000), an institutional response to improve financial cooperation in the event of future balance-of-payments crises (Daquila 2007: 264; Henning 2011: 22). Besides greater economic integration, crisis-driven institutionalisation also took place in the realm of human rights. With the rhetoric of 'Asian values' ringing hollow and the subsequent breakdown of Suharto's authoritarian regime in light of the economic crisis, the ensuing regional integration in the human rights domain can be traced by examining the formation of the ASEAN Charter and the ASEAN Inter-Governmental Commission on Human Rights (AICHR). Apart from birthing the AICHR, the Charter promised further economic and political liberalisation and, additionally, greater participation and consultation with relevant stakeholders in society (Villacorta 2011: 306).

The AFC was a necessary factor in the political transformation of Indonesia, which, in turn, had regional implications for the institutionalisation of human rights in ASEAN. The ineffectual response of the Suharto government to the economic crisis generated much resentment among Indonesians and led to mounting pressures for democratic reform (Lee 2014: 104–106) General Wiranto's withdrawal of support crucially spelt the end of Suharto's 'New Order' era, in place since 1966 (Lee 2014: 149). After Suharto, commentators widely acknowledged the internal reforms and change of direction by the Indonesian government and military towards human rights issues as a critical component in the change of heart in states – such as Singapore, Malaysia, Cambodia, Laos, Vietnam and Myanmar – which had previously been resistant to human rights discussion at the ASEAN level (Thio 1999; Tan 2011; Wong 2012). In this wave of *reformasi*, President Jusuf Habibie relaxed media controls, released political prisoners, allowed the establishment of new political parties and held free elections in 1999 (Eldridge 2002: 133). In later administrations, the need for policy legitimacy and accountability behooved Indonesian Foreign Minister Hassan Wirayuda to begin institutional reform of the Indonesian Department of Foreign Affairs (*Departemen Luar Negeri Republik Indonesia*, DEPLU) in order to make the DEPLU more responsive to feedback from Indonesian civil society and citizens (Sukma 2011: 99). Presently, as the ASEAN member with the 'widest engagement with the human rights regime' (Davies 2014), the impact of the AFC in bringing about Indonesia's democratic transition should not be underrated.

Democracy has not only flourished domestically after the demise of Suharto's regime, it has also become an important element of Indonesia's foreign policy. True, Indonesia's adherence to democratic norms and respect for human rights in the post-Suharto era are also driven by economic prerogatives, as seen in studies of EU-Indonesia relations (Camroux and Srikandini 2013). The externalisation and export of internal norms of democracy is evident from Minister Wirayuda's declaration that Indonesia 'envision[s] an ASEAN that is democratic and that respects human rights' and actively seeks to promote democracy in ASEAN (Sukma 2011: 103).

Accordingly, the idea for a Charter that would legally embody ASEAN norms and values was advanced during Indonesia's chairing of the 2003 ASEAN Summit in Bali and later incorporated in the ASEAN Security Community Plan of Action (ASC PoA) (Djani 2009: 138). Given that the Cambodian, Laotian, Myanmar and Vietnamese (CLMV) representatives of the High Level Task Force (HLTF) for drafting the ASEAN Charter were opposed to the Charter's human rights emphasis and creation of a human rights body (Ong 2009: 113; Kim 2009: 156–157; Bounkeut 2009; Bwa 2009; Thanh 2009), the role of the pro-Charter bloc comprising Indonesia, Philippines, Singapore, Thailand and Malaysia was particularly essential (Langlois 2012: 217). Amongst this bloc, the ASEAN staffer Termsak Chalermpalanupap identified Indonesia and Malaysia as the key players who 'reviv[ed] the charter idea' (Chalermpalanupap 2009: 120). Tellingly, Ambassador

Dian Triansyah Djani, the Indonesian member of the HLTF, revealed that Indonesia viewed the Charter as an important legal document because it would 'reflec[t] the norms and values of the new Indonesia' (Djani 2009: 141). Besides reflecting its own new democratic character, Indonesia's strong support for the Charter and AICHR can also be attributed to its expectation that such a regional mechanism secures, or 'locks-in', the democratic policies of the government, thereby 'insulating' them from possible reversals in the future (Jetschke and Murray 2012: 176; see also Moravcsik 2000: 228).

Accompanying these state-driven democratic reforms in Indonesia was also the increasing activism of CSOs and citizenry within Indonesia (see Kelly Gerard's chapter in this volume) and throughout the region, which facilitated and reinforced the institutionalisation of human rights. In Indonesia, CSOs were an effective, independent watchdog over domestic human rights reforms and the withdrawal of the military from politics (Aspinall 2004: 89) Citizens were also able to push the human rights agenda through the ballot box. The Habibie and Megawati administrations were voted out, among other reasons, for not living up to the *reformasi* aspirations of voters (Bertrand 2013: 58). No doubt realising the need for accountability to the masses, the Indonesian government solicited inputs from CSOs and citizens during the drafting process and eventual ratification of the Charter too (Djani 2009: 141, 147) Along with Indonesia, the citizens and CSOs of the Philippines, Malaysia and Thailand remain a substantial force to be reckoned with in their activism for human rights protections (Tan 2011: 136). The AFC, by undermining the performance legitimacy of most incumbent governments in Southeast Asia, irrevocably strengthened the public movement for greater accountability and protection of civil and political rights.

In short, the common aspirations of national publics, NGOs, think-tanks, National Human Rights Institutions (NHRIs), the ASEAN Inter-Parliamentary Assembly (AIPA) and the Working Group for an ASEAN Human Rights Mechanism (Working Group) resulted in an epistemic community that has advanced the human rights agenda at both national and regional forums (Chalermpalanupap 2009: 129). This bottom-up approach by CSOs and citizens, however, would not have been as effective if not for the AFC. The crisis changed opportunity structures by creating a more liberal atmosphere that was conducive for human rights activism For instance, in the case of the AICHR's institutionalisation, while LAWASIA, an Australian-based NGO, created the Working Group in 1995, it is unlikely mere coincidence that only in 1998 did the ASEAN Foreign Ministers 'acknowledge the Working Group and note the importance of continuing dialogues between the two parties [i.e. ASEAN and the Working Group]'.[2] The economic crisis was thus the proximate factor that triggered this state-civil society collaboration and, by extension, the further institutionalisation of human rights.

Overall, as seen most prominently in Indonesia but also among its neighbours, the AFC catalysed and enabled changes at the state and societal levels (see Appendix A) which had concomitant effects on the institutionalisation of a regional human rights regime (i.e. the ASEAN Charter and AICHR). Granted, the nature of CP rights institutionalisation in ASEAN comes across as more procedural than substantive. Its effectiveness is called into question because of ongoing human rights violations in member states (Davies 2013; Narine 2012; Emmerson 2008). Moreover, while one can cynically characterise such institutionalisation as a calculated act of bringing human rights discourse into a more sanitised and controlled environment in order to 'regulate dissent', (Gerard 2014: 155) the Charter and the subsequent creation of the AICHR still crucially enshrine and codify human rights norms. Notwithstanding these limitations, the Charter and the AICHR clearly mark an institutional landmark that has the potential to evolve and mature with time (Ciorciari 2012).[3]

Environmental governance

> 'Let us declare a war against haze'.
>
> (Susilo Bambang Yudhoyono, Former President of Indonesia)

The 'haze' – a phenomenon whereby blankets of smoke caused by slash-and-burn practices employed predominantly in the dense forests of Sumatra and Kalimantan, Indonesia spread to and impact neighbouring countries – has been a perennial thorn in intra-ASEAN relations since the late 1990s. It was considered a health, environmental and economic 'crisis' because of the severe disruptions to air traffic, tourism and public health in Southeast Asia (especially in Kuala Lumpur, southern Thailand and Singapore) in 1997, 2013 and 2015. Though member states recognised the need to establish cooperative operational procedures, the 'consensus' model of decision-making dealt a decisive failure to ASEAN's first round of attempts at seeking a regional solution to the haze. The conflicting interests of parties – particularly Indonesian recalcitrance towards the situation – meant that no inroads could be made into resolving the haze challenge via ASEAN's traditional normative processes.

The causes of environmental degradation in Southeast Asia, are multifaceted and range extensively from industrial pollution of waterways, illegal deforestation to forest fires. Nonetheless, among these multiple causes of environmental degradation, the perennial issue of haze has arguably received the most attention and has been a constant source of tension amongst ASEAN states since 1997. An almost annual occurrence for over 20 years, the haze originates in Indonesia, has been recurrent to varying degrees, and has threatened the health of citizens not only in Indonesia, but in parts of Malaysia, Brunei and Singapore. On many occasions, the haze had also brought about loss of billions of dollars in health costs and man-working hours. The causes of the haze can be attributed to a litany of reasons with human agency often being the primary cause. Forest fires have and continue to be set by individuals and corporations for short-term economic gain and this practice of adopting environmentally-unfriendly practices has been exacerbated by climatic conditions known as El Niño, which include drought, wind patterns and the periodic warming of equatorial waters (Trenberth and Hoar 1997; Smith and Dove 1997; Tay 2008).

The 1997–1998 environmental crisis had adversely affected an estimated 20 to 70 million individuals in the ASEAN region. Whilst Indonesia had been the worst hit, the economies of five ASEAN states had also suffered heavy losses with the Asian Development Bank placing estimates of the economic loss at US$6.3 billion. In Indonesia, then President Suharto had accepted moral responsibility for the 1997 fires and apologised for the damage caused to neighbouring ASEAN states. Nonetheless, despite Suharto's public apology, the haze situation had failed to improve and had persisted even after Suharto's resignation. The persistence of the haze throughout the years up to the present is clearly evident that Indonesian laws and governance have largely failed to solve the problem (Beeson 2009). In the area of regional environmental cooperation, the most significant instance of institutionalisation was the signing of the Haze Agreement in 2002 and its full ratification in 2014. The health-threatening haze – generated from forest fires in Indonesia – has perennially affected neighbouring states such as Malaysia, Singapore and Brunei and, to a lesser extent, the Philippines and Thailand. With the worst instances of the haze occurring in 1997 (at the same time as the AFC) and in 2013, it is clear that from the 1990 4th ASEAN Ministerial Meeting on the Environment (AMME) to the 2003 Haze Agreement, attempts at the regional level to successfully reduce the haze had been, at best, patchy and, at worst, ineffective (Narine 2002: 170).

The organisation's second attempt at finding a solution to the haze was through the ASEAN Agreement on Transboundary Haze Pollution (the Haze Agreement) which took effect in 2003. Differing from previous attempts, the Haze Agreement, as a legally binding document, reaffirmed the determination amongst member-countries to fight the haze. The Haze Agreement, as Simon Tay (2008: 226) notes, is an important step because it institutes a 'legally *binding* environmental regime'. But the Agreement could not be implemented because it was not ratified by the Indonesian parliament for over a decade. Indonesia's delayed ratification – which finally took place in September 2014 (Aritonang 2014) – marks a significant institutionalisation of a regional mechanism to deal with transnational environmental pollution.

The movement to combat the haze within ASEAN has also assumed novel forms with the haze becoming almost an annual phenomenon that brings about substantial costs to neighbouring states in terms of public health, air quality, economic productivity and tourism. NGOs and other citizen groups are beginning to play a more active role in raising regional consciousness and awareness of shared environmental concerns. Even states like Singapore (known for its unfriendliness towards NGOs) have started encouraging the activities of Asian and international environmental NGOs to put additional pressure on Indonesia's government and companies as a result of Jakarta's failure to stop forest fires causing health-threatening haze over much of Southeast Asia each year (Pempel 2005; Wong 2015; Tay and Lau 2015).

As Kim and Lee (2011: 964) argue, 'present ASEAN political leaders, unlike the previous generation, cannot make decisions among themselves without being subjected to democratic pressures'. Thus, in this age of heightened public accountability, NGOs and other civil society elements within individual states have been better able to directly or indirectly shape and influence official policy at a regional level. These bottom-up efforts have therefore advanced, albeit unwittingly, further regional integration in the area of environmental security.

Unlike in the issue-area of human rights, progress on the 2003 Agreement on environmental protection in Southeast Asia has been moving at a glacial pace. And unlike in human rights where Indonesia was a prime actor pushing for closer coordination and integration, Jakarta was the foot-dragger in environmental protection in the region. Environmental protection is an issue over which Indonesia has long asserted its national sovereignty. The democratisation of Indonesia and its promotion of civil and political rights likely had a salutary spill-over effect in the environmental realm as well, arguably making it more willing to acknowledge and take responsibility for the haze. Moreover, the flourishing of Indonesian environmental NGOs in a democratic milieu and their connection to the wider epistemic community has resulted in a greater capacity to monitor violations and lobby for greater compliance, thereby contributing to institutional change.

Even so, persuading ASEAN's largest member to take action against errant companies responsible for slash-and-burn practices in Indonesian forests, proves a formidable task. What can be considered incremental progress in the area of environmental rights required much egging by Indonesia's neighbours. Suharto had apologised and sought the 'cooperation of other ASEAN countries' over the haze at the seventh AMME in September 1997 (Tay 2008: 203). But circumstantial evidence suggests that the strongman was hardly bothered and even shockingly naive about the seriousness of the ongoing economic and environmental crises as pressures for regime change mounted then. Shortly after receiving a second bailout from the IMF, Suharto had exposed the extent of his delusion by announcing his desire to seek a seventh term in office (Lee 2014: 105). Thus, in reaching this stage of regional integration, the institutionalisation of environmental rights rested more on Indonesia's own timing, with domestic political considerations setting the pace, rather than the upheaval caused by the AFC or the distress caused by environmental pollution.

In the early stages of regional engagement, the ASEAN way of non-interference meant that regional provisions such as the ASEAN Cooperation Plan (1995) were often 'short on details as to exactly how its intentions would be implemented' (Tay 2008: 222). Yet, the Haze Agreement as a legally binding document is a significant improvement from past efforts with its institutionalisation of a ASEAN Coordinating Center for Transboundary Pollution Control and an ASEAN Transboundary Haze Pollution Control Fund. Most important of all, the agreement binds Indonesia to a legal framework, allowing it to 'voluntarily accept responsibility … and cooperatively, with its neighbors, clean regional skies' (Tay 2008: 226).

Ultimately, in light of Indonesia's bureaucratic inertia and the vested interests of the forestry industry (Weatherbee 2005: 274), it remains to be seen whether Indonesia's 2014 ratification will give rise to actual enforcement on the ground. The fact that ASEAN states such as Singapore have instituted *national* legislation in 2014 to bring to court and punish companies found to be responsible for the haze is a positive sign and highly indicative that no stone will be left unturned on Singapore's or on any ASEAN's member states part for that matter in assisting Indonesia's ongoing attempts to resolve the haze problem. Such actions by ASEAN member states such as Singapore should be commended as ASEAN should not be seen as explicitly or implicitly threatening Indonesia. This is because a hard-line stance will only result in further setbacks with regards to efforts to combat the haze. More importantly, the average Indonesian will be less willing to act if such action is portrayed as giving in to neighbours who are eager to accuse but are hesitant to help resolve the haze problem in any way.

Conclusion

> ...even in the UN charter, the idea of non-interference in the internal affairs of sovereign states coexists with the ideal of human rights. This coexistence may not be logically neat, but reflects the reality of international relations in the world. The ASEAN human rights body will have to find practical ways forward and its own balance. It will not necessarily evolve in a smooth trajectory or according to a strict timetable.
>
> (Ong Keng Yong, former ASEAN Secretary-General, 2009)

In the aftermath of World War II, the historian Alan Milward described European integration as 'the rescue of the nation-state' (Milward 2000). In ASEAN's case, the human rights (particularly CP rights) integration after the 1997 AFC was, for Indonesia, a 'rescue' of the democratic regime from potential retrogressions and, for other states, a rescue of their regimes from international opprobrium. As always, the charge of 'organised hypocrisy' will be levelled at the divergence between doctrine and praxis in the international arena. But, as Stephen Krasner notes, path dependence and socialisation can bring about greater institutionalisation which in turn can 'dictate actual behavior' (Krasner 1999: 226). Against this backdrop, the waning of authoritarianism in Indonesia was followed by the waxing of democratic norms in Indonesia and, eventually, beyond its shores.

While it is also true that institutions do not drive policy, they clearly circumscribe policy options. The crisis-induced upending of Indonesia's authoritarian institutions had significant implications for regional integration. The AFC in sounding the death knell for authoritarianism, marked the ascendancy of democratic norms and the institutionalisation of human rights in ASEAN. The trajectory of regional institutionalisation became increasingly path dependent after that critical juncture.

While small-*n* analysis indeed has its limitations when it comes to generalisability, single case process-tracing can disprove claims of a sufficient cause while identifying omitted variables. Studying the 1997 crises and their effect on Indonesia, a regional hegemon, is an intuitive way to test the theory of crisis in times of regional integration.

The theoretical implications of this chapter's findings are twofold. First, economic crises can and did unwittingly spur regional integration in the area of human rights, especially when the economic crisis led to political change in a major state actor (see also Wong 2015). Whether such regional integration is more procedural than substantive is beside the point. Second, this deepening of regional integration in the area of human rights is indirect. An economic crisis destabilises authoritarian regimes' source of performance legitimacy and undermines their international standing. With the domestic and international spotlight on the regimes' activities, they are more receptive to human rights concerns and inclined to regional integration of human rights as a coping mechanism.

However, the health/environmental crises in Southeast Asia in 1997 and 2013 have not similarly resulted in a substantial integration or institutionalisation of new norms in ASEAN. Indeed, the low level of institutional density in ASEAN on environmental issues, allowed states to control discussions on this agenda (and in Indonesia's case), ultimately obstruct further integration in environmental governance. As there were no economic or political gains for Indonesia to take tougher action, Indonesian politicians were able to get away with paying lip service to ASEAN solidarity while taking little or no action against the economic logging and palm oil interests responsible for the environmental degradation in Indonesia and in the wider region. Whilst the issue of haze is multifaceted and an uphill task to resolve, path dependence on the 'ASEAN Way' of tackling regional issues through intergovernmental cooperation, would mean that no state or combination of states would push for a radical multilateral solution that could swing into action each year. This would be too much of a threat to each state's sovereign rights to the control of its own territory. Instead, one can expect continued slow institutional developments at a pace comfortable to Indonesia, the resurgent regional hegemon.

Notes

1 I am grateful to Matthew Koo and Ng Song Yuan for research assistance on this chapter.

2 About Us, Working Group for an ASEAN Human Rights Mechanism. Accessed 10 February 2015. www.aseanhrmech.org/aboutus.html.

3 Ciorciari, John D. (2012). Institutionalizing Human Rights in Southeast Asia. *Human Rights Quarterly* 34, no. 3: 727–724.

References

Acharya, Amitav (1998). *Democratising Southeast Asia: Economic Crisis and Political Change*. Vol. 87. Murdoch, WA: Murdoch University Asia Research Centre.

Acharya, Amitav (1999). Realism, Institutionalism, and the Asian Economic Crisis. *Contemporary Southeast Asia*, *21*(1), 1–29.

Acharya, Amitav (2003). Democratisation and the Prospects for Participatory Regionalism in Southeast Asia. *Third World Quarterly*, *24*(2), 375.

Acharya, Amitav (2009). Arguing About ASEAN: What Do We Disagree About? *Cambridge Review of International Affairs*, *22*(3), 493–499.

Acharya, Amitav (2014). *Constructing a Security Community in Southeast Asia: ASEAN and the Problem of Regional Order*. New York: Routledge.

AFP (2013). *Indonesia says Singapore acting 'like a child' over haze*, 20 June.

Aritonang, M. S. (2014). RI ratifies haze treaty. *The Jakarta Post*, 17 September. Accessed 2 February 2015. www.thejakartapost.com/news/2014/09/17/ri-ratifies-haze-treaty.html.

Aspinall, Edward (2004). Indonesia: Transformation of Civil Society and Democratic Breakthrough, in Alagappa, Muthiah (ed.). *Civil Society and Political Change in Asia: Expanding and Contracting Democratic Space*. Stanford, CA: Stanford University Press, 61–96.

Ba, Alice D. (2009). *(Re)Negotiating East and Southeast Asia: Region, Regionalism, and the Association of Southeast Asian Nations*. Stanford, Calif: Stanford University Press.

Baig, Taimur and Ilan Goldfajn (1999). Financial Market Contagion in the Asian Crisis, *IMF Staff Papers*, Vol. *96*(2), 167–195.

Bertrand, Jacques (2013). *Political Change in Southeast Asia*. Cambridge; New York: Cambridge University Press.

Beeson, Mark (2009). ASEAN's Way: Still Fit for Purpose? *Cambridge Review of International Affairs*, 22(3), 333.

Boin, Arjen, 't Hart, Paul, Stern, Eric and Sundelius, Bengt (2005). *The Politics of Crisis Management: Public Leadership under Pressure*. Cambridge, UK; New York: Cambridge University Press.

Boin, Arjen, 't Hart, Paul and McConnell, Allan (2008). Conclusions: The Politics of Crisis Exploitation. In Boin, Arjen, 't Hart, Paul and McConnell, Allan (eds.). *Governing after Crisis: The Politics of Investigation, Accountability and Learning*. Cambridge; New York: Cambridge University Press, 285–316.

Boin, Arjen, 't Hart, Paul and McConnell, Allan (2008). Governing after Crisis. In Boin, Arjen, 't Hart, Paul and McConnell, Allan (eds.). *Governing after Crisis: The Politics of Investigation, Accountability and Learning*. Cambridge; New York: Cambridge University Press, 3–32.

Bounkeut, Sangsomak (2009). A New Turning Point in the Relations among the Southeast Asian States. In Koh, Tommy T. B., Manalo, Rosario G. and Woon, Walter C. M. (eds.). *The Making of the ASEAN Charter*. Hackensack, NJ: World Scientific Pub. Co., 159–166.

Bwa, Aung (2009). The Jewel in My Crown. In Koh, Tommy T. B., Manalo, Rosario G. and Woon, Walter C. M. (eds.). *The Making of the ASEAN Charter*. Hackensack, NJ: World Scientific Pub. Co., 27–35.

Camroux, David and Srikandini, Annisa (2013). Eu-Indonesia Relations: No Expectations-Capability Gap? In Christiansen, Thomas, Kirchner, Emil and Murray, Philomena B. (eds.). *The Palgrave Handbook of Eu-Asia Relations*. New York: Palgrave Macmillan, 554–570.

Chalermpalanupap, Termsak (2009). In Defence of the *ASEAN* Charter. In Koh, Tommy T. B., Manalo, Rosario G. and Woon, Walter C. M. (eds.). *The Making of the ASEAN Charter*. Hackensack, NJ: World Scientific Pub. Co., 117–135.

Chandra, Siddharth and Kammen, Douglas (2002). Generating Reforms and Reforming Generations: Military Politics in Indonesia's Transition to Democracy. *World Politics*, *55*(1).

Christiansen, Thomas, Kirchner, Emil and Murray, Philomena B. (eds.) (2013). *The Palgrave Handbook of Eu-Asia Relations*. New York: Palgrave Macmillan.

Ciorciari, John D. (2012). Institutionalizing Human Rights in Southeast Asia. *Human Rights Quarterly*, *34*(3), 695–725.

Corsetti Giancarlo, Pesenti, Paolo and Roubini, Nouriel (1999). What Caused the Asian Currency and Financial Crisis? *Japan and The World Economy*, Vol. II, 305–373.

Cotton, James (1999). The 'haze' over Southeast Asia: Challenging the ASEAN mode of regional engagement. *Pacific Affairs*, *72*(3), 331–351.

Daquila, Teofilo C. (2007) *The Transformation of Southeast Asian Economies*. New York: Nova Publishers.

Davies, Mathew (2013). *ASEAN* and Human Rights Norms: Constructivism, Rational Choice, and the Action-Identity Gap. *International Relations of the Asia-Pacific*, *13*(2), 207–231.

Davies, Mathew (2014). States of Compliance? Global Human Rights Treaties and *ASEAN* Member States. *Journal of Human Rights*.

Deutsch, Karl Wolfgang, Burrell, Sidney A. and Kann, Robert A. (1957). *Political Community and the North Atlantic Area: International Organization in the Light of Historical Experience*. New York: Greenwood Press.

Djani, Dian Triansyah (2009). A Long Journey. In Koh, Tommy T. B., Manalo, Rosario G. and Woon, Walter C. M. (eds.). *The Making of the ASEAN Charter*. Hackensack, NJ: World Scientific Pub. Co., 137–150.

Eaton, Sarah and Stubbs, Richard (2006). Is ASEAN Powerful? Neo-Realist Versus Constructivist Approaches to Power in Southeast Asia 1. *The Pacific Review*, *19*(2), 135–155.

Eldridge, Philip J. (2002) *The Politics of Human Rights in Southeast Asia*. London: Routledge.

Elvert, Jürgen (2011). The Institutional Paradox: How Crises Have Reinforced European Integration. In Kühnhardt, Ludger (ed.). *Crises in European Integration: Challenge and Response, 1945–2005*. New York: Berghahn Books, 49–60.

Emmerson, Donald K. (2005). Security, Community, and Democracy in Southeast Asia: Analyzing ASEAN. *Japanese Journal of Political Science*, *6*(2), 165–185.

Emmerson, Donald K. (2008). Critical Terms: Security, Democracy, and Regionalism in Southeast Asia. In Emmerson, Donald K. (ed.). *Hard Choices: Security, Democracy, and Regionalism in Southeast Asia*. Stanford, CA: Walter H. Shorenstein Asia-Pacific Research Center, 3–56.

Fawcett, Louise (2015). Drivers of regional integration: historical and comparative perspectives. In Brennan, L. and Murray, P. (eds.). *Drivers of Regionalism and Integration in Europe and Asia*. London and New York: Routledge.

Gehler, Michael (2011). Challenges and Opportunities: Surmounting Integration Crises in Historical Context. In Kühnhardt, Ludger (ed.). *Crises in European Integration: Challenge and Response, 1945–2005*. New York: Berghahn Books, 109–130.

George, Alexander L. and Bennett, Andrew (2005). *Case Studies and Theory Development in the Social Sciences*. Cambridge, MA: MIT Press, 2005.

Gerard, Kelly (2014). *ASEAN's Engagement of Civil Society: Regulating Dissent*. New York, NY; Houndmills, Basingstoke, Hampshire: Palgrave Macmillan.

Henning, C. Randall (2011). Economic Crises and Institutions for Regional Economic Cooperation. Asian Development Bank.

Henning, C. Randall (2013). Economic Crises and Regional Institutions. In Kahler, Miles and MacIntyre, Andrew J. (ed.). *Integrating Regions: Asia in Comparative Context*. Stanford, California: Stanford University Press, 170–194.

Jetschke, Anja and Murray, Philomena B. (2012). Diffusing Regional Integration: The EU and Southeast Asia. *West European Politics*, *35*(1), 174–191.

Jones, David S. (2006). ASEAN and transboundary haze pollution in Southeast Asia. *Asia Europe Journal*, *4*(3), 431–446.

Jones, David Martin and Smith, Michael L. R. (2003). ASEAN's Imitation Community. *Orbis* 46, no. 1 (2003): 93–109.

Jones, David Martin and Smith Michael L. R. (2001). The Changing Security Agenda in Southeast Asia: Globalization, New Terror, and the Delusions of Regionalism. *Studies in conflict and terrorism, 24*(4), 271–288.

Kammen, Douglas and Chandra, Siddharth (1999). *A Tour of Duty: Changing Patterns of Military Politics in Indonesia in the 1990s*. Ithaca: Cornell Modern Indonesia Project Publication No. 75.

Kao, Kim Hourn (2009). A Personal Reflection. In Koh, Tommy T. B., Manalo, Rosario G. and Woon, Walter C. M. (eds.). *The Making of the ASEAN Charter*. Hackensack, NJ: World Scientific Pub. Co., 151–157.

Katzenstein, Peter J. (1996). Regionalism in Comparative Perspective. *Cooperation and Conflict, 31*(2), 123–159.

Khoo, Nicholas (2004). Deconstructing the ASEAN Security Community: A Review Essay. *International Relations of the Asia-Pacific, 4*(1), 35–46.

Krasner, Stephen D. (1999). *Sovereignty: Organized Hypocrisy*. Princeton, NJ: Princeton University Press.

Kühnhardt, Ludger (2011). European Integration: Success through Crises, in Kühnhardt, Ludger (ed.). *Crises in European Integration: Challenge and Response, 1945–2005*. New York: Berghahn Books, 1–19.

Langlois, Anthony J. (2012). Asian Regionalism and Human Rights: The Case of the ASEAN Intergovernmental Commission on Human Rights. In *Routledge Handbook of Asian Regionalism*. Milton Park, Abingdon, Oxon; New York, N.Y: Routledge, 216–225.

Lee, Terence (2014). *Defect or Defend: Military Responses to Popular Protests in Authoritarian Asia*. Baltimore: John Hopkins University Press.

Leifer, Michael (2005). The Limits to ASEAN's Expanding Role. In Chin, Kin Wah and Suryadinata, Leo (eds.). *Michael Leifer: Selected Works on Southeast Asia*. Singapore: Institute of Southeast Asian Studies, 164–188.

Mayer, Judith (2006). Transboundary perspectives on managing Indonesia's fires. *The Journal of Environment & Development, 15*(2), 202–223.

Milward, Alan S. (2000). *The European Rescue of the Nation-State*, Brennan, George and Romero, Federico (eds.). London: Routledge.

Moravcsik, Andrew (2000). The Origins of Human Rights Regimes: Democratic Delegation in Postwar Europe. *International Organization, 54*(2), 217–252.

Narine, Shaun (2002). *Explaining ASEAN: Regionalism in Southeast Asia*. Boulder, CO: Lynne Rienner Publishers.

Narine, Shaun (2009). ASEAN in the Twenty-First Century: A Sceptical Review. *Cambridge Review of International Affairs, 22*(3), 369–386.

Narine, Shaun (2012). Human Rights Norms and the Evolution of ASEAN: Moving without Moving in a Changing Regional Environment. *Contemporary Southeast Asia: A Journal of International and Strategic Affairs, 34*(3), 365–388.

Ong, Keng Yong (2009). At Close Quarters with the Drafting of the ASEAN Charter. In Koh, Tommy T. B., Manalo, Rosario G. and Woon, Walter C. M. (eds.). *The Making of the ASEAN Charter*. Hackensack, NJ: World Scientific Pub. Co., 107–115.

Pempel, Thomas J. (2005). *Remapping East Asia: the construction of a region*. Ithaca: Cornell University Press.

Quah, Euston (2002). Transboundary pollution in Southeast Asia: The Indonesian fires. World Development, *30*(3), 429–441.

Rosenberger, Leif Roderick (1997). Southeast Asia's Currency Crisis: A Diagnosis and Prescription. *Contemporary Southeast Asia, 19*(3), December.

Smith, K. R. and Dove, M. R. (1997). Indonesian Fires: Leaders in a Haze. *Asian Wall Street Journal*, 8 December.

Soesastro, H. and M. C. Basri (1998). The political economy of trade policy in Indonesia. *ASEAN Economic Bulletin, 22*(1), 3–18.

Solidum, Estrella D. (2003). *The Politics of ASEAN: An Introduction to Southeast Asian Regionalism*. Singapore: Marshall Cavendish Academic.

Sukma, Rizal (2011). Soft Power and Public Diplomacy: The Case of Indonesia. In Yi, Suk-chong and Melissen, Jan (eds.). *Public Diplomacy and Soft Power in East Asia*. New York: Palgrave Macmillan, 91–115.

Tan, Hsien-li (2011). *The ASEAN Intergovernmental Commission on Human Rights: Institutionalising Human Rights in Southeast Asia*.

Tarling, Nicholas (2006). *Regionalism in Southeast Asia: To Foster the Political Will*. New York; London: Routledge.

Tay, Simon S. C. (2008). Blowing Smoke: Regional Cooperation, Indonesian Democracy, and the Haze. In Emmerson, Donald K. (ed.). *Hard Choices: Security, Democracy, and Regionalism in Southeast Asia*. Stanford, CA: Walter H. Shorenstein Asia-Pacific Research Center, 219–240.

Tay, Simon and Lau, Xin Yi (2015). Getting firms to take responsibility for the haze. *Today Online*, 20 October. Accessed 30 October 2015. www.todayonline.com/singapore/getting-firms-take-responsibility-haze.

Thanh, Nguyen Trung (2009). The Making of the ASEAN Charter in My Fresh Memories, In Koh, Tommy T. B., Manalo, Rosario G. and Woon, Walter C. M. (eds.). *The Making of the ASEAN Charter*. Hackensack, NJ: World Scientific Pub. Co., 95–105.

Thio, Li-ann (1999). Implementing Human Rights in ASEAN Countries: Promises to Keep and Miles to Go before I Sleep. *Yale Human Rights & Development Journal* 2.

Trenberth, K. E. and Hoar, T. J. (1997). El Niño and climate change. *Geophysical Research Letters*, *24*(23), 3057–3060.

Villacorta, Wilfrido V. (2011). Strengthening the Foundation for an ASEAN Community. In Lee, Yoong Yoong (ed.). *ASEAN Matters: Reflecting on the Association of Southeast Asian Nations*. World Scientific, 303–314.

Weatherbee, Donald E. (2005). *International Relations in Southeast Asia: The Struggle for Autonomy*. Lanham, Md: Rowman & Littlefield Publishers.

Wong, Reuben (2012). Model Power or Reference Point? The EU and the ASEAN Charter. *Cambridge Review of International Affairs*, *25*(4), 669–682.

Wong, Reuben (2015). Creeping supranationalism: The EU and ASEAN experiences. In Brennan, L. and Murray, P. (eds.). *Drivers of Regionalism and Integration in Europe and Asia*. London and New York: Routledge, 235–251.

Working Group for an ASEAN Human Rights Mechanism. About Us. Accessed 10 February 2015. www.aseanhrmech.org/aboutus.html.

10 ASEAN and the response to regional crisis

The limits of integration

Shaun Narine

Introduction

Southeast Asia was hit by financial crises in 1997–1999 and again by the global financial catastrophe of 2007–2009. In both cases, the Association of Southeast Asian Nations (ASEAN), the region's premiere multilateral institution, responded by facilitating the push for greater regional integration. Yet, in the aftermath of both crises, ASEAN has actually achieved relatively low levels of economic, political and social integration. What accounts for this limited institutional development?

This chapter argues that the answer to this question lies in the fact that ASEAN has never been a strong instrument of regional integration. As a regional institution, it has smoothed out political difficulties between its member states, but its activities have never promoted full-fledged economic, political or security integration in any substantial way. ASEAN's relationship with its member states hinges on the institution being as minimally invasive as possible in their sovereign affairs. ASEAN's focus on non-interference is a defining attribute of the institution from when it was first created in 1967. In many important ways, the same factors that made the protection of sovereignty paramount in 1967 drive ASEAN today. So long as the ASEAN states continue to believe that the preservation of their sovereignty is key to their survival as viable states, ASEAN's functional level of regional integration will remain low. This will create a gulf between ASEAN's rhetorical aspirations and its institutional capabilities. This observation contrasts with many other studies of ASEAN – particularly constructivist studies – which emphasise the norm and community-building aspects of the organisation (Acharya 2013; Busse 1999; Caballero-Anthony 2014). This study does not deny that ASEAN forms the basis of a nascent Southeast Asian community, but the commitment of regional citizens and elites to that community is seriously diluted by their focus on and commitment to more parochial identities and interests.

The chapter is divided into the following sections: Section one explains the paper's main argument, using the theoretical framework of Saurugger and Terpan to set the questions about regional integration and ASEAN that we must answer. The analytical categories identified by the framework demonstrate that the bonds of economic self-interest, political affinity and social cohesion that are necessary to further regional integration are only minimally present in the case of ASEAN. The chapter then examines the Chiang Mai Initiative Multilateralization (CMIM), a regional financial instrument that includes ASEAN and the major Asian powers – i.e. China, Japan and South Korea. CMIM is a direct product of the 1997 economic crisis and was given further impetus by the 2007–2009 global financial crisis. However, it is in its preliminary stages and remains untested and restrained by complex political concerns. In contrast to the CMIM, the ASEAN Community (AC) is a genuine effort on the part of ASEAN to further regional political, security, economic and cultural integration. However, a closer examination of the AC and its component parts reveals that it has poor prospects of success, largely because its member states continue to choose the preservation of their sovereignty over effective regional integration.

The conclusion of the chapter is that ASEAN has responded ineffectively to two major financial crises. The political, economic and social divisions that exist between the ASEAN states cannot be easily overcome. They ensure that the organisation remains a relatively loose collection of sovereign states.

Crisis and institutional change

Saurugger and Terpan specify that the object of this study is to 'analyze whether and why regional integration systems change in periods of economic and financial crises'. They note that ASEAN does not seem to be 'profoundly affected by the crises in (its) institutional structures'. The degree of *institutional density* – i.e. 'the degree to which institutions created by regional organisations constrain member states in their domestic and international politics' – is affected by 'three variables: the regional organisation's functionality, the degree of socialisation among actors and the impact of regional organisations'. 'Functionality' refers to the functions assigned by national governments to the supranational actor. 'Degree of socialisation' refers to the degree of interaction between citizens, the elites and the supranational body. 'Impact' addresses the political, economic and social influence of the integration process under examination. As expected, ASEAN shows a low level of institutional density, reflecting the weakness of these three variables in the Southeast Asian context.

ASEAN's member states have kept it at a low level of functionality. The ASEAN states assign few functions to the organisation and those that have been are often beyond the resources of the Secretariat to fulfil. The ASEAN Secretariat is underfunded and overworked, part of a deliberate strategy on the part of ASEAN's members to keep the Secretariat from becoming an alternative centre of power. ASEAN's most important functions originate with and are coordinated through the foreign ministries of the member states. This unwillingness to let the institution acquire an independent existence speaks to the ASEAN focus on protecting and enhancing the sovereignty of its members. Similarly, socialisation into a larger regional identity is generally lacking within the ASEAN states. Most surveys of regional attitudes show a high level of distrust between ASEAN elites and a low level of ASEAN awareness among the general public (Roberts 2007). If there is a sense of 'ASEAN identity' it is held by a relatively small number of academics and diplomats, but it does not extend into the general population of the member states. Finally, the impact of the organisation is relatively minimal. Regional integration has not had a significant structural impact on the ASEAN member states.

The relative weakness of ASEAN's institutional structures is not immediately apparent to the casual outside observer. Since 2003, ASEAN has made a concerted effort to create an 'ASEAN Community', an organisational rejuvenation, which its members have explicitly presented as an effort to achieve regional economic, social, political and security integration. However, the reality is less than it appears. The 'pillars' of the ASEAN Community – the three separate communities that make the whole – remain caught in the tension between the push for a stronger regional institution and the traditional desire of the member states to preserve their sovereign powers (Severino 2006).

Historically, ASEAN has never been directed at 'regional integration', despite its occasional expressions of interest in facilitating this goal. Its failure to respond to crises by effectively strengthening regional integration is not surprising. This does not mean, however, that ASEAN does not respond to crises. Throughout its history, ASEAN has reacted to external political, economic and security impetuses by *trying* to strengthen its institutional structures. These efforts have usually been led by one or more ASEAN states and have sometimes resulted in a somewhat more active and complex ASEAN (Narine 2008). However, these pressures and crises have never been enough to push the organisation to a deep level of integration. When push has come to shove, the other member states of ASEAN have resisted the pressure for change from the more motivated members. Collectively, ASEAN has lacked the political will to make the organisation an effective instrument of regional integration (Narine 2009). This lack of will reflects real political, social and security limitations within member states. This pattern of unfulfilled aspiration continues today.

The ASEAN Plus Three and the Chiang Mai Initiative Multilateralization (CMIM)

In 1997, the ASEAN states met with China, Japan and South Korea to coordinate East Asia's approach to the first Asia-Europe Meeting (ASEM). The Asian economic crisis (1997–1999) had just begun and the Asian states took advantage of their meeting to discuss the financial turmoil rocking the region. This meeting was the origin point of the ASEAN Plus Three (APT), a regional organisation that has since evolved into the most consequential and potentially effective Asian multilateral institution in the twenty-first century. The APT consists of ASEAN and its three wealthier, more powerful Northeast Asian neighbours (Terada 2012). The APT's members saw it as a regional response to the financial instability of the Western-dominated international financial system. During the crisis, Japan had suggested that the Asian states work together to create an 'Asian Monetary

Fund', a regional mechanism that could provide up to $100 billion dollars in emergency support for the crisis-affected states. This initiative was firmly opposed by the US, which wished to prevent Japan from taking a regional leadership role and to block any challenge to the American-dominated International Monetary Fund (IMF), which was managing the crisis. Japan later provided the Miyazawa Initiative to help regional states, but the idea of an AMF never entirely died. It gained greater regional support among the affected states as it became clear that the IMF had mismanaged the crisis by forcing crisis-devastated states to pursue policies that made the situation worse. The IMF's failure underscored the need for an Asian financial instrument to provide insurance to regional states against inevitable future financial upheavals (Narine 2003).

The APT initiated a number of measures designed to strengthen East Asian regional financial and economic systems and cooperation. These included the Asian Bond Markets Initiative (ABMI), the Asian Bond Fund (ABF) and the Economic Policy and Review Dialogue (EPRD). The most substantial development was the Chiang Mai Initiative (CMI), later the Chiang Mai Initiative Multilateralization (CMIM) (Grimes 2009a, Ciorciari 2011).

The Chiang Mai Initiative (CMI) of 2000 was a currency swap arrangement, designed to make the extensive foreign reserves of the wealthier East Asian states available to their poorer neighbours. The swap arrangements would allow states in financial crisis to exchange their own currency for foreign currencies. This move was in response to the fact that the 1997 crisis started as an attack on regional currencies by Western currency speculators. The 2000 CMI expanded the existing ASEAN Swap Arrangement (ASA) from $200 million to $1 billion and included bilateral swap arrangements between the ASEAN members of the ASA and China, Japan and South Korea. The CMI allowed China, Japan and South Korea to offer support to the ASEAN countries and each other in the event that a currency crisis occurred again. A series of bilateral swap arrangements (BSAs) were organised under the CMI umbrella. The different BSAs allowed a country in crisis to swap US dollars from its CMI lender for an equivalent amount of its own currency. At the end of the swap period, the borrowing country had to return the dollars with interest, set at the IMF borrowing rate (Ciorciari 2011).

Over the course of the next several years, the amount of money available through the BSAs expanded rapidly. By October 2003, 13 BSAs totalling roughly $35 billion had been negotiated. The CMI's challenge to the existing international financial system was highly constrained. Under the terms of the CMI, the IMF remained the arbiter of international financial management. Even so, states could claim up to 10 per cent of the total amount of a swap without linkage to an IMF programme for 180 days. To obtain the rest of the swap, the country needed to be under an IMF programme or about to enter one. At first, most of the BSAs were one way; one party would provide funds while the other would receive. In 2005, the Istanbul Agreement specified that the BSAs would be converted to two-way arrangements. Some BSAs were also asymmetrical, reflecting the fact that developed economies have more capability to give than their developing economy counterparts. Most BSA arrangements involved providing US dollars to economies in crisis, though China insisted on using local currencies, which are calculated in the dollar equivalent.

In 2005, the APT Finance Ministers agreed to 'multilateralise' the CMI, in order to improve regional financial cooperation. In May 2007, in Kyoto, Japan, the finance ministers ordered their deputies to develop 'a multilateral reserve arrangement under a single operating contract'. This meant that the CMIM would no longer be a series of discrete BSAs but, instead, would allow any of its members to draw upon the organisation in time of need, in accordance with set guidelines. In 2008, in Madrid, Spain, the finance ministers agreed to increase the CMI to at least $80 billion and that 80 per cent of the total would be contributed by the Plus Three countries, with the remaining 20 per cent contributed by the ASEAN states. By May 2009, the total size of the facility was increased to $120 billion. The ministers worked out individual country contributions and their borrowing multipliers. The ministers also agreed that the most fundamental issues of the CMIM – questions such as membership, changing borrowing multipliers and contributions, terms of lending, etc. – would be decided by consensus. Other issues, such as lending, renewal and default, would be decided by majority vote. The major impediment to the completion of the CMIM was that China and Japan were competing for the right to be the country to make the largest contribution to the new organisation (Japan and China vie to be top contributor to regional fund 2009).

The global financial crisis of 2007–2009 finally provided the impetus to break the impasse between the two Asian powers. China and Japan agreed to a formula that made them equal contributors to the CMIM and equal in voting weight. Each country contributed 32 per cent to the organisation. China's 32 per cent includes Hong Kong's contribution. This formula allowed both China and Japan to claim that they are the single largest contributor to the CMIM. In agreeing to this formula both China and Japan are significantly 'underweight' in their representation in CMIM (Ciorciari 2011). If the contributions had been based on GDP or the size of foreign reserves, both China and Japan would have contributed far more and have had even greater voting influence in the organisation. ASEAN was concerned about this possibility and insisted on a formula that reduced the singular influence of the two great powers. In the final tally, South Korea contributed 16 per cent of the CMIM and ASEAN collectively contributed 20 per cent. Concerned with being overwhelmed by the economic power of its northern neighbours, ASEAN negotiated a majority two thirds voting system.

The Chiang Mai Initiative Multilateralization (CMIM) came into effect on 24 March 2010. The central banks of the APT agreed to contribute $120 billion to a multilateral swap facility when called upon to do so, setting aside the bilateral swap model of the CMI. The total amount available to CMIM was quickly increased to $240 billion.

In order to reassure its Western partners that CMIM is not a nascent AMF, CMIM's members deliberately limited its objectives. It is designed to address balance of payments and short-term liquidity difficulties for its members and to 'supplement existing international financial arrangements'. The institution has no physical offices, save for the ASEAN +3 Macro-economic Research Office (AMRO), located in Singapore and a minimalist institutional structure. The APT Finance Ministers use consensus to decide major issues, such as changes in financial contributions, the rules of the regime or which economies can participate. The APT Finance Ministers meetings take place on the sidelines of the regular Asian Development Bank meetings. Below the finance ministers is the Executive Level Decision-Making Body (ELDMB), consisting of deputy-level finance and central bank officials from the APT states. This body oversees AMRO, votes on whether to activate specific swaps and handles the day-to-day operations of the CMIM.

CMIM is sustained by contributions from the central banks of its member states. The banks only transfer funds to CMIM once a swap request has been approved. In contrast to other regional financial arrangements, CMIM does not pool or manage the contributions from its members. This arrangement avoids tension between central banks that have different investment priorities, but is another example of the organisation accepting weak institutional structures in order to avoid conflict between its member states. The borrowing rules of CMIM are straightforward. Each participating economy may borrow a specified multiple of its contribution to CMIM. As of 2013, the maximum amount that any country can borrow without an IMF programme in place is 30 per cent of its total available sum. Borrowers can renew their loans every 90 days for up to 720 days. The central banks participating in a swap deliver the money directly to the borrower on a bilateral basis, rather than going through a central administrator.

The relationship between the IMF and CMIM is evolving rapidly. When the CMI was first created, only 10 per cent of its funds could be dispersed without an IMF plan in place. In 2005, this allocation was increased to 20 per cent. Shortly after CMIM was inaugurated, the limit was increased 30 per cent, with the objective of increasing the exemption to 40 per cent by 2014, though this has not yet happened.

Institutional density vs power games?

The dynamics around the IMF-CMIM relationship illustrate the complexity of intra-East Asian political dynamics. All the members of the APT are aware of the political traps involved in lending to each other. The Plus Three countries wish to ensure that their money is lent in a fiscally and economically prudent manner. At the same time, the smaller economies of the APT – the ASEAN economies – bristle at the idea of being subject to conditions determined by the powerful states of the region. Once again, the ASEAN countries are concerned with protecting their sovereignty and are sensitive to being under the economic (and, by extension, political) domination of the large regional states. The IMF link is a way to ensure a certain amount of discipline on the part of the borrowers without the lenders having to take the unpopular and politically difficult position of setting conditions. The IMF is willing, able and

Table 10.1 CMIM contributions and purchasing multiples

Countries		*Financial contribution (billion USD)*		*Share (%)*		*Purchasing multiple*	*Maximum swap amount (billion USD)*
Plus Three		192.00		80.00			117.30
Japan		76.80		32.00		0.5	38.40
PRC	PRC	76.80	68.40	32.00	28.50	0.5	34.20
	Hong Kong, China		8.40		3.50	2.5	6.30
Rep. of Korea		38.40		16.00		1	38.40
ASEAN		48.00		20.00			126.20
Indonesia		9.104		3.793		2.5	22.76
Thailand		9.104		3.793		2.5	22.76
Malaysia		9.104		3.793		2.5	22.76
Singapore		9.104		3.793		2.5	22.76
Philippines		9.104		3.793		2.5	22.76
Vietnam		2.00		0.833		5	10.00
Cambodia		0.24		0.100		5	1.20
Myanmar		0.12		0.050		5	0.60
Brunei Darussalam		0.06		0.025		5	0.30
Lao PDR		0.06		0.025		5	0.30
Total		240.00		100.00			243.50

Source: CMIM Agreement, available at AMRO website. Table from Siregar and Chabchitrchaidol 2013: 6.

accustomed to playing the role of international enforcer. The linkage to the IMF also assuaged the fears of the United States and other Western powers that the Asians were looking at creating an alternative form of international financial institutionalism (Grimes 2009a).

When the economic crisis of 2007 began, a number of Asian countries faced short-term liquidity shortfalls. South Korea and Singapore made arrangements for loans from the US Treasury rather than going to CMIM. Some observers explain this action by arguing that, after its mishandling of the Asian economic crisis, the IMF is so politically toxic in the Asia Pacific that no Asian state could take the political risk of approaching it (Katada 2012, Beeson and Broome 2008). This was especially true in South Korea, where the IMF 's actions during the crisis had created a social catastrophe. Other observers argue that the actions of South Korea and Singapore demonstrated their lack of faith in the CMIM (Grimes 2009b). Rethel argues that this failure helped to convince Asian states of the need to consolidate the CMIM and further refine the institution (Rethel 2014). If the former explanation is correct, then CMIM must reduce its connection to the IMF or else many of its members may never use it at all.

Reducing the IMF link could also, potentially, be used by the Northeast Asian states to leverage greater representation for themselves in the established world financial institutions, i.e. the IMF and the International Bank for Reconstruction and Development (IBRD). The Western powers running the IMF will be much more likely to take Asian interests and perspectives into account if they wish to keep Asia fully engaged in the existing structure. Asian states have been pushing for the reform of the IMF to reflect the changing global distribution of economic power. In 2006, China and South Korea were among four countries given more IMF shares because their economic clout was grossly underrepresented within the fund. The IMF leadership has officially disavowed the traditional policy of giving the directorship of the IMF to a European. As wealthy Asian states gain greater say in the IMF, however, they will be implicated in IMF policies that may be applied to Asia in the future. Thus, the problem of setting conditions on their neighbours may be unavoidable. Moreover, the ability to leverage the CMIM will depend on playing up the idea that it is the first step towards an independent Asian financial institution that can, potentially, challenge the IMF. CMIM presently lacks the resources to be such a threat, though it could become more.

From the perspective of ASEAN and regional integration, a few points about CMIM stand out. First, it is a very limited effort at regional integration, and one that is only peripherally based in ASEAN itself. ASEAN serves as an institutional anchor but the organisation has not significantly reformed as a result of CMIM. Second, most of the resources for its operation come from non-ASEAN states. Thus, it is difficult to argue that CMIM is an example of ASEAN regional integration. It is an East-Asian-wide effort at financial insurance. This is still far from constituting a form of genuine integration. The financial and political limits that its members place on CMIM underline their considerable wariness of allowing the institution to expand.

The ASEAN community

By the early 2000s, ASEAN was concerned that it was losing its appeal to foreign investment and its vitality as a regional organisation. It commissioned a study by the international consultants McKinsey and Company to study the issue. The final report argued that ASEAN's fragmented economies discouraged international investment. ASEAN began to study the process of enhancing its regional economic integration. ASEAN had pursued regional integration in the past, notably in the 1970s and again when ASEAN pursued AFTA in the 1990s, but these efforts had been unsuccessful or, with AFTA, limited in effect. At the 2002 ASEAN Summit, Singaporean Prime Minister Goh Chok Tong suggested that the next stage in ASEAN integration be called the 'ASEAN Economic Community', evoking the European Economic Community of years past (Severino 2006). While the ASEAN states had no desire to integrate on the scale of the EEC, they were more open to the idea of serious economic integration than in the past. In the aftermath of the 1997–1999 crisis, China and other Asian states had become more attractive than ASEAN as destinations for foreign investment. Moreover, after its failure to manage the East Timor crisis and the regional haze (resulting from man-made fires in Indonesia), ASEAN needed to demonstrate that it was still a meaningful regional institution.[1]

As ASEAN pursued the idea of an Economic Community, it put into motion plans to create an ASEAN Political and Security Community (APSC) and an ASEAN Socio-Cultural Community (ASCC) and announced its intention of creating an ASEAN Community at the Second Bali Summit in 2003 (Weatherbee 2005, Freistein 2005). The APSC was suggested by Indonesia. At that time, Indonesia was the Chair of ASEAN, but it was concerned that its relative economic weakness would leave it on the sidelines during discussions of the AEC. Indonesia suggested creating an ASEAN Security Community (ASC) as a way to enhance intra-ASEAN security cooperation. The other ASEAN states were sceptical of Indonesia's motives and the plausibility of creating a security community. Many also felt that Indonesia had not properly consulted with them. Nonetheless, they supported the idea because they believed it would benefit Southeast Asia (Severino 2006, Roberts 2012).

If the idea of the ASEAN Security Community (later changed to the ASEAN Political and Security Community) was instigated by a single state and seemingly with relatively little consideration, the idea of an ASEAN Socio-Cultural Community (ASCC) was even more last minute. The Philippines suggested that the ASCC be created in order to show that ASEAN was not just an elite-driven institution focused on politics and security but that it also cared about the health, education and social environments of ordinary citizens. The ASCC is the least developed of the ASEAN Community 'pillars' but it is of critical importance. It attempts to address the need for an 'ASEAN identity', a crucial factor if true regional integration is ever to occur (Severino 2006).

Over the next few years, ASEAN issued a set of 'blueprints' for each of the three pillars of the ASEAN Community. The blueprint for the AEC came out in

2007; the blueprints for the APSC and ASCC followed in 2009. In 2007, as part of the ASEAN Community building process, ASEAN introduced the ASEAN Charter, a document that, for the first time, incorporated and codified ASEAN's established practices and treaties and gave the organisation legal personality (Caballero-Anthony 2008, ASEAN 2008). The Charter introduced the ASEAN Intergovernmental Committee on Human Rights (AICHR), a body that monitors ASEAN members' human rights behaviours and which fits under the auspices of the APSC. However, as the Charter made clear, there were significant limitations on how far down the road to regional integration ASEAN was willing to go. The Charter emphasised the need for ASEAN to respect state sovereignty and allow for national diversity before it focused on democracy or human rights. The blueprints laid out ambitious plans and aspirations for regional collective action and institutions. However, the blueprints for the APSC and the ASCC, in particular, presented visions that were more idealistic than realistic. Many of the actions they advocated to advance their own agendas actually lay within the sovereign authority of member states and outside of the purview of ASEAN. The apparently contradictory focus of the Charter and the blueprints on expanding ASEAN activity even as they reinforced and prioritised ASEAN's established practices of non-intervention demonstrated the tension between the rhetoric of the ASEAN Community and where it was going in practice (Severino 2010).

The ASEAN economic community

The efforts to pursue the ASEAN Economic Community were significantly more advanced than the other two pillars. The AEC blueprint defined a number of distinct goals necessary to attain a regional market, such as lowering barriers to labour mobility and investment. However, reviews of how far ASEAN has actually come in the intervening years since the blueprint was introduced are unenthusiastic. Using AFTA, ASEAN has been highly successful in lowering intra-ASEAN tariffs. However, non-tariff barriers remain the largest problem facing regional trade and there is little indication that the AEC has made any substantial dent in them. Intra-ASEAN trade has flourished between regional businesses but many Southeast Asian businesses seem unaware of the various regional initiatives and, even if they are aware of them, are not prepared to invest the time and money necessary to utilise trade agreements. Experts who have reviewed the AEC's plans agree that relatively little progress has been made in achieving its desired results (Das *et al.* 2013).

In addition, the ASEAN states' economies remain primarily oriented towards the outside world. The AEC recognises this and is designed to attract foreign capital. ASEAN trade has increased substantially over the decades, but in percentage terms it has remained fairly constant, at around 25 per cent, a figure that reduces dramatically when Singapore is factored out. Even so, it is difficult to build the political commitment needed for strong regional economic integration when the most important trading partners of the states involved are outside the region. For states with limited resources, regional economic integration may not be a top priority.

The ASEAN political security community

The various measures encouraged by the ASEAN Political and Security Community (APSC) include promoting 'democracy, the rule of law and good governance' as well as 'human rights and fundamental freedoms'. It promises to build cooperation, shared norms and better societies within ASEAN (ASEAN 2009). There are some indications of progress in these areas. However, as noted, many of these initiatives fall under the sovereign authority of member states. While nothing stops ASEAN from encouraging its members to adopt certain policies and practices, going further than this requires a debate about intra-ASEAN coordination and accepting intrusive ASEAN, region-wide policies that ASEAN members have sought to avoid. Even more, the indications are that ASEAN states are unwilling to seriously alter the established focus on non-intervention and respect for state sovereignty.

The most serious example of the differences between ASEAN's rhetoric around the APSC and its actual practice was the conflict between Thailand and Cambodia over Preah Vihear (PV). Preah Vihear is an ancient temple and part of the larger Angkor Wat temple complex in Cambodia. In 1962, the International Court of Justice awarded most of PV to Cambodia; however, a small area adjacent to the temple remained under dispute, claimed by both Thailand and Cambodia. In 2008, Thai nationalists used an agreement for peaceful co-development between the Thai government and Cambodia to charge the sitting Thai government with having violated Thailand's constitution. This measure was part of a political campaign by nationalist forces to undermine the government of the day, which was associated with deposed Thai premier Thaksin Shinawatra. The sitting government was deposed by Thailand's constitutional court in an action that was tainted by an anti-Thaksin political agenda. Thailand and Cambodia then embarked on a series of confrontations over PV that resulted in the exchange of gunfire and heavy weapon fire, the displacement of tens of thousands of fleeing villagers on both sides of the border and the deaths of between 12–18 soldiers between 2008–2010 (Roberts 2012). The conflict came to an end when a new government – once again, affiliated with Thaksin – came back to power in Thailand in 2011 (International Crisis Group 2011).

One of ASEAN's most enduring claims is that it is responsible for creating peaceful political and economic interactions between its member states. While tensions and disputes between member states have continued since 1967, they had not led to sustained violence until Preah Vihear. During most of this conflict, ASEAN sought to avoid dealing with the dispute directly. Indeed, Singaporean foreign minister George Yeo argued that ASEAN should avoid even trying to manage the conflict rather than risk failing. For the first part of the dispute, Vietnam was ASEAN's Chair and was intent on keeping the issue off ASEAN's agenda. Indonesia took over as ASEAN Chair in 2011 and was much more active in trying to manage the conflict. Indonesian Foreign Minister Marty Natalegawa shuttled back and forth between the antagonists. Despite these efforts, Cambodia tried to take the issue to the UN Security Council, given the inability of ASEAN to act effectively. The UNSC sent the issue back to ASEAN, but agreed to continue monitoring the situation. Many outside observers, including the United States, warned Thailand that its actions risked damaging ASEAN. Even so, the dispute only died down after a change of government in Thailand (Sothirak 2013, Traviss 2012).

The PV case study showed that the idea of an APSC remains little more than an ideal, despite the fact that some of ASEAN's most important institutional structures, including the ASEAN Foreign Ministers Meeting, the ASEAN Regional Forum and the ASEAN Defence Ministers Meeting all fall under the APSC. Faced with a real threat to regional peace perpetrated by two of its members and instigated by one of its founding members, ASEAN was hard-pressed to even agree on the need to deal with the problem. The conflict indirectly demonstrated the continuing importance of a non-intervention principle.

In 1998, Thailand promoted the idea of 'flexible engagement', a change in ASEAN's approach that would allow the organisation to criticise member states' domestic policies if those policies had cross-border and/or regional effects. The other ASEAN states rejected this suggestion, settling for 'enhanced interaction', which made it acceptable for individual ASEAN states, but not the organisation, to comment on the disruptive activities of members (Narine 2002). At the time, Thailand was confident in its own democracy and willing to push for principles that could enhance democratic expression within ASEAN. Today, Thailand is wrestling with serious political instability. The country's elites refused to accept the outcome of democratic elections that saw the consistent elections of pro-Thaksin governments. They fomented political instability that led their military allies to stage a coup. The military government is consolidating its hold on power. Thailand demonstrates the fragility of democracy in Southeast Asia and illustrates the extent to which the ASEAN states remain deeply engaged in the process of state-building (Chambers 2010, Strate 2013). Under these circumstances, deep integration cannot take place.

The idea of an 'ASEAN socio-cultural community'

In respect to the ASCC, the prospects for regional integration are even weaker than in the realms of politics and security. An important survey on 'affinity and trust in Southeast Asia', conducted by Christopher Roberts between May 2004 and July 2007, demonstrates that ASEAN has been unsuccessful in creating a strong sense of regional identity in Southeast Asia. The first part of the survey consisted of over 100 in-depth interviews with people constituting the academic and governmental elites in most ASEAN countries. The second part is a communal survey of 819 people conducted in all the ASEAN capital cities except Yangon. The survey indicates the considerable distance that ASEAN has yet to go in inculcating a sense of region and identification, not just among the general public within the ASEAN states but even at the elite level. In some instances, more work needs to be done among the elites than other groups (Roberts 2007).

In the communal survey, at least 40 per cent of the respondents recognised ASEAN countries to be part of their region. However, when asked to identify which countries were part of their region, most respondents did not extend that identification to all the ASEAN states. The survey indicated a low level of understanding of what ASEAN is among the general publics and 37.5 per cent of respondents said they could trust all the ASEAN countries. However, 36.1 per cent were unsure and 26.4 per cent answered 'no'. The three countries that were mostly untrusting of their neighbours were Myanmar, Singapore and Indonesia. While the reasons for Myanmar's distrust may be obvious (particularly given the survey's timeframe), it is disturbing that Singapore and Indonesia fall into this category. Both are original members of ASEAN, and have played prominent roles in the institution's creation and evolution. However, as Roberts notes:

> ...the most disconcerting statistics arose from the respondents within the 'elite survey' sample. When forced to provide only a 'yes' or 'no' answer to the question of 'trust', 59.8% of regional elites said they couldn't trust other countries in Southeast Asia to be 'good neighbours'. Furthermore, when the sample was split between the government respondents and the academic respondents, it was the academics who were the most cynical with 66.7% answering 'no' to the question of trust. When asked if they could envision circumstances causing armed conflict within ASEAN within the next 20 years, 50% of elites indicated no, while 22.3% indicated yes and 27.7% were unsure. Regarding whether the principle of noninterference is as important now as a decade ago, 46.7% replied yes, 39.1% no and 14.1% unsure; 61.1% of government respondents replied yes to the question. Perhaps somewhat paradoxically, 54.8% of the elite sample felt that diplomatic interventions between ASEAN states could be justified. Of these, 66.7% of academic respondents replied yes, while 50% of government officers responded in the affirmative. The survey also indicated a low-level support among elites for democracy, with 75% saying that democracy was not personally important to them.
>
> (Ibid.)

The amount of time a country has been a member of ASEAN does not appear to have significantly affected the extent of trust between the communities and elites of Southeast Asia. Roberts suggests that further economic development and institutional capacity is necessary before higher levels of policy coordination and interest harmonisation can take place within ASEAN. The survey demonstrates the need for educational programmes and other initiatives to address the issues of trust and familiarity across the region, as advocated by the ASCC.

> Nevertheless, and in order to avoid the trappings of disillusionment, it should be accepted that the process of adding assets of community and regional identity will likely occur over the course of many decades rather than by ASEAN's current goal of 2015.
>
> (Roberts 2007)

The limits of integration

This book questions how and why regional institutions respond to financial crises. Do these crises help or hinder the process of regional integration? With respect to ASEAN, the organisation's original goals never really included regional integration. When it was created in 1967, ASEAN was a non-aggression pact between its member states. Its founding members were most concerned with protecting their sovereignty and avoiding intra-regional conflict as they pursued political and economic development. As it evolved over the decades, ASEAN became the foundation for regional diplomacy and security interaction. Its most important role during the Cold War was to coordinate ASEAN's opposition to Vietnam's invasion and occupation of Cambodia. However, ASEAN was unable to further any substantive efforts at regional integration. Indeed, ASEAN's focus on the Vietnam-Cambodia situation may actually have distracted it from building stronger formal regional ties. ASEAN did make some effort to strengthen intra-ASEAN economic ties during the Cold War, but these efforts were notable for their failure.

In the post-Cold War era, ASEAN was spurred by its desire to retain its regional diplomatic primacy by building new institutional structures dealing with regional trade (the ASEAN Free Trade Area – AFTA – in 1992) and regional security (the ASEAN Regional Forum-ARF – in 1994). These endeavours met with limited success, but they never bound the ASEAN states together in any deep way. Indeed, ASEAN's leaders explicitly rejected the idea that ASEAN had any aspirations to be like the European Union and most regional observers emphasised Southeast Asia's many territorial disputes, competing identities, religious and cultural differences, and historical grievances as reasons why meaningful regional integration was not a serious ASEAN institutional goal (Narine 2002, Alagappa 1998).

The Asian economic crisis of 1997–1999 demonstrated to the ASEAN states that, whether they liked it or not, their economic fates were intertwined (Narine 2002). But the fact that the states were interconnected, at least in the eyes of the outside world, did not immediately inspire a desire to make those bonds even stronger and deeper. The impetus to organise CMIM was driven by the desire to protect the sovereign authority of its participating states from the whims of the unstable international financial system. Learning to cooperate for mutual gain and to create a necessary regional insurance policy is different than pursuing a regional integration strategy. As we have seen, the efficacy of CMIM as a financial instrument has not been tested. It hinges on the participation of the three major non-ASEAN states that are its major contributors. CMIM makes the foreign currency reserves of the richest states in the region available to their poorer neighbours. As such, it is not an act of *Southeast Asian* regional integration. Indeed, the prominence of the APT, the CMIM's mother institution, may well undermine the integrative potential of ASEAN as individual Southeast Asian states are pulled into the orbit of their Northeast Asian economic partners. It may be possible to argue that CMIM is a very preliminary step towards some kind of larger East Asian integration. But, if so, the Asian states have yet to lay the political foundation for such an effort.

CMIM remains intertwined with the IMF, a fact that may create political complications for its operation. The ASEAN states have no desire to economically or politically integrate with Japan, China and South Korea, the major regional economic and political powerhouses. In such a union, the ASEAN states would be overwhelmed. Thus, the one institutional arrangement that is a direct product of the 1997–1999 crisis is not a true instrument of regional integration, if we understand integration to include the lowering of economic, political and social barriers between participating states. It took the second financial crisis of 2007–2009 to convince Japan and China to reach an agreement on the organisation's funding formula. Even then, CMIM was not used by any of the regional states during the crisis. Many observers believe that the $240 billion available to CMIM is not enough to deal with any crisis comparable to the 1997 catastrophe. To date, CMIM is an unutilised, probably under-financed, regional financial instrument that has, at most, symbolic value.

ASEAN's desire to create an ASEAN Community appears, on the surface, to be a much clearer example of a deliberate and serious attempt to further true regional integration. Indeed, from a cursory examination, everything about the ASEAN Community suggests it is explicitly an instrument of economic, political and socio-cultural integration. However, a deeper examination shows that this is more apparent than real.

First, the ASEAN Community idea was not a direct result of the 1997 economic crisis. Instead, it began as an effort by Singapore to create an ASEAN Economic Community. This was spurred by the belief that ASEAN was losing foreign direct investment (FDI) to China. The loss of FDI was a product of the 1997 crisis, though it is also a situation that would surely have developed without the crisis; the emergence of China as major regional and world economy would have attracted FDI one way or the other. The AEC is a clear effort at regional integration. However, as noted, it has run into numerous obstacles. The AEC may be able to address those obstacles over time, but the process will be long and gradual and will continue to run into the demands of domestic political considerations and the reality that the ASEAN states remain convinced that they are too fragile to risk giving up too much power to regional institutionalism. Moreover, the economies of the individual states are oriented outside of Southeast Asia. The AEC may, eventually, become a reasonably substantial institution. But it will be a very gradual process.

The ASEAN Political Security Community (APSC) and the ASEAN Socio-Cultural Community (ASCC) stand on much shakier ground. As we have seen, the APSC was introduced by Indonesia largely to give greater content to its chairmanship of ASEAN in 2003. Most Southeast Asian states continue to seek outside powers with which to form security relationships. The APSC blueprint calls for many actions that impinge on state sovereignty. The ASEAN Intergovernmental Committee on Human Rights (AICHR), which falls under the auspices of the APSC, is highly circumscribed in what it can investigate and how much it can accomplish. These limitations are deliberate. The APSC creates a picture of a regional institution that gives with one hand and takes away with the other. Its founding documents speak to an aspiration to create stronger regional ties and more binding institutional structures even as they reinforce ASEAN's traditional focus on state sovereignty and the need for states to make their own social and political choices.

The ASEAN Socio-Cultural Community (ASCC) is the most extreme example of an institutional afterthought. As we have seen, the ASCC, like the APSC, also recommends institutional actions and objectives that intrude on the sovereign responsibilities of its member states. Most of the evidence suggests that the ordinary people of ASEAN are either unaware of the institution or consider it one very minor identity among many others. Regional elites are largely distrustful of each other and, with the exception of a few people in academia and regional foreign affairs departments, share little sense of regional identity. Creating such an identity is an essential part of creating a true ASEAN Community, but it remains a distant long-term project.

ASEAN's responses to the two regional financial crises are logical, given the actual nature of the organisation. Historically, ASEAN has never successfully pursued an integration strategy. Its member states valued their sovereignty above all else; maintaining and promoting that sovereignty was ASEAN's primary goal. ASEAN's failure to respond effectively to the Asian economic crisis of 1997 seriously damaged the organisation's international standing. But this was because the international community had unrealistic expectations and perceptions of what ASEAN was and what it could achieve. In fact, ASEAN lacked the resources, institutional structures and purpose necessary for it to deal with the financial crisis. ASEAN's efforts in 2002 onward to restructure and revitalise the institution were an effort to restore some of its lost prestige and international economic profile. The ASEAN Community may be an effort to create, for the first time, an integrated regional community. In practice, there is little reason to think this goal can be achieved.

Conclusion

In 1967 its members created ASEAN to enhance regional diplomatic community and prevent future conflict between states that had just come out of a destructive regional confrontation. Regional states were concerned to protect their sovereignty and understood that making a commitment to non-interference in each other's affairs would further this goal. In 1967, all of the ASEAN states were concerned about protecting themselves from internal insurgency and political instability. Decades later, the same basic concerns continue to animate ASEAN. Over the past 47 years, ASEAN states have gone through periods of upheaval that have underlined their fragility as functioning states. Thailand is an excellent example of this: in the 1990s, Thailand was at the forefront of efforts to promote democracy within ASEAN, confident in the durability of its own democratic credentials. Today, Thailand is ruled by a military dictatorship after a coup that ousted a fairly-elected government. Muslim insurgency in the South only adds to the political instability wracking the country. Indonesia, by contrast, has become the standard-bearer for democracy in ASEAN. This is a remarkable turnaround, given that Indonesia was ruled by one man for more than 30 years, until 1998. However, even Indonesia continues to experience upheavals and uncertainty about the shape of its democracy. These experiences highlight how fragile democratic development in Southeast Asia can be. For the regional states to seriously pursue concrete integration strategies, they would first need to be convinced that pooling their political and economic resources would strengthen their abilities to function as independent states. This is unlikely to happen. For the states of Southeast Asia, their major economic and security relationships are with states outside of the region. These fundamental facts act against successful regional integration.

Note

1 In 1997, during the height of the economic crisis, man-made forest fires in Indonesia blanketed large parts of Southeast Asia in intense smog and pollution. ASEAN's non-interference principle made it difficult to address the catastrophic pollution (Cotton 1999). In 1999, Indonesian military-backed militias unleashed a campaign of violence across East Timor after Timorese voted for independence from Indonesia. ASEAN could not intervene to end or even address the violence. A UN interventionary force, led by Australia, eventually brought an end to the conflict (Narine 2004).

References

Acharya, Amitav (2013). Contingent Socialization. In Kahler, Miles and MacIntyre, Andrew J. (eds.). *Asian Regionalism in Integrating Regions: Asia in Comparative Context*. Stanford: Stanford University Press, 221–241.

Alagappa, M. (1998). International Politics in Asia: the Historical Context. In Alagappa, M. (ed.). *Asian Security Practice*. Stanford: Stanford University Press, 65–111.

ASEAN (2008). *The ASEAN Charter*. Jakarta: ASEAN Secretariat.

ASEAN (2009). *ASEAN Political-Security Community Blueprint*. Jakarta: ASEAN Secretariat.

Beeson, M. and Broome, A. (2008). Watching from the sidelines? The decline of the IMF 's crisis management role. *Contemporary Politics*, *14*(4), 393–409.

Busse, Nikolas (1999). Constructivism and Southeast Asian Security. *The Pacific Review*, *12*(1), 39–60.

Caballero-Anthony, M. (2008). The ASEAN Charter: an opportunity missed or one that cannot be missed? In Singh, D. and Maung Than, T. M. (eds.). *Southeast Asian Affairs 2008*. Singapore: Institute of Southeast Asian Studies, 71–85.

Cabellero-Anthony, M. (2014). Understanding ASEAN's Centrality: Bases and Prospects in an Evolving Regional Architecture. *The Pacific Review*, *27*(4), 563–584.

Chambers, P. (2010). Thailand on the Brink: Resurgent Military, Eroded Democracy. *Asian Survey*, *50*(5), 835–858.

Ciorciari, J. D. (2011). Chiang Mai Initiative Multilateralization: International Politics and Institution-Building in Asia. *Asian Survey*, *51*(5), 926–952.

Cotton, James (1999). The 'Haze' over Southeast Asia: Challenging the ASEAN Mode of Regional Engagement. *Pacific Affairs*, *72*(3), 331–351.

Das, S. B., Menon, J., Severino, R. and Shresthra, O. L. (eds.) (2013). *The ASEAN Economic Community: A Work in Progress.* Singapore: Asian Development Bank.

Freistein, K. (2005). ASEAN after the Bali Summit 2003: From Paralysis to New Life? *European Journal of East Asian Studies*, *4*(2), 177–203.

Grimes, W. (2009a). *Currency and Contest in East Asia.* Ithaca: Cornell University Press.

Grimes, W. (2009b). The Global Financial Crisis and East Asia: Testing the Regional Financial Architecture. *EAI Fellows Working Paper Series* (20).

International Crisis Group (2011). *Waging Peace: ASEAN and the Thai-Cambodian Border Conflict.* International Crisis Group.

Japan and China vie to be top contributor to regional fund2009-last update [Homepage of Intellasia] (2009). [Online]. Accessed 11 April 2009. www.eastasiaforum.org/2009/05/11/the-chiang-mai-initiative-china-japan-and-financial-regionalism/.

Katada, S. (2012). Regional financial cooperation. In Beeson, Mark (ed.). *Routledge Handbook of Asian Regionalism.* London: Routledge, 129–137.

Narine, S. (2002). *Explaining ASEAN: Regionalism in Southeast Asia.* Boulder: Lynne Rienner Publishers.

Narine, S. (2002). ASEAN in the Aftermath: The Consequences of the East Asian Economic Crisis. *Global Governance*, *8*(2), 179–194.

Narine, S. (2003). The Idea of an 'Asian Monetary Fund': The Problems of Financial Institutionalism in the Asia-Pacific. *Asian Perspective*, *27*(2), 65–103.

Narine, S. (2004). Peacebuilding in Southeast Asia: an Assessment of ASEAN. In Keating, Thomas and Knight, W. Andy (eds.). *Building Sustainable Peace*. Edmonton: University of Alberta Press, 213–239.

Narine, S. (2008). Forty years of ASEAN: a historical review. *The Pacific Review*, *21*(4), 411–429.

Narine, S. (2009). ASEAN in the twenty-first century: a sceptical review. *Cambridge Review of International Affairs*, *22*(3), 369–386.

Rethel, L. (2014). Regionalising Financial Development in East Asia. In Eun, Y. and Haastrup, T. (eds.). *Regionalising Global Crises. The Financial Crisis and New Frontiers in Regional Governance.* Basingstoke: Palgrave, 60–75.

Roberts, C. B. (2007). Affinity and Trust in Southeast Asia: A Regional Survey. In Katsumata, H. and Tan, S. S. (eds.). *People's ASEAN and Governments' ASEAN.* Singapore: Rajaratnam School of International Studies, 84–92.

Roberts, C. B. (2012). *ASEAN Regionalism.* London: Routledge.

Severino, R. C. (2006). *Southeast Asia in Search of an ASEAN Community.* Singapore: Institute of Southeast Asian Studies.

Severino, R. C. (2010). The Year in ASEAN: The Charter, Trade Agreements, and the Global Economic Crisis. *Southeast Asian Affairs*, 60–68.

Siregar, R. and Chabchitrchaidol, A. (2013). Enhancing the Effectiveness of CMIM and AMRO: Selected Immediate Challenges and Tasks. ADBI Working Paper 403. Tokyo: Asian Development Bank Institute. Accessed 3 April 2015. www.adbi.org/working paper/2013/01/17/5454.enhancing.effectiveness.cmim.amro.

Sothirak, P. (2013). Cambodia's Border Conflict with Thailand. *Southeast Asian Affairs*, 87–100.

Strate, S. (2013). A pile of stones? Preah Vihear as a Thai symbol of National Humiliation. *South East Asia Research*, *21*(1), 41–68.

Terada, T. (2012). ASEAN Plus Three: becoming more like a normal regionalism? In Beeson, M. and Stubbs, R. (eds.). *Routledge Handbook of Asian Regionalism.* London: Routledge, 364.

Traviss, A. C. (2012). Temple of Preah Vihear: Lessons on Provisional Measures. *Chicago Journal of International Law*, *13*(1), 317–344.

Weatherbee, D. E. (2005). *Southeast Asia: the Struggle for Autonomy.* Lanham: Rowman & Littlefield.

11 Crises, civil society and regionalism in Southeast Asia

Kelly Gerard

Introduction

The regional economic crisis of the late 1990s had a far-reaching and enduring legacy on Southeast Asian regionalism, both for political elites leading the Association of Southeast Asian Nations (ASEAN) and civil society groups contesting this political project. The regional economic crisis generated a legitimacy crisis for ASEAN, and political elites responded with an ambitious reform programme, the central component being the establishment of a single market – the ASEAN Economic Community – that commenced at the end of 2015. ASEAN elites sought to re-legitimise this political project by promoting the concept of 'people-oriented'[1] reform and including civil society organisations in regional policy-making. For civil society, the crisis generated political upheavals across affected states that galvanised advocacy. The reform of ASEAN alongside elites' claims to widen political structures fuelled the regionalisation of activism, with organisations increasingly collaborating across borders and issues in targeting ASEAN.

This chapter considers how the crisis has shaped the relationship between civil society organisations and ASEAN elites. Examining the form and impacts of civil society consultations[2] in regional policy-making, it critically engages with this apparent shift to widen ASEAN's political structures. Drawing from interviews conducted with representatives from ASEAN, its member governments and civil society organisations, the chapter charts the role of the crisis in prompting ASEAN elites' pursuit of a market-building agenda, and the promotion of this political project as being 'people-oriented'. The chapter highlights how these reforms prompted the regionalisation of advocacy, with organisations collaborating with the aim of shaping ASEAN's reform in accordance with their objectives. However, by examining who can participate in ASEAN's consultations, the nature of this participation, and the issues discussed, the chapter highlights the barriers to participation and the limited potential for civil society organisations to shape policy. While a range of actors now seek to influence regional policy-making, only a select few are permitted to contribute, with the inclusion of these groups being determined by their alignment with ASEAN elites' market-building agenda. The chapter thus argues that the notion of 'people-oriented' reform is an attempt by ASEAN elites to legitimise the development of the ASEAN Economic Community while marginalising dissenting actors.

This argument is developed as follows. First, the chapter outlines the critical political economy approach adopted here to examine the regional economic crisis and its impact on the relationship between ASEAN elites and civil society organisations. Second, it provides an overview of the crisis and its role in shaping the trajectory of regionalism in Southeast Asia. Third, the chapter highlights the crisis' impact on advocacy, charting the regionalisation of campaigns and platforms. Fourth, the article describes the limitations of ASEAN's engagement of civil society organisations, demonstrating that their inclusion is directed towards legitimising the development of the single market, rather than creating spaces for groups to contest policy or advance alternatives.

Conceptualising regionalism and civil society

Prevailing studies of ASEAN largely assume a zero-sum relationship between state and regional governance. This is reflected in explanations of ASEAN's form and trajectory alternating between outcomes being understood as a consequence of states' apparent unwillingness to hand over power to a supranational entity or ASEAN's limited capacity to override some state functions. This analytical dualism arises from an implicit methodological nationalism in regionalism studies, where states are conceptualised as autonomous, coherent and fixed entities that 'stand above and "do things" to their societies and engage in relations with other states in a relatively autonomous fashion' (Jones 2012: 31; see also Hameiri and Jayasuriya 2012: 178). Such a conception of the state problematically amplifies the significance of state borders by assuming them to be a boundary for political power. As a consequence, this approach overlooks how domestic political projects can be interwoven with regional governance.

This chapter draws from a branch of materialist state theory in recognising the relationship between domestic and regional governance as mutually constitutive. It conceptualises states as complex social relations, meaning their form is structured through conflicts between social forces seeking to advance their interests at the expense of others'. According to Jessop's strategic relational approach to governance, the state is regarded 'neither as a unitary political subject nor as a passive, instrumentalisable thing but as *a complex social relation*' (Jessop 2004). Understanding states as socially constituted acknowledges that state power is always wielded in ways that privilege particular interests over others. States are thus forever evolving through the manner in which state power is wielded, rather than being the fixed 'thing' that prevails in regionalism scholarship, given that 'the nature of statehood, citizenship and state-society relations ... changes through conflict between coalitions that cut through the formal state-society divide' (Hameiri 2013). Recognising that strategies to build networks of state power can extend beyond borders, state-building and regionalism are understood as often part of the same political project, namely the 'spatial and institutional organisation of political rule' (Hameiri 2013: 320).

This conception of states as social relations thereby draws into the analysis the role of social and political conflict in shaping the form and trajectory of both domestic and regional governance. Regional institutions, their form and their practices are thus understood to be the product of distinct political amalgams that allocate power in asymmetric ways. Hence, institutional forms and practices may persist not because of historical momentum – as argued by historical institutionalists – but because 'they are integral to a specific set of power relations' that political elites seek to maintain (Rodan *et al.* 2006: 7). In the case of ASEAN's recent attempts to widen political participation to include civil society organisations, these are thus understood as being established within system-level processes of social and political conflict,[3] as described in subsequent sections.

Civil society is, of course, a highly contested term. Armstrong and Gilson (2010) attribute the term's rise to prominence during the 1970s and 1980s in reference to forces that challenged authoritarian states and ensured that society continued working at the grassroots level in Eastern Europe, resulting in the term being viewed positively. Like other 'good words', civil society was subsequently appropriated by a range of actors, resulting in its meaning becoming 'increasingly malleable and fuzzy' (2010: 5). Recognising the term's strong normative associations, the chapter conceptualises civil society according to the historical, political and socio-cultural setting for which it is concerned (see Armstrong and Gilson 2010: 6). It employs Alagappa's definition in his study of the non-state public sphere in Asia where civil society is considered

> a distinct public sphere of organisation, communication and reflective discourse, and governance among individuals and groups that take collective action deploying civil means to influence the state and its policies but not capture state power, and whose activities are not motivated by profit.
>
> (2004: 9)

This definition is relevant in the Southeast Asian context because it does not exclude advocacy groups that are established by or affiliated with the state, nor does it ignore ascriptive groups where membership is based not on consent but on religion, language or ethnicity. Conceived as an arena for political engagement, civil society provides a useful analytical lens for examining political change (Nesadurai 2010: 5). The increasing use of the term by state actors and activists in Asia also creates compelling reasons for exploring how it is used and why (Alagappa 2004: 2; Nesadurai 2010: 5), notably by ASEAN elites in promoting 'people-oriented' reform in response to the regional economic crisis.

ASEAN after the crisis

The regional economic crisis was sparked by the devaluation of the Thai Baht, primarily as a result of aggressive speculation by currency traders. The financial contagion spread throughout the region, as asset prices, currencies and stock markets slumped. Growth rates plummeted, and states took on hefty debts in their attempt to halt this decline. The IMF assisted affected countries, however its prescriptions of cutting public spending, removing currency controls and allowing interest rates to rise plunged the region deeper into recession (Stubbs 2002: 448). Most heavily hurt by the crisis was the region's poor. The crisis led to a sharp increase in poverty in those countries that were hardest hit, namely Thailand, Indonesia and Malaysia. The rapid contraction in growth led to a spike in prices for food and consumer goods, widespread unemployment and a decline in the value of real wages. Especially vulnerable were those employed in low or semi-skilled employment in the export-oriented industrial and service sectors (Jones and Marsden 2010). The roots of the crisis have been argued to lie in trends that begun as early as the mid-1980s, where deregulation and privatisation policies directed towards integrating Southeast Asian economies into the global economy entrenched patronage networks. Through the process of deregulation and the privatisation of public infrastructure, power was diffused to domestic cartels that were subsequently able to influence (and in some cases, capture) sections of states' policy-making apparatuses (see Robison *et al.* 1987).

Alongside the crisis' economic impacts, domestic upheavals were experienced in affected countries, sparked by calls for greater accountability and transparency in governments. The most significant of these was the collapse of the Suharto regime in Indonesia after 30 years of rule. This occurred alongside the *Reformasi* movement in Malaysia that was led by the dismissed deputy Prime Minister Anwar Ibrahim; protests in Thailand that forced Chavalit Yongchaiyudh to resign, eventually making way for Thaksin's rise with his establishment of the Thai Rak Thai Party in 1998; while Joseph Estrada also came to power in the Philippines in 1998, winning by a wide margin on a populist platform. The economic and political effects of the crisis were, however, highly uneven across ASEAN member states, and responses thus also varied. Elites in ASEAN's more developed countries pursued some social and political reforms so as to draw investors back to the region and restore domestic stability, with these reforms being resisted by oligarchic forces; its newer members faced little imperative for reform because of the weakness of opposition forces in these countries (Jones 2012, 2015).

For the institution of ASEAN, the economic crisis prompted a legitimacy crisis. ASEAN's conspicuous absence from the recovery, alongside the involvement of the IMF, prompted questions and criticisms regarding ASEAN's practices and purpose, with these criticisms publicly acknowledged by its elites (see Ahmad and Ghosal 1999). In the context of domestic political upheavals in some countries and widespread criticisms of ASEAN, its political elites embarked on an ambitious reform programme. Central to this was the establishment of the ASEAN Economic Community, a single market that commenced at the end of 2015 and entail the free flow of goods and services and freer movement of capital and labour.

This market-building programme was complemented by ASEAN's restructure in accordance with regulatory transformations in its member states. From the 1980s states' new political projects were increasingly organised around a regulatory form of governance, superseding the developmental state strategies that emerged in the post-war era (Jayasuriya 2003a: 353). Rather than directly intervening, the regulatory state functions as a facilitator, or 'as a guardian of the market order' (Jayasuriya 2003b: 205). Regulatory state projects are characterised by strategies directed towards mitigating risks and ensuring market credibility, rather than protecting domestic capital and labour, such as measures to give central banks greater autonomy and independence, separating them from political processes so as to 'insulate and quarantine the economy from the corrosive influence of political interests' (Jayasuriya 2000: 324). In alignment with these domestic reforms, ASEAN was increasingly organised around a regulatory framework, where through regulatory networks, states harmonise standards and norms across a region, which are implemented and policed at the local level (Jayasuriya 2004, 2009). These regional regulatory networks thus create spaces within states where actors are involved in regulating regional concerns, underscoring the importance of examining regional and domestic governance as interwoven, rather than discrete, processes. Importantly, regulatory regionalism 'is not the emergence of supranational authority but the rescaling of governance and policy making to regional spaces located within the state or alongside the established institutions of domestic rule' (Hameiri 2009: 431). This regional regulatory framework is embodied in the networks that have been established across a widening set of issues. One example is the meeting of ASEAN Finance Ministers and Central Bank Deputies, first held in November 1997 in Manila to discuss a regional response to the crisis. The outcome of this meeting was the 'Manila Framework', which was a regional monitoring and surveillance mechanism for capital flows and economic conditions. These meetings were expanded in 2012 to include the participation of central bank governors. ASEAN has established regulatory networks governing non-traditional security issues, such as the ASEAN Ministerial Meeting on Transnational Crime, the Regional Knowledge Network on Forest Law Enforcement and Governance, and the Regional Knowledge Network on Forests and Climate Change. These networks bring together representatives of the relevant state departments and research institutions in harmonising domestic rules and regulations. Elliot notes ASEAN elites made 'explicit strategic and political claims for the advantages of transgovernmental network arrangements. Networks, they claim, will bring fluidity to the policy-making process by helping to streamline the policy agenda' (2012: 49).

This regulatory framework also advanced ASEAN elites' agenda of promoting the region's competitiveness and attracting global capital flows following the crisis. Regulatory regionalism 'should not be viewed as a departure from the disciplines of the global economy, but as an attempt to instantiate the disciplines of neoliberalism within a regional framework' (Jayasuriya 2003a: 206). ASEAN elites' response to the crisis, along with APEC and the Asian Development Bank, was drawn from the belief that the region's economic recovery would come about through the return of foreign investment (Wesley 1999: 62). The ASEAN Economic Community is intended to make the region more competitive for global capital flows, particularly in the context of neighbouring economic powerhouses, India and China. ASEAN's regulatory regional framework thus furthers its market-building programme, and is entwined with the regulatory transformation in state management taking place among its members.

This process of regional regulatory reform is not uncontested, as rescaling the governance of an issue will privilege particular interests at the expense of others, and hence conflicts can arise as actors seek to control whether an issue is governed at the national, regional or other scale (Hameiri and Jones 2012). These contestations are evident in the highly partial and uneven process of liberalisation that is taking place in developing the single market. Jones (2015) explains ASEAN's variegated integration by charting the political economy of the grouping, and some of the conflicts that have emerged around this attempt to rescale governance. Establishing an integrated regional market would entail extensive regulatory reforms, substantially impacting on the distribution of power and resources among the region's politico-business alliances. The region is characterised mainly by a large informal sector and some small and medium-sized enterprises and these operate alongside a fairly small number of low-value-added large conglomerates that emerged with state support. As elaborated by Rodan *et al.* (2006), the process of state-led development in Southeast Asia has seen the fusing of the state and business interests, such that the latter has developed a vast influence over public policy. This degree of influence has meant that the process of liberalisation taking place through the ASEAN Economic Community is highly variegated across sectors, with relevant coalitions competing across governance scales over how to organise the economy, and these struggles resulting in greater levels of economic integration in some contexts and not in others. For example, on the movement of skilled professions, the establishment of a regional certification scheme for architects that permits movement across ASEAN states has emerged alongside a protectionist arrangement for medical professions, reflecting the political economy of each sector where each country's bargaining position in developing a regional arrangement has been determined by whether the national bodies in each country had an interest in supporting professional labour migration (see Sumano 2013).

Political elites attempted to re-legitimise this reform agenda for ASEAN through the considered embrace of some liberal agendas. This included limited measures to strengthen institutional capacity and accountability, such as the ASEAN Charter that entered into force on 15 December 2008 and was a nod to a more rules-based form of governance. There have also been attempts to promote some rights through the establishment of relevant agencies, such as the ASEAN Intergovernmental Commission on Human Rights.[4] Finally, ASEAN's reform programme invoked the rhetoric of a 'people-oriented' ASEAN and the inclusion of civil society organisations in regional policy-making. This commitment first appeared in Vision 2020, released in 1997, where member states committed to creating a 'community of caring societies' in 2020, where 'the civil society is empowered' and countries are 'governed with the consent and greater participation of the people' (ASEAN 1997). The role of civil society in ASEAN's reform agenda was affirmed in the Vientiane Action Programme, signed in 2004, where leaders endorsed the 'effective participation of family, civil society and the private sector in tackling poverty and social welfare issues', noting that 'approaches and mechanisms to closely involve other ASEAN stakeholders, including the private sector and civil society, must also be addressed' (ASEAN 2004). With the Charter of 2008 state leaders agreed: 'ASEAN may engage with entities which support the ASEAN Charter' (ASEAN 2007). Thus, in the years following the crisis consulting with civil society became a consistent part of ASEAN rhetoric, leading Acharya to portend the possibility of 'participatory regionalism' developing in Southeast Asia (2003).

This rhetoric of widening participation gained a more concrete form from the early 2000s. The longstanding form of civil society participation that has existed since 1979 is the affiliation system, where organisations can apply to become affiliated with ASEAN, and affiliation carries with it some participatory opportunities. However, from 2005 ASEAN sanctioned two additional opportunities for civil society involvement, namely informal consultations on specific issues and annual sectoral forums to facilitate dialogue between civil society representatives and officials. Alongside these channels, ASEAN officials began interacting with civil society organisations through forums established by external actors, such as the ASEAN People's Assembly and the ASEAN Civil Society Conference. The subsequent section examines civil society responses to the crisis and to ASEAN's commitments to widen its political structures.

Regionalising activism

Prior to the regional economic crisis, civil society organisations paid little attention to ASEAN given its limited impact on their activities. Also deterring advocacy was ASEAN's historical practice of a highly elitist and exclusive form of governance that earned it the moniker of a 'club of dictators', evident in ASEAN's narrow interactions with non-state actors throughout the 1970s. The first non-state actor it formally engaged was the ASEAN Chamber of Commerce and Industry, established in 1972 and comprising the apex business chamber of each member state. The affiliation system was then established in 1979, described further on, where ASEAN engaged some professional bodies, first certifying the Federation of ASEAN Public Relations Organisations and the ASEAN Bankers Association (ASEAN 2009). Affiliated organisations in subsequent years also included the ASEAN Kite Council and the ASEAN Vegetable Oils Club, making it a source of ridicule for civil society organisations and journalists, such as Suryodiningrat who argued it displays 'the intent by which ASEAN perceives its subjects: with ridicule and condescension' (2009).

The late 1980s bought novel challenges for political elites in member states: the uncertainty accompanying the end of bipolarity and the declining presence of the US in the region presented leaders with new complexities, alongside the dislocation and disruption being experienced in these recently industrialising societies. To address these changing social and political contexts, member states began engaging economic and security technocrats through the ASEAN-ISIS network, a 'track 2' arrangement comprising academics, think-tank and business representatives, and politicians and military officials in their private capacities. The network was formally established in 1988, and it later expanded with ASEAN to include institutes from its more recent members. These consultations with the ASEAN-ISIS network, alongside consultations with business interests and professional associations, characterised the extent of ASEAN's engagement with non-state actors prior to the regional economic crisis.

ASEAN's 'people-oriented' rhetoric after the crisis along with the establishment of new participatory channels suggested that this trajectory was changing. This apparent shift occurred alongside the expansion of ASEAN's activities into issues that had typically been the purview of civil society organisations, such as environmental management, human rights and migration. Some groups subsequently sought to shape ASEAN's form and trajectory in alignment with their objectives, and ASEAN's 'people-oriented' rhetoric suggested that their contributions to policy-making would be welcomed. ASEAN's reform agenda was therefore an important catalyst for the regionalisation of advocacy.

Civil society organisations in the region have historically been highly atomised, which Rodan (2012) attributes to the prevalence of non-democratic ideologies that militated against the development of broad-based coalitions, as occurred in Western Europe. Rodan notes that in Western Europe 'the agency of independent labour organisations was indispensible to universal suffrage and expanded political pluralism' (2012: 313). Despite Western Europe often being used as the 'yardstick' for political development, there was nothing natural about the role of organised labour in this case; it was the consequence of specific historical conditions. Rodan emphasises the differences in the Southeast Asian case, where the vestiges of past conflicts, particularly the suppression of independent civil societies during the Cold War, as well as ongoing capitalist development have defined conflicts over forms of political representation. These conflicts fragmented social forces so that while the number of civil society organisations increased, cohesive collective action was not sustained. These conflicts, dissimilar from those in Western Europe, did not result in the creation of structures linking civil societies to formal political institutions, such as alliances between working and middle classes in the pursuit of social justice and redistribution agendas and the reform of the structural sources of social inequality.

The Cold War and accompanying suppression of independent civil societies was a decidedly inhospitable context for the political Left, and this did not change with the end of the war. Rapid and predatory capitalist development from the late 1980s in Southeast Asia bought a different set of conflicts over forms of political representation. Those whose fortunes were improved with the region's economic development began demanding political participation, which saw the renewal of civil societies. However, these new demands for political representation were largely compatible with market reforms. Activism was detached from radical socio-political change and attempts to reform the structural sources of social inequality, instead centring on the protection of rights, liberty and representative forms of government (Hewison and Rodan 2011: 25). Clammer attributes this trend in Southeast Asia to the interweaving of civil society and state interests:

> the problem of the civil society sector (non-governmental groups and institutions of a non-business nature) is both that its members are increasingly consumers and that the state that it is attempting to relate to is one increasingly pre-occupied with its own relationship to consumer capitalism.
>
> (2003)

Hence, the Southeast Asian civil society sector has historically been highly atomised and the recent regionalisation of activism in response to ASEAN's reform agenda after the regional economic crisis marked a shift in this trajectory.[5] Groups began collaborating across countries and issues. Their common experiences organising around issues arising from member states' narrow pursuit of growth provided fertile ground for collaboration. Issues that have been the consequence of this approach to state management, such as land evictions, deforestation, the rights of migrant workers, election monitoring, child trafficking and sex tourism, provided rallying points for the development of regional platforms. Collaborating through networks permitted groups to pool resources, this being significant given the few resources with which Southeast Asian civil society organisations frequently operate (Chong 2011).

The regionalisation of activism is evident in the establishment of regional networks and the development of ASEAN-focused activities in existing networks. Examples of networks that have been established solely to engage ASEAN or have developed ASEAN-focused advocacy capacities (such as by having a staff member or 'desk' that organises ASEAN campaigns) include the Southeast Asian Committee for Advocacy (SEACA), the Southeast Asia Women's Caucus on ASEAN, FORUM-ASIA, Asia Pacific Refugee Rights Network, Asian Partnership for the Development of Human Resources in Rural Asia (AsiaDHRRA), Focus on the Global South, Land Watch Asia, Child Rights Coalition, Migrant Forum in Asia and ALTSEAN-Burma. These networks often form an organisational umbrella under which national and local groups operate. They have been central in organising opposition to ASEAN's market-building programme. Activities have taken numerous forms, including workshops, seminars and study tours, and producing and disseminating information on the efficacy of advocacy efforts in Southeast Asia. For example, SEACA has published numerous edited volumes documenting advocacy in Southeast Asia, including *Breaking Through: Political Space for Advocacy in South East Asia*, edited by Paredes *et al.* (2007). Regional networks have also produced and disseminated guides on how to engage ASEAN, such as FORUM-ASIA's handbooks that are designed to inform organisations of ASEAN policy, including *Rights Now: A Training Manual on ASEAN Human Rights Mechanisms* (FORUM-ASIA 2010).

Not all organisations consider ASEAN an advocacy target, with a vast spectrum of views regarding the benefits and potential of targeting ASEAN.[6] Opinions range from those that view engaging ASEAN as equivalent to their co-optation, to organisations that not only view engagement beneficial but also devote resources to encouraging others to do the same. As noted by Chavez, 'ASEAN has largely been inaccessible to civil society, and is not known for initiatives that directly target broad sections of the ASEAN population. Many groups therefore question the value of engaging the ASEAN Charter process, or ASEAN itself' (2006: 2). Scepticism of advocacy targeting ASEAN also reflects its high costs, given the resources required to monitor ASEAN's 1,000+ meetings each year, the long period with which advocacy must be framed and the limited resources that organisations often work with.

The Solidarity for Asian People's Advocacy (SAPA) network was a crucial actor during the early stages of the development of advocacy targeting ASEAN. SAPA was formally established at its first regional consultation on 3–4 February 2006 in Bangkok, and comprises approximately 100 organisations, both national and regional. Its aims are twofold: to promote campaigns on development issues in the region, and to advance civil society engagement with multilateral organisations (Dano 2008: 68). It was founded in recognition of the need for a forum that allows civil society organisations to collaborate and share resources so they can more effectively engage the increasing number of multilateral processes in Asia. As suggested in its title, its activities cover the entire Asian region, and it is organised around three sub-regions – South Asia, Northeast Asia and Southeast Asia – with working groups targeting the relevant multilateral processes for each sub-region. Its members work on disparate issues, including women's rights, migrant rights, human rights, sustainable farming practices, child prostitution, people trafficking and the protection of endangered species, but they are united by their desire to 'enhance the effectiveness and impact of civil society advocacy by improving communication, cooperation and coordination among non-governmental organisations operating regionally' (PAAR 2011).

SAPA has been a crucial organising force for Southeast Asian activists seeking to target ASEAN. Ramirez attributes SAPA's success in creating a broad alliance across organisations to its leadership:

> Highly noticeable in the SAPA process is the emergence of a new generation of CSO [civil society organisation] leaders who are more prepared to cross political lines and traditions and to form broad-based partnerships. These leaders recognise new friendships as essential in sustaining a movement that must present a united front before ASEAN, while, at the same time, acknowledging that each has its own agenda.
>
> (2008: 8)

SAPA has played the lead role in the organisation of the ASEAN Civil Society Conference,[7] which has become the central parallel summit for groups seeking to influence ASEAN policy (see Gerard 2013). Additionally, by drawing on the research capacities of its various members, SAPA has been able to present a coherent alternative regional project, articulating a concerted position for an alternative regionalism that constitutes 'a counter-hegemonic challenge to the dominant ASEAN framework of conservatism, illiberal political governance and neo-liberal economics' (Nesadurai 2011: 172). SAPA's structure has also been a central component of its success. The SAPA Working Group on ASEAN forms an organisational umbrella under which its various tasks forces operate, and it was the key civil society actor in the consultations that ASEAN conducted during the drafting of the Charter (Ramirez 2008: 7). It comprises approximately 40 organisations and 'advocates for better participation and decision making by the people in ASEAN policies' (ThinkCentre 2009). The SAPA Working Group on ASEAN established a physical space with the opening of the ASEAN People's Centre in Jakarta on 15 January 2009 to promote engagement between civil society organisations and ASEAN, given that the ASEAN Secretariat is based in Jakarta (Chandra 2009: 7).

Within the SAPA Working Group on ASEAN, there are various task forces organised around specific ASEAN processes. One is the SAPA Task Force on ASEAN and Human Rights, formed in August 2007 as a means of uniting human rights groups to lobby ASEAN in its development of the ASEAN Intergovernmental Commission on Human Rights. Similarly, the SAPA Task Force on ASEAN and Migrant Workers was formed in April 2006 to unite relevant groups in lobbying the ASEAN Committee on the Implementation of the ASEAN Declaration on the Promotion and Protection of the Rights of Migrant Workers (SEARCH 2010: 4). Others include the SAPA Task Force on ASEAN and Freedom of Information, and the SAPA Task Force on ASEAN and Burma. By bringing together organisations targeting specific ASEAN processes, with these task forces then grouped under the banner of the SAPA Working Group on ASEAN, the SAPA network has contributed in unifying society organisations in their attempts to influence ASEAN policy. The subsequent section examines the boundaries of civil society participation in ASEAN policy-making.

Participation as representation, not contestation

The longstanding form of participation for civil society in ASEAN – the affiliation system – dates back to 1979. In this system, civil society organisations that meet specified criteria can apply for affiliation which brings with it some forms of participation in ASEAN processes. In its push to engage civil society in policy-making, ASEAN established two new participatory channels, alongside the affiliation system. First, from 2005 some ASEAN bodies began holding ad hoc consultations with civil society representatives on specific issues, the most high-profile being those conducted during the drafting of the Charter. Second, beginning in 2006 ASEAN also established annual sectoral forums to encourage dialogue between officials and civil society organisations, termed the GO-NGO forums ('GO-NGO' referring to Government Organisation – Non-Governmental Organisation). These have been established on migrant labour, social welfare and development, rural development and poverty eradication, agriculture and forestry, equal opportunity for people with disabilities, and children's issues.

These three participatory channels established by ASEAN offer limited opportunities for civil society groups to contest policy and shape official processes as a result of three characteristics. First, there are strict controls over who can participate. For example, in the case of the GO-NGO forums, an informal system of affiliation operates where each country compiles a list of relevant organisations that they wish to invite to participate. Every member of the ASEAN Committee of Permanent Representatives considers each list, and if any of the nominated organisations are deemed contentious by a member state, they are removed and the remaining groups are invited to participate.[8] Hence, all participants must receive the endorsement of all member states, making participation in these forums highly exclusive. Many of the participants in these forums are subsequently GONGOs (government-organised non-governmental organisations), these being organisations that are established and/or maintained by states. The distinction between a GONGO and an independent organisation varies, as does the extent of governmental control over an organisation's activities, however groups with a more contentious agenda and grassroots groups are generally not represented. Participation is largely restricted to nationally accredited organisations, this being biased towards groups with formalised and legalised systems of operation and those that do not contest national policies and maintain the favour of their governments.

Second, there are strict controls over the nature of participation in these spaces. For example, the only form of participation guaranteed through the affiliation system is the submission of written statements to the ASEAN Committee of Permanent Representatives. All other activities, such as presenting information to an agency, attending meetings or obtaining access to documents, must be requested in writing, and there are no mechanisms for recourse if an application is rejected. The limited scope for participation in ASEAN activities through the affiliation system has meant that it includes only one organisation that is widely respected in the civil society community, namely AsiaDHRRA. Professional bodies dominate the list of affiliated organisations, such as the ASEAN Association of Radiologists.

Third, spaces for civil society participation in ASEAN are determined by the issue under discussion, which further limits the range of political activities by activists. Issues aligned with ASEAN's market-building agenda, such as rural development and poverty eradication, have been the subject of forums to promote interaction between civil society organisations and ASEAN officials. However, groups working on issues deemed contentious by officials because they directly challenge powerful interests – such as land evictions in Cambodia, or the enforced disappearance of environmental activists – have been excluded from all forums for civil society engagement established by ASEAN. These three characteristics of participatory channels established by ASEAN – determining who participates, the nature of participation and the issues discussed – narrow the possibilities for seeking to influence ASEAN policy.

Alongside these three participatory channels established by ASEAN, as part of its reform agenda officials also began to interact with civil society through mechanisms established by external actors, such as the ASEAN People's Assembly and the ASEAN Civil Society Conference.[9] However, ASEAN has not institutionalised these forums, which means that state and ASEAN officials retain the ability to utilise these activities in accordance with their interests. For example, the ASEAN-ISIS Colloquium on Human Rights (AICOHR) has been held annually since 1994 and is organised by the Philippine branch of the ASEAN-ISIS network of think-tanks. The AICOHR was intended to build confidence amongst participants, comprising government officials, academics, staff from the ASEAN-ISIS network and civil society representatives. This was because at the time of its establishment, human rights was a highly sensitive issue for ASEAN elites, who asserted that it impacted on national sovereignty. Elites initially used the AICOHR to contest the perceived universality of human rights, which they argued was a Western construct. They sought to refute this by advocating for 'Asian values', based on the notion that human rights are shaped by a country's experiences. While these ideas were debated during the AICOHR's early years, representatives from all of the ASEAN states' Foreign Affairs Ministries consistently participated in the AICOHR, with the newer members of Vietnam, Laos and Cambodia participating from the second meeting and Myanmar participating from the sixth (Kraft 2006: 83–85). In later years the debate moved from base-lining studies to discussions of specific human rights concerns in the region. Meanwhile, from the seventh AICOHR an increasing number of civil society representatives also began to participate (Kraft 2006: 85). As civil society participation increased and the debate shifted away from base-lining studies, many countries stopped sending state representatives. More recently, the only officials in attendance are from ASEAN's post-authoritarian states, such as at the fourteenth AICOHR where Enrique Manalo, Philippine Undersecretary for Policy in the Department of Foreign Affairs, delivered the keynote address on behalf of Alberto Romulo, Philippine Foreign Affairs Secretary. As officials are invited to attend, and their participation is not decreed by states or ASEAN, they have been able to utilise this forum in accordance with their objectives, attending or withholding their attendance as it suits their interests. Withholding their attendance has the important effect of quashing activists' efforts to communicate their views.

Evidently, these characteristics of participatory channels limit civil society organisations from using them to contest ASEAN policy or advance alternatives. Their structure militates against the inclusion of groups that are not supportive of ASEAN's market-building agenda. By inviting some civil society representatives to contribute their views while restricting their ability to contest policy, political elites in ASEAN have created opportunities for representation, but not contestation.

A 'people-oriented' ASEAN?

With the regional economic crisis having sullied its reputation, ASEAN elites sought to re-legitimise this political project with domestic and foreign audiences through an ambitious reform programme. The central component of this agenda has been the establishment of the ASEAN Economic Community, a project that furthers the regulatory reforms underway in member states. ASEAN elites promoted the reform of this political project by committing to include civil society organisations in policy-making. These commitments were followed by the establishment of two new participatory channels for civil society organisations, namely the GO-NGO forums and ad hoc consultations held by some agencies, and these existed alongside the longstanding form of participation, the affiliation system.

Civil society organisations did not previously seek to engage ASEAN in light of the historically limited impacts of the grouping's activities on their objectives as well as ASEAN's highly exclusive and elitist governance, which prior to the crisis saw it engage only private business interests, professional bodies, and economic and security technocrats. ASEAN's reform following the regional economic crisis had the important effect of driving the regionalisation of activism, with groups collaborating across countries and issues to try to influence ASEAN policy in accordance with their objectives, particularly in light of elites' commitments for civil society inclusion. The regionalisation of activism has taken the form of advocacy targeting ASEAN through existing and new networks, notably SAPA, and the organisation of platforms, in particular the ASEAN Civil Society Conference.

In responding to the questions raised by the editors of this volume, this chapter has argued that it is not the degree of regional integration that leads to higher civil society support for regionalism. Participation, on the contrary, relates not to the degree of institutional density of a regional organisation, but to social and political conflict. Examining the shift in ASEAN to consult civil society organisations in policy-making, the chapter demonstrated that this institutional change is an attempt by political elites to socially embed a project that conflicts with the objectives sought by the increasingly organised and vocal Southeast Asian civil society sector.

While a greater range of actors now seek to influence regional policy-making and ASEAN elites have committed to their inclusion, as demonstrated in this chapter, participatory channels are structured to include particular interests that are congenial to market-building reforms and marginalise non-compatible groups. By determining which civil society organisations can participate, the nature of their participation and the issues discussed, political elites have structured these participatory channels to advance their interests, and in doing so, to manage the criticisms presented by civil society groups. This approach to widening participation in ASEAN enables political elites to advance domestic political projects where they intersect with regional aims, while marginalising dissenting voices, thereby underscoring the importance of examining regional and domestic governance as interwoven rather than discrete processes. ASEAN elites' engagement of civil society organisations thus serves to legitimise the establishment of the single market by promoting an inclusive approach to policy-making, while channels for participation are organised to marginalise the project's critics.

Notes

1 ASEAN initially embraced the term 'people-centred', however when the Charter came into force in 2008 it included the term, 'people-oriented', signifying a subtle weakening of ASEAN's proclaimed people-focus (see Chandra 2009: 10).

2 This chapter draws substantively on Gerard 2014; see pp. 9–11 for description of research methodology.

3 On alternative approaches to explaining ASEAN's problematic engagement of civil society organisations and their limitations, see Gerard 2015a.

4 These agencies' mandates speak of both promoting and protecting particular rights, however various loopholes limit their capacity for rights protection. See Gerard 2014a.
5 This shift was preceded by regional advocacy campaigns on two specific issues: first, in support of Timorese independence; and second, in support of political reform in Burma. See Jones 2012; Gerard 2014b.
6 Interview with Indonesian human rights activist, Jakarta, 19 October 2011; interview with Indonesian gender equality activist, Jakarta, 18 October 2011.
7 This forum has been held under various titles over its existence, including the 'ASEAN People's Forum' and the 'ASEAN Civil Society Conference/ASEAN People's Forum'. This chapter refers to these events using their original title, the 'ASEAN Civil Society Conference'.
8 Interview with ASEAN Secretariat official, Jakarta, 22 November 2011.
9 The ASEAN People's Assembly was first held in 2000 and established by the ASEAN-ISIS network as a forum for dialogue between civil society organisations and government officials, while the ASEAN Civil Society Conference was first held in 2005, led by regional civil society organisations in collaboration with the Malaysian government, given that Malaysia was the ASEAN Chair in that year. For a detailed discussion of these two events, see Gerard 2013.

References

Acharya, Amitav (2003). Democratisation and the Prospects for Participatory Regionalism in Southeast Asia. *Third World Quarterly*, *24*(2), 375–390.

Ahmad, Zakaria Haji and Ghosal, Baladas (1999). The Political Future of ASEAN After the Asian Crisis. *International Affairs*, *75*(4), 759–778.

Alagappa, Muthiah (2004). Introduction. In Alagappa, Muthiah (ed.). *Civil Society and Political Change in Asia*. Stanford: Stanford University Press, 1–24.

Armstrong, David and Gilson, Julie (2010). Introduction: Civil Society and International Governance, in David Armstrong, Valeria Bello, Jule Gilson and Debora Spini (ed.) *Civil Society and International Governance: The Role of Non-state Actors in Global and Regional Regulatory Frameworks*. Oxford: Routledge, 1–12.

ASEAN [Association of Southeast Asian Nations] (1997). *ASEAN Vision 2020*. Jakarta: ASEAN Secretariat.

ASEAN (2004). *Vientiane Action Program*. Jakarta: ASEAN Secretariat.

ASEAN (2007). *Activities of the HLTF on the Drafting of the ASEAN Charter (HLTF): January–October 2007*. Jakarta: ASEAN Secretariat.

ASEAN (2009). *Register of ASEAN-Affiliated CSOs*. Accessed 20 November 2013. www.asean.org/archive/6070.pdf.

Chandra, Alexander C. (2009). *Civil Society in Search for an Alternative Regionalism in ASEAN*. Winnipeg, Manitoba: International Institute for Sustainable Development.

Chavez, Jenina Joy (2006). Building Community: The Search for Alternative Regionalism in Southeast Asia, in *Revisiting Southeast Asian Regionalism*. Bangkok: Focus on the Global South, 1–10.

Chong, Terence (2011) Executive Summary, in Terence Chong and Stephanie Elies (eds.) *An ASEAN Community for All: Exploring the Scope for Civil Society Engagement*. Singapore: Frederich-Ebert-Stiftung.

Clammer, John (2003). Globalisation, Class, Consumption and Civil Society in Southeast Asian Cities, *Urban Studies*, *40*(2), 403–419.

Dano, Elenita (2008). *Building People-oriented and Participatory Alternative Regionalism Models in Southeast Asia.* Manila and Bangkok: Asian Farmers Association for

Sustainable Rural Development and AsiaDHRRA. Accessed 10 March 2010. http://asiadhrra.org/wordpress/wp-content/uploads/2008/03/alternative_regionalism.pdf.

Denoon, David B. H. and Evelyn Colbert (1998). Challenges for the Association of Southeast Asian Nations (ASEAN). *Pacific Affairs*, *71*(4), 505–523.

Elliott, Lorraine (2012) ASEAN and Environmental Governance: Strategies of Regionalism in Southeast Asia. *Global Environmental Politics*, *12*(3), 38–57.

FORUM-ASIA (2008). *SAPA: New Strategies to Embrace Arising Human Rights Challenges in Asia*. Accessed 1 August 2011. www.forum-asia.org/index.php?Itemid=132&id=1481&option=com_content&task=view.

FORUM-ASIA (2010). *Rights Now: A Training Manual on ASEAN Human Rights Mechanisms*. Accessed 3 September 2011. www.forum-asia.org/?p=5551.

Gerard, Kelly (2013). From the ASEAN People's Assembly to the ASEAN Civil Society Conference: The Boundaries of Civil Society Advocacy. *Contemporary Politics*, *19*(4), 411–426.

Gerard, Kelly (2014a). ASEAN and civil society activities in 'created spaces': the limits of liberty. *The Pacific Review*, *27*(2), 265–287.

Gerard, Kelly (2014b). *ASEAN's Engagement of Civil Society: Regulating Dissent*. New York: Palgrave Macmillan.

Gerard, Kelly (2015). Explaining ASEAN's engagement of civil society in policy-making: smoke and mirrors. *Globalizations*, *12*(3), 365–382.

Hameiri, Shahar (2009). Beyond Methodological Nationalism, but Where to for the Study of Regional Governance? *Australian Journal of International Affairs*, *63*(3), 430–441.

Hameiri, Shahar (2013). Theorising Regions through Changes in Statehood: Rethinking the Theory and Method of Comparative Regionalism. *Review of International Studies*, *39*(2), 313–335.

Hameiri, Shahar and Jayasuriya, Kanishka (2012). Regulatory Regionalism in Asia. In Beeson, Mark and Stubbs, Richard (eds.). *Routledge Handbook of Asian Regionalism*. Abingdon, Oxon: Routledge, 177–185.

Hameiri, Shahar and Jones, Lee (2012). The Politics and Governance of Non-traditional Security. *International Studies Quarterly*, *57*(3), 462–473.

Hewison, Kevin and Rodan, Garry (2011). Southeast Asia: The Left and the Rise of Bourgeois Opposition. In Robison, Richard (ed.). *Routledge Handbook of Southeast Asian Politics*. Abingdon, Oxon: Routledge, 25–39.

Jayasuriya, Kanishka (2000). Authoritarian Liberalism, Governance, and the Emergence of the Regulatory State in Post-Crisis East Asia. In Robison, Richard, Beeson, Mark, Jayasuriya, Kanishka and Kim, Hyuk-Rae (eds.). *Politics and Markets in the Wake of the Crisis*. London and New York: Routledge, 315–330.

Jayasuriya, Kanishka (2003a). Introduction: Governing the Asia Pacific: Beyond the 'New Regionalism'. *Third World Quarterly*, *24*(2), 199–215.

Jayasuriya, Kanishka (2003b). Embedded Mercantilism and Open Regionalism: The Crisis of a Regional Political Project. *Third World Quarterly*, *24*(2), 339–355.

Jayasuriya, Kanishka (2004). Introduction: The Vicissitudes of Asian Regional Governance, in Jayasuriya, Kanishka (ed.). *Asian Regional Governance: Crisis and Change*. London: RoutledgeCurzon, 1–18.

Jayasuriya, Kanishka (2009). Regulatory Regionalism in the Asia-Pacific: Drivers, Instruments and Actors. *Australian Journal of International Affairs*, *63*(3), 335–347.

Jessop, Bob (2014). Multi-level Governance and Multi-level Meta-governance. In Bache, Ian and Flinders, Matthew (eds.). *Multi-level Governance*. Oxford: Oxford University Press, 49–74.

Jones, Lee (2012). *ASEAN, Sovereignty and Intervention in Southeast Asia.* New York: Palgrave Macmillan.

Jones, Lee (2015). Explaining the Failure of the ASEAN Economic Community: The Primacy of Domestic Political Economy, *The Pacific Review.*

Jones, Nicola and Marsden, Hannah (2010). Assessing the Impacts of and Responses to the 1997–98 Asian Financial Crisis Through a Child Rights Lens: Including Children in Policy Responses to Previous Economic Crises. *UNICEF Social and Economic Policy Working Paper*, December 2010.

Kraft, Herman Joseph (2006). ASEAN-ISIS and Human Rights Advocacy: The ASEAN-ISIS Colloquium on Human Rights (AICOHR). In Soesastro, Hadi, Joewono, Clara and Hernandez, Caroline G. (eds.). *Twenty Two Years of ASEAN-ISIS: Origin, Evolution and Challenges of Track Two Diplomacy*, 75–87. Jakarta: CSIS.

Nesadurai, Helen (2010). Labor and Grassroots Civic Interests in Regional Institutions. *ABD Working Paper Series on Regional Economic Integration*, No. 63. Manila: ABD.

Nesadurai, Helen (2011). The ASEAN People's Forum (APF) as Authentic Social Forum: Regional Civil Society Networking for an Alternative Regionalism. In Beeson, Mark and Stubbs, Richard (eds.). *Routledge Handbook of Asian Regionalism.* Oxford: Routledge, 166–176.

PAAR [People's Agenda for Alternative Regionalisms] (2011). *ACSC/SAPA (Southeast Asia).* Accessed 1 August 2011. www.alternative-regionalisms.org/?page_id=57.

Paredes, Joel, de Guzman, Marissa and Rillorta, Eltheodon (eds.). (2007). *Breaking Through: Political Space for Advocacy in Southeast Asia.* Manila: South East Asian Committee for Advocacy.

Ramirez, Marlene (2008). AsiaDHRRA and ASEAN: A Case Study of the Process of Civil Society Engagement with a Regional Intergovernmental Organisation. Paper presented at the FIM Forum, Montreal, 8–9 February.

Robison, Richard, Hewison, Kevin and Higgott, Richard (eds.). (1987). *Southeast Asia in the 1980s: The Politics of Economic Crisis.* London: Allen and Unwin.

Rodan, Garry (2012). Competing Ideologies of Political Representation in Southeast Asia. *Third World Quarterly*, *33*(2), 311–332.

Rodan, Garry, Hewison, Kevin and Robison, Richard (2006). Theorising Markets in Southeast Asia: Power and Contestation. In Rodan, Garry, Hewison, Kevin and Robison, Richard (eds.). *The Political Economy of Southeast Asia: Markets, Power and Contestation.* Oxford: Oxford University Press, 1–38.

SEARCH [South East Asia Regional Cooperation in Human Development] (2010). *Promoting a Process of Change: The Task Force on ASEAN Migrant Workers.* Accessed 28 September 2011. www.searchproject.ca.

Stubbs, Richard (2002). ASEAN Plus Three: Emerging East Asian Regionalism? *Asian Survey* 42(3): 440–455.

Sumano, Boonwara (2013). Explaining the liberalisation of professional migration in ASEAN. PhD thesis, School of Politics and International Relations, Queen Mary, University of London, London.

Suryodiningrat, Meidyatama (2009). Facing the People, ASEAN's Strategic Deficit. *The Jakarta Post*, 5 March. Accessed 6 October 2009. www.thejakartapost.com/news/2009/03/05/news-analisys-facing-people-asean%E2%80%99s-strategic-deficit.html.

ThinkCentre (2009). ASEAN People's Centre Launched in Jakarta to Advance Civil Society Advocacy. *ASEAN Watch*, 22 January. Accessed 10 June 2012. www.thinkcentre.org/article.cfm?ArticleID=2970.

Wesley, Michael (1999). The Asian Crisis and the Adequacy of Regional Institutions. *Contemporary Southeast Asia*, *21*(1), 54–73.

12 Regional integration in times of crisis

Power, institutional density and the people – a conclusion

Sabine Saurugger and Fabien Terpan

Global economic and financial turmoil has occurred over the last ten years and put stress on regional governability. European, Asian, Latin American – as the chapters of this collective volume have shown, but also African, North-American or Arab regional organisations have been confronted with a series of challenges. These included: finding new institutional designs to tackle questions of financial and economic difficulties, assure the internal survival of their member state economies, and addressing legitimacy problems. These crisis situations also provided opportunities in some cases. For instance, they allowed civil society organisations, as well as new institutions to emerge and, reinforce cooperation. These challenges were thus means to strengthen integration, but in some cases also weakened cooperation.

Understood as phenomena that question the standard operating procedures of systems by creating a feeling of urgency, crisis situations lead stakeholders to react. And while regionalism is intimately linked to crisis situations which prominently figure amongst the main variables leading to the initial integration process (wars that make people understand the need for peaceful cooperation, external enemies threatening the peaceful development of countries, economic difficulties shared by a number of countries which require cooperation (Fioramonti 2012, Dosenrode 2012)), this collective volume has taken this question a step further. Our aim has been to systematically analyse whether financial and economic crises in particular influence regional integration. For this, we studied three empirical puzzles:

First, if change occurs, does it strengthen regional integration or conversely, do crises lead to progressively weaker regional integration? Second, is the strengthening or weakening of regional integration a consequence of the crisis or rather an endogenous process in which the crisis has very little influence? Finally, why do citizens react differently in all three regions, varying from increasing scepticism with regard to integration projects to continued indifference?

The sections of this book concentrating on European, Latin American and Asian integration schemes have specifically analysed these questions with regard to three aspects: The chapters looked at power relations between the member states and the regional organisations in different policy domains (economic, financial, environmental policy areas). They analysed institutional change in regional integration and have shown how formal and informal institutions are set up as well as their workings. They have also, through in-depth case studies and the use of large-scale databases, analysed change in individual citizens' attitudes or in collective actors attitudes towards regional integration.

Our starting point was based on comparative regionalism's typology of region-ness, or degree of regionalisation (Hettne 1997, 2001; Schulz *et al.* 2001): core regions, such as the European Union, which are extremely well structured and allow their members to play an influential role on the world stage; intermediate zone regions, such as Latin American regions, which imitate core regions and strive to compete with them in the global economy; and, finally, peripheral zone regions, such as ASEAN, where political and economic institutions remain fragile and where member states' sovereignty is the main explanatory factor for regional activity or inactivity.

The results found in the chapters of our collective volume, however, are not as clear-cut as this typology suggests. What we have seen is a more nuanced picture, in which core regions, intermediate regions and peripheral regions do not systematically react to the challenge of economic and financial crises along the expectations presented in the Table 12.1. Hence, member states of intermediate zone regions such as Brazil initially used regional integration to increase its level of economic development. When economic and financial crisis situations occurred, they only paid lip service to regional integration and did not further strengthen regional institutions. In peripheral regions such as ASEAN, citizens' and civil society interest in their regional organisation increased through crisis situations and they engaged more thoroughly in participating in the process of regional integration. On the contrary, in core regions such as the EU, citizens and civil society actors grew more sceptical towards regional integration as economic and financial crisis situations occurred.

One of the reasons for these nuanced research results stems from the fact all the volume's authors adopt an actor-centred view that allows them to see how actors use crisis situations in order to change institutions, or even prevent change. Crisis situations relax the structural constraints that keep institutions in place. The routine way of working and thinking – or in other words, cognitive frames – loses credit and room for alternatives suddenly emerges. But these changes can only become possible if actors use the opportunity for change. They can also block change, by adopting strategies of inertia or framing problems in such a way that change becomes undesirable.

Table 12.1 Institutional change according to regional integration type

	Power relations among member states	*Institutional density*	*Citizens' and collective non-state actors' attitude towards regional integration*
Core regions	+++	+++	+++
Intermediate regions	++–	++–	++–
Peripheral regions	+–	+–	+–

Relative power of actors

We have argued in a first series of hypotheses that the higher the relative power of actors (cognitive, economic, political as well as military power) before a crisis occurs, the higher the probability that these actors influence institutional change in a situation of crisis. The authors have shown that actors possess different forms of power (Strange 1996). Beyond their economic power, measured in GDP (Gross Domestic Product), participation in interregional trade, level of direct foreign investment, contribution to the regional organisation's budget, their power also depends on their voting weight in the organisation, and the number and elite-level presence of their civil servants in the organisational structure. Furthermore, they can defend a specific cognitive frame that, at a particular moment, becomes the dominant paradigm that rules the way problems and solutions are interpreted. This becomes particularly visible in Degner's and Lequesne's chapters when we look at how the EU responded to the economic and financial crises (increased austerity and more formal rules) based on an understanding of the solutions framed by Germany. The Eurozone crisis is perceived as the most severe crisis the EU has ever faced, threatening the EU's political and economic system based on a common currency with the – unorganised – return to national currencies. Uncertainty about the causes and the consequences of the crisis, but also about the best solution to face it characterises the situation.

The chapters studying the impact of the financial and economic crisis on all three regional integration areas unanimously underline the importance of member states strengthening or weakening the integration process, as well as their role in the development of solutions to the crisis. Member states are identified as the major motors of regional integration during and after a crisis. The central state actor in the EU crisis – together with its partner France, as we will see below – is Germany. Having recovered from its economic slowdown after reunification – the German government has played both a dominant and a leadership role in the Eurozone crisis. The economic crisis makes Germany the *de facto* hegemon of Europe not through an explicit political project to dominate Europe, but because of its economic position and the impossibility for the other member states to impose credible and convincing alternatives, as Lequesne argues. Its position at the EU level was however reinforced by the broader concern of German institutions and the German public about EU representation and legitimacy. In Latin America, Brazil takes the lead before and during the crises that shake the continent, due to its economic power more than to its voting power in MERCOSUR. In the context of Asian regional integration, Indonesia is identified as the leader.

The member states' power, however, is unevenly distributed. In the European realm, the Franco-German coalition – the so-called Franco German couple – is a central actor for change, as both Lequesne's and Degner's chapters show, contrary to MERCOSUR, UNASUR or ASEAN where individual member states influence the path of integration. Coalitional dynamics might be central to understanding the change of agents' strategies in periods of crises, only if they are based on longstanding coalitions, forged before the outbreak of the crisis, which was the case in Europe with the Franco-German tandem. In times of crisis, member states coalition did not emerge unexpectedly but were based on already existing cooperation structures.

One crucial research result of the comparative studies is the differential impact citizens and domestic constituencies more generally seem to have on the regional strategies followed by the member states, in the different regions, to confront crisis situations. While all chapters concentrating on member state strategies in the context of European integration insist on the significant influence of citizens or powerful domestic actors such as parliamentary factions, central banks, well-organised economic interest groups and major banks (Degner, Lequesne, Hülsemeyer) in shaping these member state interests, Asian and Latin American member states seemed to be much less continuously influenced by citizens in between general elections. In their case studies concentrating on Latin America, Dabène and Parthenay point out that regional policies as response to crisis situations mainly stem from presidential decisions, underlining that Latin American policies are characterised by presidential politics. Citizens influence member states' positions through elections. Changes in member state positions, however, occur through changes in government, as we see in the context of the second Latin American Integration in the 1980s that was triggered, according to Dabène and Dri, through the continent's election of many leftist presidents. Dri shows that party politics explain the change in the position of Brazil's government with regard to the institutional development of MERCOSUR.

In the case of the Asian region, Kelly argues that civil society organisations had a very limited overall influence on ASEAN member states' position, though the regional organisation itself created room for debate. Thus crisis situations seem to open up the possibility for civil society organisations to engage with regional integration organisations. Nevertheless, the case studies on ASEAN show, that this concerns only a few civil society organisations: only a few NGOs were permitted to contribute to decision-making processes and only if their views were aligned with ASEAN elites' market building agenda.

In the European context, on the contrary, the relations between national constituencies and governmental positions at the EU level are important for defining the member states' preferences during the crisis. In his chapter analysing whether governmental positions changed over time during the crisis, Hülsemeyer argues that there seems to be a correlation between the change in the German government's position vis-à-vis the German financial contribution to the European Stability Mechanism (ESM) as well as on the Greek bailout. German public opinion indeed appears to be constraining government decisions during the Eurozone crisis. Similarly, Lequesne stresses, in concordance with the conceptual framework developed in the introduction, that institutional change is not so much the result of how regional institutions constrain member states, but how member states were able to frame the crisis domestically. Thus, in the European Union, both member states and institutions influence decision-making in times of crisis.

Degner, however, questions whether public opinion has a consistent impact on the German government's position. He points to the fact that this influence is not consistently high but varies: while a stable majority of Germans continuously opposed bailout payments for over-indebted Euro area members, the German government considered, in June 2010, that setting up the newly created European Financial Stability Facility (EFSF) was an absolute necessity.

Finally, we also see that crisis situations trigger a shared understanding of the effects of institutional engineering by powerful actors, more specifically member states. Degner thus argues in his chapter that the crisis largely discredited the existing system of EU fiscal and economic governance. He cites German Chancellor Merkel who called the SGP provisions an 'insane' ('schwachsinniges') instrument for fiscal crisis management, and called for the revision of both EU treaty provisions and EU secondary legislation, which other member states, and in particular France agreed upon. This is illustrated by the agreement amongst heads of state and government to set up an institutional emergency mechanism for Euro area members in need and to enlarge the existing legal framework to ensure fiscal sustainability in the Eurozone and enhance its capacity to act in times of crisis.

With regards to ASEAN, the promotion of human rights as a consequence of the 1997 financial and economic crisis became possible once Indonesia considered the inherent institutional development necessary. Investing in environmental protection however, was hindered by Indonesia's conception of economic development, shown by its reluctance to undertake firm action against recalcitrant individuals and companies.

While the majority of authors in this collective volume insist on the importance of historically developed state powers in strengthening or, on the contrary, slowing down regional integration, they come to differentiated conclusions about whether the existing institutional structures enable or hinder the exercising of these powers. Indeed, in the EU, institutional density frames the solutions developed by member states in response to the crisis. On the contrary, while institutional frames exist in the context of UNASUR, MERCOSUR or ASEAN, they exert a comparatively weaker influence in framing the solutions to the crisis. State power seems to be the main driver of institutional change; whether institutional density plays a complementary role remains a controversial issue.

Institutional density

Actors, more specifically decision-makers, citizens and collective non-state actors, evolve in more or less institutionalised contexts, understood as different degrees of 'institutional density'. We have defined 'institutional density' as a dynamic concept, implying fluidity and movement: Hence it represents the degree to which institutions, created by regional organisations, constrain, both member states in their domestic and international politics, and individual (public opinion) and collective groups of citizens (civil society organisations and interest groups). We have argued that regional integration processes are discontinuous ('stop-and-go') processes led by the governments of the member states, agencies, and non-state actors as well as the established organisations themselves. This 'processes perspective' helped us to measure the 'structural perspective', in other words the levels of influence exercised by the specific regional integration structures under scrutiny on the internal functioning of the member states as well as non-member states – in political, economic, or social terms. In other words, the idea that the more integrated the institutional structures are, the less room for manoeuvre the national actors have, is embedded in the reasoning behind path dependency and institutional 'lock-ins' (Mahoney 2000). In this sense, historical institutionalism arguably predicts that in the event of an exogenous shock, the pre-crisis level of integration will, to a large extent, determine actors' attitudes.

Based on the above, we have argued that the higher the institutional density in a situation of crisis, the higher the continued engagement of both institutions and member states in regional integration. This means, on the one hand, the higher the institutional density in a situation of crisis, the higher the probability that agents will push integration forward. And, on the other hand, the higher the institutional density in a situation of crisis, the higher the probability that path dependence will occur.

Empirical results show that all the regional organisations analysed in this collective volume, whether particularly well developed institutionally such as the EU or presenting a looser network of constraining norms such as ASEAN, UNASUR, SICA or MERCOSUR, lacked an institutional emergency mechanism to provide funds in order to restore public finances in member states threatened by economic and financial breakdown. In the EU, member states and institutions possessed neither the institutional ability to reduce macro-economic imbalances in the Euro area, nor a harmonised system for financial market supervision – the supervision of banks and financial markets was carried out at the domestic level. However, as we have seen earlier, the cooperation amongst member states, the European Commission and the European Central Bank (ECB) has led to a reinforcement of the EU's institutional density. New economic and financial surveillance mechanisms have been created whose implementation and control was transferred, partially or completely to supranational institutions such as the Commission, the EU Court of Justice and the European Central Bank.

In Latin America, the institutional network regulating economic cooperation is denser but also incommensurably more fractured than in the EU: the Community of South American Nations (CSN), the South American Common Market (MERCOSUR), the Union of South American Nations (UNASUR), the Andean Community (CAN), the Caribbean Common Market (CARICOM), the Central-American Integration System (SICA) to mention but the most visible ones, deal with questions of economic integration. In Central America, this institutional network has led to a true patchwork of organisations since the early 1990s. These regional organisations, however, do not provide the same dense web of constraining norms as the European Union. As in the EU, the reaction to the economic and financial crisis that started in 2008, emerged first and foremost amongst intergovernmental actors (with the difference that no supranational organisation seemed to be involved in the agenda setting): there were meetings of heads of state, as well as economic and foreign ministers calling for macro-economic stability and fiscal responsibility and implementing a series of emergency mechanisms. Heads of state and government called upon the Central American Bank for Economic Integration (CABEI) to initiate support programmes for food production and the labour market. Central American governments implemented individual measures at the domestic level, very similar to what we observe in the EU. The difference with European integration is that the crisis did not lead to a formal, coordinated and resilient institutional response to tackle the economic, financial but also social problems that arose from the crisis.

In other words, crisis situations may lead to norm construction or the deepening of a regional organisation's institutional density. Clarissa Dri argues along these lines in her analysis of MERCOSUR's institutional engineering after the 1997–1999 economic debt crisis where the regional organisation created an international secretariat and reinforced its dispute settlement mechanism. First and foremost, however, in Latin America and in Asia, crisis situations allow issues to be put on the agenda. In his chapter Dabène shows three policy areas – trade, defence and democratic institutions – in which issues were put on the institutional agenda through external incentives (US diplomacy and pressure) as well as through internal strategies pushed forward by UNASUR member states, and most notably by the Brazilian government in economic crisis situations. In terms of external pressure, the US government managed to circumvent UNASUR's trade strategies, established and defined during the 1999–2001 economic crisis that affected Latin America by extending the NAFTA model mostly through bilateral agreements.

The institutional density of UNASUR might increase in the current economic and financial crisis, but shows no sign of doing so yet. The UNASUR institutional framework is based on a Council of heads of state, a Council of foreign ministers, a Council of delegates and a secretariat. Whenever policy issues arise, during or in between crisis situations, UNASUR forms sectorial councils and issue committees to deal with policy questions that emerge, and these remain in place after the problem is solved. Other regional organisations such as MERCOSUR have reacted in a very similar way. Committees were created, hence densifying the institutional network, without necessarily strengthening integration, as those committees remain, more often than not, empty shells, as Parthenay illustrates in his case study on regional organisations in Central America. Central American regional organisations have constantly been under reform and encounter a systematic problem of compliance. This seems to be a consequence of the considerable asymmetry of the member states' economic development in particular in the Central American region. At the same time, however, the case studies on Latin America also show that institutional systems, once established, are remarkably resilient in times of economic and financial turmoil. Regional integration does not improve, but does not break down either.

In ASEAN, the reaction to the crisis was similar to what we observed in Latin America insofar as one of the first reactions was to establish a financial emergency mechanism.

The case studies on the reaction of ASEAN to the crisis also show that the low level of institutional density was not an obstacle for member states to come up with innovative solutions, as long as they were carried by the powerful member state of the organisation. Wong underlines that the low level of institutional density was a blessing in disguise for the development of human rights norms as there was no path to be followed. Hence NGOs in favour of human rights could act as policy entrepreneurs as long as they were supported by Indonesia after the fall of the authoritarian Suharto regime in Indonesia. More generally, the setting up of a human rights' commission by ASEAN led to the argument that the institutionalisation of ASEAN had become significant enough to be considered as integration. Together with the development of the ASEAN Plus Three (ASEAN +3) initiative and the Chiang Mai Initiative Multilateralization (CMIM), this was seen as a possibility for a deviation from the ASEAN norm of non-interference in the aftermath of the 1997–1998 financial crisis as economic ministers proposed a regional framework that would allow 'mutual surveillance of each others' economic policies' (Acharya 1998).

In his analysis of the situation, Shaun Narine presents a more sceptical picture of the degree of development ASEAN has reached. Contrary to Wong who states that though ASEAN did not drive policy, it did circumscribe policy options, Narine argues that ASEAN's relationship with its member states hinges on the institution being as minimally invasive as possible in their sovereign affairs, before, during and after a economic crisis. His argument is based on the fact that CMIM has no physical offices, except for a research office located in Singapore, the finance ministers of its member states meet at the sidelines of regular Asian Development Bank Meetings. CMIM does not manage the financial contribution of its members and most of its resources come from non-ASEAN member states.

The reasons for these different institutional reactions can be found as we argued in the density of institutional norms that characterise regional organisations: it is clear that where neither secretariat nor established norms (whether they are formal or informal) or specific permanent institutions exist, member states are less constrained on developing their own solutions to the crisis. However, three additional elements have been pointed out, and it is crucial to include them in an explanation of why regional organisations react differently to economic and financial crises. First, the relative difference in member states' economic development influences the framing capacity of regional institutions. If this difference is too great, the internal coherence does not exist for institutions to frame policy answers. This is particularly the case if no redistributional element has been introduced. Although the rough data stemming from the IMF and Eurostat[1] for 2014 shows that the relative differences between GDP/capita data in both ASEAN and EU member states is high (ASEAN = 100: Singapore = 1,031.4; Brunei = 928; Indonesia = 85; Laos 51.4; EU = 100: Sweden and Germany = 124; Poland = 68; Romania = 54), and the absence of a redistributive instrument in ASEAN may explain why individual member states, such as Singapore or Indonesia can influence policy solutions so strongly.

Table 12.2 Economic and financial crises and institutional change in regional organisations

	European regional integration	*Latin American regional integration*	*Asian regional integration*
Crisis emergence: immediate response	Emergency funds	Emergency funds	Emergency funds
Institutional engineering	Institutional strengthening (new norms, based on path dependency, are established)	No institutional strengthening	No institutional strengthening
Resilience	Regional organisation remains in place	Regional organisation remains in place	Regional organisation remains in place

A second element that needs to be taken into account is the level of compliance with norms. It does not seem enough for a regional organisation to have established a series of legal constraints: if the member states do not comply with them, which is the case in SICA, institutions have a limited capacity to frame solutions.

Finally, the original integration goals have been added as an element explaining why institutions do not influence solutions: if original integration goals are absent, or extremely limited, as in the case of ASEAN, member states' perception of sovereignty and territorial disputes prevail in situations of crisis.

Explaining citizens' attitudes

Economic and financial crises represent crucial challenges for citizens: if we agree with the assumption that a functioning democratic political system creates the environment in which its population may not only coexist peacefully but also create an economically stable situation in which wealth is more or less equally distributed, crises disrupt this equilibrium and lead to instability: a higher unemployment rate, welfare benefit cuts, increased distance between rich and poor populations, social unrest. The well-being of societies is jeopardised. Hence, economic and financial crises are not just a matter of scarce liquidity and overexposure of national governments and private banks, but they also reveal the limitations of regionalisation models. Regional integration processes impact national societies. It is therefore crucial to understand how these societies experience regional integration, but also how they contribute to regional integration processes through individual citizens, parties or non-state actors. In order to analyse both individual and groups of citizens' attitudes towards regional integration in crisis situations, and the possible influence this attitude exerts on the strengthening or loosening of integration processes, the chapters studied how individual and groups of citizens' attitudes impact institutional change and how these attitudes are influenced by regional integration.

While a large number of studies exist which analyse the question of European citizen's attitudes towards integration, and more particularly the impact of the economic and financial crisis (Serricchio *et al.* 2013; Hobolt and Wratil 2015), few studies do so with regard to Latin American or Asian regional integration (for exceptions see Roberts 2007). We have already pointed out in the introduction that the conclusion of these Europe-centred studies is that the economic crisis did not have a substantial impact on bringing economic factors back in as an important contributor to citizens' attitudes towards integration, although the most pronounced increase in Euroscepticism has taken place in the countries most affected by the crisis. Overall purely economic explanations seem to have very limited analytical leverage. If economic and financial crises do not seem to have a strong influence on attitudes towards regional integration, other factors must explain why the level of support remains more or less stable. Linking this result to institutional density explanations, we argued in the introduction that: the higher the institutional density, the higher citizens support for increased regional integration in times of economic crisis (more formal and informal cooperation).

The empirical results of this research differ again with regard to the three regional integration schemes under scrutiny in this book. While the correlation between high citizen support during crises and high institutional density seems to exist in the European context (Belot and Guinaudeau, Hülsemeyer), this correlation does not exist in the case of Latin American and Asian regional integration. We have seen earlier that domestic public opinion more or less significantly constrains member state positions in times of crisis in the European Union. It is difficult to conclude from the empirical material at our disposal what precisely accounts for this difference though. Neither of the four chapters – Belot and Guinaudeau, Hülsemeyer, Lequesne and Degner – use the same theoretical basis: Degner situates himself in a neoliberal framework, Lequesne combines neofunctionalism and intergovernmentalism, Hülsemeyer as well as Belot and Guinaudeau are situated in a postfunctionalist logic, although all four chapters apply the hypotheses developed by our neo-institutionalist framework developed in the introduction. Hence, the answer to the question of why public opinion sometimes, but not always, influences policy positions with regard to regional integration needs more scrutiny.

More generally, Belot and Guinaudeau start in their chapter from a very crucial assumption: in European Union politics, academics as well as policymakers nowadays consider citizens' support as a necessary condition for the strengthening and deepening of regional integration. From the other chapters, however, it follows that neither Asian nor Latin American regional integration considers this as a *sine qua non* requirement. While we observe in Latin America a wide range of entrepreneurs from the civil society calling for another kind of regional integration to be promoted as Parthenay shows in his chapter, the influence on decision-makers remains relatively limited.

By adopting a longitudinal analysis, Belot and Guinaudeau cover a period of over 40 years with several economic crises in European integration. Starting from a review of contrasting research results, the authors combine the level of institutional density with the length of membership and the socialisation effect membership produces. Their study shows that although the level of support for European integration at member state level and the trend over time sometimes diverge, the two biggest declines in support occurred in the aftermath of the Maastricht Treaty and in the context of the economic and financial crisis starting in 2008. They qualify the drop in support as impressive, as it affects all countries. The wide time span allowed them to confirm that this development is not part of a long-term trend, but that it coincides with the crisis. Hence, in the European Union, the worsening of economic conditions is key to understanding the crisis in support. These findings contradict numerous studies that observe economic considerations to be of limited leverage when it comes to explaining citizen support for European integration (Hobolt and Wratil 2015). In their study Belot and Guinaudeau are insisting on a methodological caveat: trends in EU support are also shaped by other factors. Hence the higher the institutional density the more citizens tend to adjust their support for EU membership to the economic context, a result observed in particular with regard to monetary policy: the effects of macro-economic conditions on public support for the EU is substantially stronger amongst the 17 member states of the Eurozone than amongst countries outside the Eurozone such as the UK, Sweden, Denmark or Poland, a result we unsurprisingly also find in Lequesne's study, albeit more on the member state than on the citizen level. This important research results explains the limited impact of economic and financial crises in ASEAN, UNASUR and MERCOSUR. The existing public sphere in the EU and the instruments of the EU's democratic accountability, although constantly criticised for its limited impact, are comparatively immensely more developed than in the other regional organisations under scrutiny here.

Even less comparative empirical evidence exists with regard to the influence of regional integration on collective groups, such as civil society organisations during crisis situations. In the EU, although interest group studies have reached a new level of visibility (see Klüver *et al.* 2015), their reaction to crisis situations, whether in EU studies or in comparative regionalism studies is not yet well understood. Empirical anecdotes illustrate the importance of this question: anti-crisis measures introduced by national governments and regional organisations have led to uprising over the last ten years. 'Occupy Wall Street' represented this movement in the US, the *indignados* or *indignées* movement in Argentina and Brazil, Spain, France, Italy and Greece – whereas in Spain and Greece the movement transformed into parties or became part of the established party system and today is part of the ruling government at national (Greece) or local (Spain) level. The Arab Spring movements, although with rather limited effect in the long term, reacted to financial and economic difficulties by calling for – and successfully implementing – a broad-reaching uprising. In line with the hypothesis on citizens' attitudes, we have argued that economic and financial crises increase the willingness of civil society organisations to engage in integration (in specific policy fields), if institutional density is high. On the contrary, the less integrated a region is, the less inclined civil society organisations feel to engage in more activism at the regional level.

The results of the case studies on MERCOSUR and ASEAN show that the difference in institutional density does not account for civil society engagement with regional integration. Neither NGOs nor parties are more inclined to support regional integration in times of crisis, whether the institutional density be high or low. Civil society actors are engaged in changing the path of regional integration in contemporary politics in Latin America, Asia and the EU. The reasons for this change seem to lie in the fact that global politics have opened up to civil society participation since the end of the Cold War (Rosenau and Czempiel 1992). This thus has less to do with the density of constraining norms or the feeling of allegiance with regional organisations than a broader global development. With regard to MERCOSUR, it is the ideological influence of the regional organisation's member state – Brazil's – parties that account for the engagement with regional integration in times of crisis. Hence, the impact of crises in reinforcing or eluding integration not only depends on institutional structures but also on the beliefs and interests of political agents. The way political parties perceive the crisis according to their central ideological lines influences how they choose to deal with regionalism in crisis periods. This implies that endogenous mechanisms are an important source of change in MECOSUR. The Brazilian Workers Party (PT) as well as the Social Democratic Party (PSDB) were willing to open national markets in the 1980 and identified regional integration as the most promising strategy. In 2008, however, the strategy changed and PT invested in the construction of an 'emerging and solidary power' image for Brazil. When Brazil was perceived as autonomous enough, the regional path was no longer a priority. This questions the last hypotheses, according to which the more integrated a region is, the greater the support of civil society's organisations. The lack of institutional density in 2008 left a wide space for PT's nationalistic currents to circumvent the regional treatment of the crisis. Contrary to the situation in the 1980s, the following economic crises were not able to trigger regionalism in an efficient and stable manner. In other words, the institutional density of MECOSUR was not significant enough to trigger continued engagement with integration.

The ASEAN financial and economic crises led to a process of re-legitimation of ASEAN which included limited measures to strengthen institutional capacity and accountability, such as the ASEAN Charter or the ASEAN Intergovernmental Commission on Human Rights, as Wong pointed out. This reform programme called for a 'people oriented' ASEAN and the inclusion of civil society organisations in regional policy-making.

While civil society participation has existed since the end of the 1970s, new instruments have been initiated with regard to the civil society affiliation system. From 2005 ASEAN added two additional opportunities for civil society involvement, namely informal consultations on specific issues and annual sectorial forums to facilitate dialogue between civil society representatives and officials. Alongside these channels, ASEAN officials began interacting with civil society organisations through forums established by external actors, such as the ASEAN People's Assembly and the ASEAN Civil Society Conference.

However, these interactions only offered limited opportunities for civil society groups to contest policy and shape official processes as a result of three characteristics, as Kelly Gerard underlines in her chapter: strict monitoring of who can participate coexists with strict controls of the nature of participation in these organisations. Finally, areas for civil society participation in ASEAN are determined by the issue under discussion, which further limits the range of political activities by activists. Hence it seems that it is not the degree of regional integration that leads to higher civil society support for regionalism, as assumed in the introduction. Participation, on the contrary, is an elite-induced process, relating not to the degree of institutional density of a regional organisation, but to social and political conflict. Kelly demonstrated that the institutional change induced by ASEAN is 'an attempt by political elites to socially embed a project that conflicts with the objectives sought by the increasingly organised and vocal Southeast Asian civil society sector'.

Conclusion

Global economic and financial crises have regional impacts. They influence the power relations between member states, the institutional density of regional organisations and, finally, change the level of allegiance and interest of citizens and civil society organisations.

The chapters in this collective volume have forcefully underlined the power of member states in developing initial answers to the specific crisis situations. In the very first moments of the crisis in all three regional areas, member states coordinated the initial analysis of problems. Heads of states and governments, finance and economy ministries gave the first indications on how to understand the crisis. What we have seen is that member state power is in particular based on the historical power of member states, and the perception of this power by others: in the EU, Germany, but also the Franco-German couple influenced the initial framing; Indonesia is considered as a central motor for or obstacle to a certain number of developments; and, finally, Brazil was identified as a crucial actor and policy framer in the initial crisis situation. We have also seen, throughout the chapters that the institutional density of a central factor in a second period of the crisis to offer specific possibilities for framing. Here, the cases of ASEAN, UNASUR and MERCOSUR show that the lower the institutional density of the less possibility to initiate resilient solutions. The EU, showing the highest level of institutional density, is the only regional organisation where permanent solutions were decided and implemented. While the initial solutions introduced the regional organisations under scrutiny were similar and concentrated on financial emergency funds, no resilient institutional norms were developed and implemented in other regional realms than the EU. Institutional density also framed domestic reactions to the crisis: where institutional density was high, as in the EU, collective citizens' demands and positions are mediated, or tempered through the regional organisations institutional density. While the demands influence member states positions, they do so marginally the higher the institutional density of the organisation. Where institutional density is low, domestic change can lead to a clear change in member state positions towards regional integration as we saw in the case of Brazil moving from an initial attitude towards regional deepening to a position advocating its slowdown.

Finally, with regard to the attitude of civil society towards regional integration in times of crisis, the chapters have underlined that interest and participation in regional integration is part of a more global development whereby civil society organisations increasingly search to take part of regional developments. This can be observed in all three regional areas that have been analysed. However, contrary to the European Union where a regional allegiance exists, questioned during the crisis situation, neither ASEAN no UNASUR or MERCOSUR have created a regional identity that increases or decreases during regional economic and financial crises.

The impact of economic and financial crisis on regional organisations varies, as the chapters have shown, due to member states' economic, cognitive or historical power, the regional organisation's institutional density, as well as the degree of engagement citizens have with this region. Hence the institutional changes observed do not entirely fit the comparative regionalism's typology of regionness, but are more nuanced according to the three variables developed in our model. One of the most important and overarching results of this study goes however beyond member state power, the degree of institutional density or citizen's engagement: it is the incredible resiliency of regional integration that we witness in all the regions even in times of financial and economic turmoil.

Note

1 http://ec.europa.eu/eurostat/tgm/table.do?tab=table&init=1&language=en&pcode=tec00114&plugin=1. Accessed on 27 August 2015.

References

Acharya, A. (1998). *Democratising Southeast Asia: Economic crisis and political change* (No. 87). Asia Research Centre on Social, Political and Economic Change, Murdoch University, Western Australia.

Dosenrode, S. (ed.) (2012). *Regions and Crises: New Challenges for Contemporary Regionalisms*. Farnham: Ashgate.

Fioramonti, L. (ed.) (2012). *Regions and Crises: New Challenges for Contemporary Regionalisms*. Basingstoke: Palgrave Macmillan.

Hettne, B. (1997). Development, security and world order: a regionalist approach. *The European Journal of Development Research*, *9*(1), 83–106.

Hettne, B. (2001). Regionalism, security and development: A comparative perspective. *Comparing regionalisms: Implications for global development*, 1–53.

Hettne, B. (2003). The New Regionalism Revisited. In Soderbaum, F. and Shaw, T. M. (eds.). *Theories of New Regionalism: A Palgrave Reader*. New York: Palgrave Macmillan.

Hobolt, S. B. and Wratil, C. (2015). Public opinion and the crisis: the dynamics of support for the euro. *Journal of European Public Policy*, *22*(2), 238–256.

Klüver, H., Braun, C. and Beyers, J. (2015). Legislative lobbying in context: towards a conceptual framework of interest group lobbying in the European Union. *Journal of European Public Policy, 22*(4), 447–461.

Mahoney, J. (2000). Path Dependence in Historical Sociology. *Theory and Society, 29*(4), 507–548.

Motsamai, D. and Qobo, M. (2012). Regionalism in Africa: Development Crises and the Growing Influence of Emerging Powers. In Fioramonti, L. (ed.). *Regions and Crises. New Challenges for Contemporary Regionalism*. Basingstoke: Palgrave, 145–162.

Roberts, C. B. (2007). Affinity and Trust in Southeast Asia: A Regional Survey. In Katsumata, H. and Tan, S. S. (eds.). *People's ASEAN and Governments' ASEAN.* Singapore: Rajaratnam School of International Studies, 84–92.

Rosenau, J. N. and Czempiel, E. O. (eds.) (1992). *Governance without government: order and change in world politics*. Cambridge: Cambridge University Press.

Schulz, M., Söderbaum, F. and Öjendal, J. (eds.) (2001). *Regionalization in a Globalizing World. A Comparative Perspective on Forms, Actors and Processes*. London: Zed Books.

Serricchio, F., Tsakatika, M. and Quaglia, L. (2013). Euroscepticism and the Global Financial Crisis. *JCMS: Journal of Common Market Studies, 51*(1), 51–64.

Index

Page numbers in *italics* denote tables, those in **bold** denote figures.

www.ingramcontent.com/pod-product-compliance
Ingram Content Group UK Ltd.
Pitfield, Milton Keynes, MK11 3LW, UK
UKHW011004180926
475701UK00004B/551
* 9 7 8 1 1 3 8 4 8 8 1 4 4 *